Miracle at TENWEK

Miracle at TENWEK

THE LIFE OF *Dr. Ernie Steury*

GREGG LEWIS

Foreword by FRANKLIN GRAHAM

Discovery House Publishers

Books, music, and videos that feed the soul with the Word of God

Box 3566 Grand Rapids, MI 49501

© 2007 by The Christian Medical & Dental Associations
All rights reserved.

Discovery House Publishers is affiliated with RBC Ministries,
Grand Rapids, Michigan.

Discovery House books are distributed to the trade exclusively by
Barbour Publishing, Inc., Uhrichsville, Ohio.

Requests for permission to quote from this book should be directed to:
Permissions Department, Discovery House Publishers,
P.O. Box 3566, Grand Rapids, MI 49501.

Cover photo courtesy of World Gospel Mission.
Photo section photos courtesy of World Gospel Mission,
the Steury family, and Lisette Lewis.

Interior Design by Sherri L. Hoffman

Library of Congress Cataloging-in-Publication Data

Lewis, Gregg, 1951-
Miracle at Tenwek : the life of Dr. Ernie Steury / by Gregg Lewis.
p. cm.
Includes bibliographical references and index.
ISBN-13: 978-1-57293-222-7 (alk. paper) 1. Steury, Ernest M., 1930- 2. Missionaries, Medical—United States—Biography. 3. Missionaries, Medical—Kenya—Biography. 4. Tenwek Hospital (Kenya) I. Title.
R722.32.S72L49 2007
610.73092—dc22
[B] 2007019457

Printed in the United States of America
07 08 09 10 11 12 / SB / 10 9 8 7 6 5 4 3 2 1

Dedication

In keeping with what certainly would have been Ernie's wishes:

This book is dedicated with gratitude to the national and missionary staff of Tenwek Hospital who served alongside Ernie over the years with faith, sacrifice, and compassion. He always wanted them to get all the credit they deserved.

CONTENTS

Foreword by Franklin Graham 9

Chapter 1: Daktari 11
Chapter 2: Finding God's Will 17
Chapter 3: New Focus, New Direction 25
Chapter 4: Medical Training 41
Chapter 5: Coming to Tenwek 49
Chapter 6: Challenges of Life in Africa 65
Chapter 7: So Many Need Our Help 77
Chapter 8: Dealing with Kipsigis Traditions 91
Chapter 9: Meeting Needs and Embracing Opportunities 105
Chapter 10: The Servant Leader 113
Chapter 11: Family Life in Kenya 129
Chapter 12: The Lord Provides 145
Chapter 13: Dreams Coming True 173
Chapter 14: Power for Tenwek 191
Chapter 15: Envisioning the Future 211
Chapter 16: A Time for Farewell 241
Chapter 17: Kenya Is Still in Our Hearts 261
Chapter 18: Worth It All 279

Afterword 301
Author's Note 307
Additional Information 309

Foreword

When I first met Ernie Steury on an East African hillside almost thirty years ago, I never imagined the ultimate impact our meeting would have on my life. Ernie was medical director of Tenwek Hospital in a small community outside of Bomet, Kenya. When he started his work there in 1959, Tenwek was little more than a rural clinic and dispensary. Today, its 300-bed facility is widely recognized as one of the premier mission hospitals in the world. What I loved and appreciated most about Tenwek is that it had, and still has, one of the most effective evangelical outreaches of any hospital I have ever visited. And Ernie's tireless leadership was responsible for making that so.

Ernie never turned anyone away. Even when they ran out of space, which happened often, the hospital still admitted patients—even if Ernie had to put them under beds or on the floor in the chapel. And Ernie was never content just to treat physical needs. He and his medical team made sure the Gospel was clearly presented to every patient. Time and time again, through the direct influence of the hospital's doctors and nurses, or during the follow-up by Tenwek's chaplaincy ministry, this transmitted into lasting spiritual, as well as physical, healing. Until over the years, tens of thousands have come to know the Lord Jesus Christ as Savior through the ministry of Tenwek Hospital, its missionary and African staff, and the visionary community health and development programs Tenwek established under Ernie Steury's direction.

My first visit with Ernie in Kenya spawned a decades-long relationship between us which presented numerous opportunities for Samaritan's Purse and the Billy Graham Evangelistic Association to partner with Tenwek in various building and ministry projects. From World Medical Mission we sent hundreds of physicians on short-term mission assignments to work alongside Ernie and his team in their hospital ministry.

So I had frequent opportunities to witness the impact Ernie's example had on many others who encountered this gentle man in person. He was so unassuming and modest that it was amusing to learn of the reaction of many visiting physicians we sent to work with him. Ernie was always so interested in learning and improving his own knowledge and skills that he'd pick the brain of every new doc who showed up—asking about their latest training back in the States, how they did this procedure, how they would handle that problem. They'd be flattered by the opportunity to share their expertise. Then they would go into the OR with Ernie and have their socks blown off with what he could do and what he had done as a surgeon. In no time these doctors would realize they were in the presence of one of God's very special servants. By his incredibly competent, compassionate, consistent, committed example, Ernie taught hundreds of colleagues what it meant to be both a Christian physician and a missionary doctor.

This book fleshes out the remarkable yet real-life ministry of Ernie Steury at a time in history when the world's need for medical missions is perhaps greater than it's ever been before. Ernie's life story provides us all with an inspiring example of what can be accomplished through one individual who says yes to the call of the Holy Spirit upon his life. This humble giant of a man committed his own life to serving God and providing basic health care to a remote African tribe. By God's grace he lived to see the medical ministry of Tenwek Hospital and its many outreach programs impact the lifestyle and health of hundreds of thousands of people throughout the highlands of southwest Kenya and eventually become a model for medical missions around the world.

I am proud to have known Ernie and grateful to have called him my friend. For me he was, and always will be, a true model of Christian servanthood. My prayer is that God will use his story and this book to impact many more for a life of service to the King.

FRANKLIN GRAHAM
PRESIDENT AND CEO
BILLY GRAHAM EVANGELISTIC ASSOCIATION
SAMARITAN'S PURSE

Chapter 1

DAKTARI

"Daktari! Daktari!

Dr. Ernie Steury smiled as he handed the day-old infant back to her mother before he looked up to see the messenger rushing across the maternity ward. The young Kenyan woman, one of the hospital's nursing assistants, kept calling as she came: "Daktari! Daktari!"

"What is it?" Ernie wanted to know.

"Come quickly!" She was breathing hard. "They need you . . . in outpatient . . . A boy . . . with an arrow wound . . . He is hurt . . . very bad, Mosonik (MOH´-SOH-NIK)."

"Then let's go!" Ernie responded, hurrying out of the maternity ward and across the Tenwek Hospital compound. Rushing into the outpatient clinic thirty seconds later, he found a missionary nurse checking the vital signs on a fifteen-year-old Kipsigis (KIP-SUH-GEEZ) boy. The patient was obviously in pain and going into shock. In the Kipsigis language, Ernie asked the boy's name.

"Kiprotich."

Then Ernie asked what had happened.

The young man's father, who had hitched a ride to the hospital for his son on the back of an old pickup truck, told a familiar story. Early that morning, his boy and some others in their village were taking the family cows out to graze for the day when they'd been ambushed by a band of Maasai warriors intent on stealing the cattle. The herders resisted, but futilely. The Maasai, who were better armed, also had the advantage of surprise and greater numbers. During the fight, Kiprotich was wounded.

Ernie had heard similar stories many times before. There were frequent raids and skirmishes over livestock all along the border of the Kipsigis and Maasai territories. The Maasai believed that the creator gave their tribe dominion over all cattle; thus, they considered every cow on earth to be rightfully Maasai property—a worldview neither accepted nor appreciated by neighboring tribes.

Even as he listened to the account of the early morning attack, Ernie began examining a deceptively small abdominal wound. He'd seen enough of those to know it was far worse inside than it looked on the outside. He knew that Maasai arrows, primitive as they might seem, were ingeniously designed to inflict maximum damage to their target. Each arrow was a hollowed-out shaft into which was inserted a long metal point. When the arrows hit their target, the wooden shaft simply fell off, while the metal head penetrated deep into the target. The sharpened point contained numerous wicked barbs that ripped flesh going in and tore even more flesh coming out if it was pulled out quickly.

Noting the angle of the entrance wound at the front of the abdomen, Ernie feared the boy's internal organs were seriously damaged. He couldn't imagine how this youngster had survived a two-hour ride in a *matatu* (a covered pickup truck or van used for public transportation) over primitive, rutted roads. Ernie knew there was massive internal bleeding; the patient's low blood pressure indicated there wasn't much time left. He quickly started two large IVs and began infusing fluid into the boy as rapidly as it would go.

An X-ray confirmed that Ernie would have a surgical challenge. The four-inch-long metal point of the arrow had gone almost all the way through the boy before lodging near his spine.

Ernie wanted a second pair of trained hands to help with this surgery. So he sent word for a young colleague to join him as he personally wheeled the patient to the operating room. He also mobilized the hospital's walking blood bank (staff who had volunteered to donate blood whenever an emergency arose). Ernie knew he would need many units of blood for this boy.

After administering a spinal and waiting for the anesthetic to take effect, Ernie did what he did with every patient before he operated: He prayed. He took the boy's hand and spoke slowly and clearly in the Kipsigis language to make sure his patient understood. "Lord, we need your help today, and we know you are here with us. We pray for Kiprotich Arap[1]

1 *Arap* is Kipsigis for "the son of."

Rono and ask that you would be with him and show your great love for him by helping to heal his body . . . "

When he finished his prayer, Ernie smiled and patted the boy's arm as he reassured him again, "We'll take care of you the very best we can."

Ernie scrubbed in as the nurses finished prepping the patient for surgery. When he stepped back to the side of the table and took his scalpel in his hand, his focus became so intense on his patient that he barely noticed the others in the room: his colleague standing across the table waiting to assist as needed, the scrub nurse handing over the instruments as he called for them, and the circulating nurse, who gathered and delivered additional gauze, sutures, instruments, units of blood, or whatever was requested during the operation.

As soon as he opened the abdomen, Ernie could see the damage he had feared. The arrowhead had ripped through multiple loops of intestine. Ernie clamped off the intestine around each tear to prevent further contamination as he worked his way down into the abdomen, searching for the primary source of bleeding.

With his colleague holding the intestines aside, Ernie had at least a small field of vision and finally spotted the tip of the arrow. As the younger doctor suctioned out the constant flow of blood, Ernie began packing sponges around the projectile in an attempt to spot the source of all that bleeding.

"We've got a big problem!" he announced in English.

The arrow had embedded itself in the abdominal aorta—the largest blood vessel in the body—just above where it divided into the two main arteries leading to the legs. Ordinarily, a perforated aorta would result in a patient's bleeding to death within a minute or two. This boy had survived a long, jolting ride to the hospital only because the embedded arrowhead itself was partially plugging the hole. The very thing that had created his mortal wound was also keeping the boy alive.

Ernie called for the vascular instrument set. But it didn't contain a clamp large enough to fit over the abdominal aorta. He now faced a surgical catch-22: He couldn't leave the arrowhead in because the patient was slowly and steadily bleeding to death, yet if he removed the arrow, the resulting fountain of blood would obscure his view of the puncture and the boy would bleed out before he could repair the artery.

"Lord, help us!" Ernie prayed aloud as he took a few seconds and tried to think. What he needed, but the small mission hospital didn't have, was a very special large vascular clamp. A regular surgical clamp would irreparably crush the aorta. He could repair this immediate wound, but the aorta would rupture within a day when the crushed tissue broke down.

Suddenly Ernie had an idea: "Get me a piece of red rubber catheter!" (a small diameter flexible tube). "And a piece of suction tubing!" With one hand he pinched the aorta to the arrow to lessen the bleeding that obstructed his vision. With the other hand he dissected away the peritoneum (the thin, plastic-wrap-like membrane covering the abdominal organs) a few inches above the arrowhead and worked his finger down and around the aorta where it ran along the spine. Once he cleared an opening, Ernie instructed his colleague to slowly feed one end of the catheter down into the abdomen. Then, completely by feel, Ernie gently maneuvered the end of the catheter through the hole he had made in the peritoneum and around the backside of the aorta.

After he fed the leading tip of the catheter through, he pulled it up with a hemostat and brought both ends together. Next, he called for a short piece of half-inch-diameter suction tubing, threaded the parallel ends of the catheter up through that, and then slid the suction tubing down the rubber catheter to create a soft noose that he tightened gently around the aorta. Finally, he clamped the suction tube to the catheter to hold the noose firmly closed.

Only then could Ernie release the direct pressure, remove his left hand, and find out if his wild idea was going to work. Once his colleague had suctioned most of the blood out of the patient's abdomen, they could see that the makeshift vascular clamp had slowed the blood loss to a manageable level. As expected, clamping the aorta had caused the patient's blood pressure to spike dangerously high, and there was now no blood flowing to the lower extremities. With little time and only one chance to get it right, Ernie had already made sure he had a vascular suture on a needle holder ready. Then he removed the arrow, grabbed the needle and suture, and sewed in two layers as quickly as possible to close the aorta. The moment he finished, he slowly loosened the rubber noose to let the blood flow again and watched to make certain he had a dry bed with little or no bleeding.

After pulling out the catheter, Ernie applied some gel foam to help clot formation and placed drains from the puncture site through the abdominal wall. During the next hour he carefully sewed up each of the holes in the intestine, gradually working his way out by closing up one layer after another of the boy's abdominal wall.

The boy received large doses of broad-spectrum antibiotics to control the infection already beginning from the spillage of his bowel contents. After ten days of tender loving care in the hospital, as well as many prayers, Kiprotich Arap Rono walked out of Tenwek Hospital, went home to his village, and soon made a complete recovery.

Ernie Steury added the tip of that arrow to his extensive collection of foreign objects—including numerous arrowheads, spear points, and assorted projectiles—that he had removed from patients over the years. Every one was a story in itself.

Tenwek Hospital added one more memorable surgical account to its case file of remarkable success stories. Another patient saved, another life forever changed.

And yet again a grateful Kipsigis family went home with their own tale to add to the already legendary reputation of the American doctor known throughout the highlands of western Kenya as Mosonik (Kipsigis for "Left-Handed One").

But that remarkable story didn't start in Kenya. It began half a century earlier, and half a world away, with an Indiana farm boy who never imagined how his life would intersect with a wounded Kipsigis boy on an operating table in an overcrowded mission hospital in a remote corner of Africa. Yet somehow this American doctor named Ernie Steury, without any formal training as a surgeon, without adequate instruments, without even a constant electrical supply, saved thousands of lives, transformed health care in the highlands of Kenya, and built one of the most successful medical mission facilities in the world.

Chapter 2

FINDING GOD'S WILL

The Early Years

The entire community of Berne, Indiana, always took special note and celebrated the first baby born in Adams County each year. In 1930 that honor was claimed on January 3 with the birth of Ernest M. Steury, the seventh child born to David and Mary (Habegger) Steury.

Except for its timing, nothing about another birth in a large Midwestern farm family at the outset of the Great Depression seemed especially noteworthy, but a large family was not the only thing the Steurys shared in common with members of their rural northeastern Indiana community. Like most of their neighbors, the Steurys had a fine Swiss name and shared an old-world heritage. Though proud Americans for decades, Ernie's family still spoke only Swiss-German, which also remained the preferred language of conversation and commerce for most folks living in and around the nostalgically named towns of Geneva and Berne. Indeed, Ernie never learned English until he enrolled for first grade in the one-room country school a mile and a half down the road from the family's farm. Ernie recalled, "I spent more time standing in the corner than I did at my desk during the first and second grades. Not because I intended to misbehave; I simply didn't understand many of the instructions given to me."

Life was hard for the Steurys, as it was for most people during those difficult years. Yet a steady progression of stairstep children was as much a blessing as hardship. More mouths to feed also meant more hands to help and more love to go around.

David and Mary's family—Esther, Clara, Franklin, Clint, Florine (Flo), Ruth, Ernie, and eventually Mary-Alice and Shirley—fared better than most. Not only did they have a regular supply of meat, eggs, milk, and vegetables they raised on a fertile fifty-acre plot two and a half miles north of Berne, but Mr. Steury found steady enough work in town as a carpenter to pay for most of his family's other needs. With added income earned in nearby factories by the two oldest Steury sisters, the family got along fine in the way of food, shelter, and clothing.

"We wore a lot of homemade clothes, but we also managed to purchase warm winter snowsuits out of the Sears and Roebuck catalog," recalled several of Ernie's siblings. "Even after the older two girls married and moved out, the upstairs of our small frame farmhouse sometimes felt a little cramped. The girls crowded into two big beds in the larger room while the three boys (and sometimes a hired hand) shared two double beds in another.

Like children in most farm families, the Steury children all had their own daily chores—inside the house and out. From an early age, Ernie helped his older sister Ruth fill the wood box by the kitchen stove and gather eggs. By the time Ruth and Ernie reached school age, the two of them regularly climbed the silo to get silage for the cows, shoveled oats for the horses, and tossed hay down from the barn loft for all the animals. When they were finished, they would often snag one of the pulley ropes hanging from the barn rafters, climb the ladder into the loft, wrap their legs around the rope as they sat on the pulley, hold tight to the rope, and swing down out of the loft in a long arc that almost scraped the barn floor before carrying the rider up and out through the open barn doors into bright sunshine and fresh air, before swinging back into shadows heavy with the rich fragrance of clover and cows. Back and forth, in and out, they would swing in ever decreasing arcs, until they dragged their feet on the barn floor to stop and then haul the pulley rope up the ladder to start all over again.

The barn also served as a setting for Ernie's first safaris. His dad, who hated the mess birds made when they nested in the rafters, supplied Ruth and Ernie with all the BBs they needed to significantly reduce the sparrow population. The two of them also used a burlap bag to seine nearby ditches and ponds for tadpoles and other interesting creatures.

The Steurys walked to school most of the year. But in winter the children sometimes ice skated to and from school on frozen roadside ditches. And once in a while, when it stormed, their father would show up at the end of the school day with a team of horses pulling a toboggan-like sleigh piled high with blankets enough to keep everyone warm and cozy.

While food for the body didn't worry the Steurys as much as it did many other families during the Depression, spiritual nourishment, and where his family found it, played a pivotal role in young Ernie Steury's life. When he was born, and for the next few years, the entire Steury clan worshipped regularly in a strict, new-order, Amish Christian church. The bishop (what these Amish called their minister) had a reputation for being extremely dour, and even harsh. Listeners heard little good news in the gospel he preached. Faith was important enough for Ernie's family that they attended church every week. But their religion seemed a solemn and joyless duty.

Not too surprisingly, some families left that congregation over the years. The Steurys stayed in part because the bishop was married to one of their relatives. Many of the other folks who remained in that congregation often grumbled and chafed under the bishop's leadership. They and the Steurys seemed caught in a vicious cycle: The more people left the church, the more judgmental and harsh the bishop was toward those who remained.

For many of the bishop's congregation, the final straw came after the man's first wife died and he remarried another woman only weeks later. Even greater questions about his character were raised by the discovery that the bishop had been operating his own whiskey still back in the woods. Scandalized by their minister's moral failing (which was also a crime in that era of national prohibition), the congregation disbanded and locked its doors.

Before and after Ernie's disillusioned family left that first church, his spiritually sensitive mother, who had always felt there was something missing in Sunday worship, listened regularly to a variety of religious radio broadcasters. Mary Steury wrote one of these evangelists to invite him to Berne. When the Reverend C. Quentin Everest accepted her invitation, she arranged to open the family's old empty church for him to conduct special evangelistic meetings.

The entire Steury family attended the first revival service. And they kept going back every night thereafter to hear a message of good news they'd never understood before. When those services ended, the Steurys determined to find a church in Berne where they could hear similar preaching on a regular basis. The first Sunday, they attended an Evangelical Mennonite church. Then back home around the dinner table, David and Mary took a little straw poll with their children to see if they wanted to continue attending there. Ernie and his siblings voted no, saying some of the boys in their Sunday school class were too rude and unruly. So the next week the family visited the First Missionary Church. Again David and Mary polled the children, who gave a vote of approval. First Missionary Church it was from then on.

There they met Reverend Clarence Wiederkehr, who soon became their close friend as well as pastor and spiritual shepherd. Instead of angrily accosting his listeners every Sunday, as their previous pastor had, Reverend Wiederkehr preached a hope-filled gospel of love and grace. He explained that no one could ever be good enough to earn divine forgiveness and favor; no one could *earn* salvation. But that was okay, because God had sent His Son, Jesus, to pay the price. His salvation was free—a generous and loving gift of grace, available to anyone who simply accepted and believed in Jesus. To those who did, God then gave the gift of His Holy Spirit to empower them to live an abundant, victorious, and joyous life for Him.

Reverend Wiederkehr made the Christian life seem so different, so much more appealing than what they had been taught before, that in short order all the Steurys old enough to understand the sermons went down to the altar and prayed to accept this loving and accepting Jesus he talked about. And immediately the Steury home became a better and happier place as a result of this new understanding and belief.

It wasn't as if their personalities were transformed. David remained a rather stoic, undemonstrative man. Yet the people closest to him, especially those among his immediate family and friends, saw in him a genuine change of heart once the Steurys began attending their new church.

Mary was a lot more affectionate than David ever was. Yet they both loved the Lord very much and let the children know that they wanted all of them to follow Him as well. Ernie and his siblings recall their mother being a great prayer warrior. Among their most meaningful memories is the sound of their mother's voice drifting sweetly through the house, repeatedly singing her favorite song, "My Jesus, I Love Thee," as she did her housework, cooked the meals, and attended to the rest of her daily routines.

The Steury children not only received Christian instruction and encouragement at home from their parents; they also benefited from regular biblical training from their own church and the greater Berne community. Every summer, most of the churches in town banded together to offer one big, ecumenical vacation Bible school. Every morning for five straight weeks, they engaged, entertained, and awarded children for learning as many Bible verses as possible.

Ernie Steury's early teen years were spent fulfilling expectations. After his father suffered a tragic fall off a barn roof, leaving him an invalid who subsequently suffered from periodic bouts of depression, Ernie learned the constant, ever-changing challenge of maintaining a working farm to provide for the family. The hours spent at school and on schoolwork often seemed a welcome break from the physical toil of farming. He found little time or opportunity for any real social life outside of school except at church.

Church, always a central part of Ernie's life, became especially important after he made his decision to accept Jesus Christ as his Savior. At age twelve he was baptized in the Wabash River. During worship services at the First Missionary Church in Berne, boys sat on one side of the balcony, the girls on the other. But there was more chance for friendly interaction during activities of the church youth group, called the Gleaners. Ernie, though one of the group's most active members and an eventual leader, always seemed shy, even awkward, around the girls.

Ernie dated a little, played an active role at church, and did very well in most school subjects. But what really excited him, what inspired his dreams for the future, was an avid interest in electronics and ham radios. He learned all he could about the subject in vocational classes at school and devoured any articles on the subject in *Popular Mechanics.*

Seeking a Vocation

Maybe it was the natural sense of adventure many teenage boys experience as they approach manhood or maybe it was the influence and example of all the young men Ernie knew who had served in World War II. Whatever the motivation, upon his graduation from Monroe High School in 1948, Ernie decided the most appealing (and affordable) route to an exciting and rewarding career in electronics would begin with military service. He would enlist and let Uncle Sam pay for his training.

He visited and talked to a recruiter in Fort Wayne. He read the brochures. And he decided the U.S. Navy offered the best training in his chosen field. Once he passed the aptitude tests with flying colors, Ernie signed up for basic training at Great Lakes Naval Station in Chicago, with his local recruiter's promise that he could then go on for introductory, and eventually advanced, technical programs in electronics.

Ernie couldn't wait. It was all he could think about, all he could talk about with family and friends for weeks. The day finally arrived. He said his goodbyes and caught a ride to the navy recruiting office in Fort Wayne, where he signed his final enlistment papers and waited with twenty-five other young men for the bus to Chicago.

As the coach pulled to a stop at the curb outside, the recruiter opened the door and stood there. Suddenly, an uneasy feeling began to grow in the pit of Ernie's stomach, though maybe it had been there all along and he had just ignored it until he stood in the storefront recruiting office that morning. He told himself that this was just an uneasy feeling common to boys leaving home for the first time. But the troubling sensation kept getting stronger, and he became more and more unsettled.

Abruptly, the line began moving. Even as those at the front of the procession hurried out the door, crossed the sidewalk, and filed up the steps onto the bus, Ernie experienced an almost overwhelming sense that he was about to make a serious mistake. Approaching the door where the recruiter stood with all his enlistment paperwork in hand, Ernie stopped and asked the officer, "Is it too late to back out?"

Undoubtedly the man had encountered a lot of boys with second thoughts who had asked the same question. He replied that nothing was final and binding until the recruits were officially sworn in upon arrival at the training base.

Ernie digested that information just long enough for the guy in front of him to step up into the bus. Then he made an instantaneous decision.

When Ernie turned and walked away, a surprised and distressed recruiter called after him: "Don't you ever think about joining the U.S. Navy again!" Then he let loose an angry stream of invectives, some of which Ernie had never heard before and none of which did anything to change his mind.

By the time he got back to Berne, Ernie was almost as angry with himself as the recruiter had been. In the moment he decided not to get on that bus, he had been absolutely convinced in his heart that he was doing the right thing. Now he wasn't so sure.

His thoughts and feelings were all confused. He knew it was going to be embarrassing when everyone found out he'd backed out at the last minute after being excited and talking about his plans for so long.

How could he explain to other people what had happened when he didn't understand it himself?

Feeling weighed down more by his disappointment than by the belongings slung over his back, Ernie trudged slowly up the steps into his house to face the family, still wondering, *Why am I doing this?*

Within minutes he learned his return was the answer to all the desperate prayers his mother had been praying since he'd left that morning. But his mother's joy did little to diminish his own feelings of confusion.

Again and again in his mind he replayed the scene at the recruitment office. How could he have turned and walked away like that? He'd been so excited about the prospects for his future. Now he realized those dreams were gone forever as he recalled the recruiter's angry threat, *"Don't you ever think about joining the U.S. Navy again!"* "I was convinced," Ernie recalled years later, "I'd just blown the biggest and best opportunity of my life. Why? For what? I didn't know what I was going to do now. I didn't even know how to explain what had happened to my surprised and curious family and friends. Embarrassed and upset, I fled out into the fields to be alone and help my brother harvest corn. The rest of that day I remember yanking the husks off those ears and then hurling them into the wagon just as hard as I could throw them.

"For some time I was angry at the people around me, angry at the world, maybe even a little angry at God. But mostly I was angry at myself for what I'd done. For what I'd not done that morning. And for not having any idea why."

Only gradually over the coming years would Ernie Steury learn that his seemingly sudden and impulsive change of mind was also the answer to the prayers of countless other people he didn't yet know.

But the first clues to the mystery of his "why" question would begin to be revealed in the coming days.

Chapter 3

New Focus, New Direction

Those next few days, Ernie Steury tried to spend a lot more time out in the fields on the family farm than he did on the familiar streets of Berne, Indiana. He avoided every encounter he could with friends and relatives because he dreaded having to respond to their surprise and their questions: "I thought you joined the navy, Ernie! What happened?"

He never knew what to say. He still didn't understand why he'd suddenly turned his back on his dream of a career in electronics and come home.

It didn't help that his mother acted so pleased to have him back, convinced and content that God had answered her prayers. *If that is true,* Ernie asked God, *could you at least let me know what is going on? It would be nice to have some explanation for people.* But the Lord seemed a lot slower to answer his prayers than his mom's.

According to Ernie, "I just didn't know what I was going to do. All I really knew was farming. And I hadn't been planning on doing that."

Within the next couple of weeks, the First Missionary Church held a series of special services. Ernie, realizing it was time to get back out in public, decided to go. "One night," he later recalled, "the evangelist preached about making a complete commitment to Jesus Christ, letting him be Lord of your life and allowing the Holy Spirit to fill you and take control. 'To die out to self,' the man said.

"That evening, at the close of the service, I went down to the altar in front of the church. I told the Lord, *I don't know what you want me to do. But whatever you can do with my life, here it is!"*

The irritation and unhappiness he had been feeling since he came home from the recruitment office in Fort Wayne was replaced by what

Ernie acknowledged was "a tremendous sense of joy" and a surprising sense of peace.

Having told God he would do what He asked, Ernie began praying daily for guidance. Over the next few weeks, as he diligently sought some answer about his future, he realized he'd never done so before. "I had never truly considered God's will for my life," Ernie admitted. "When I'd decided to pursue a career in electronics and to join the navy for training, those were *my* ideas. Not the Lord's. I gradually realized that was *why* they didn't work out. God had other plans for me! But what?"

Over the next few weeks, as he prayed, Ernie became burdened about those who had never heard the gospel. The First Missionary Church there in Berne, Indiana, had always emphasized the importance of missions and supported numerous missionaries. Ernie had listened with interest and met many of the missionaries who had come to speak there over the years, but suddenly he found himself thinking about overseas service more often, more seriously, and in a whole new way. Ernie gradually began to consider, for the first time in his life, the idea of missions as a career.

Ernie went to talk to Reverend Pritchard Amstutz, the relatively new pastor of the First Missionary Church. He explained how he'd been praying for guidance. "And I believe God is calling me to become a missionary," he confessed. "If that is true, what would I need to do to prepare myself?"

Reverend Amstutz recommended his own alma mater to Ernie. Asbury College, only a couple hundred miles away in Wilmore, Kentucky, was a small Christian liberal arts college that had produced hundreds of ministers and missionaries over the years. Ernie had never before heard of the school, but the more he learned about it, the more he felt certain that was where the Lord would have him go.

So he applied and was accepted to begin in the fall of 1949. With his dad's physical injuries and bouts of depression, his mom's trying to keep up mortgage payments on the farm, two younger sisters still at home, and the rest of his siblings just starting their own families, Ernie knew his parents wouldn't be able to help much with his education.

So he spent the next few months working for his brother Frank and other farmers who needed an extra hand. He also took whatever odd jobs he could find around town, first at Graber Poultry and Produce, then Fulton Glass Company, and eventually at the Dunbar Furniture Company. Wherever Ernie could find work to earn money for college tuition and books, he was ready to go.

In the fall of 1949, Ernie's sister and brother-in-law, Clara and Eli Sprunger, drove him to central Kentucky. Most of his possessions fit in one old steamer trunk. So it didn't take Ernie long to unpack and settle in for his freshman year. He felt confident that he was now following God's plan for his life. Whenever anyone asked, he quickly replied that he was majoring in religious studies—preparing to do evangelism and church-planting ministry as a missionary in Africa.

He took an on-campus job working every day in the school cafeteria to help pay the bills. Ernie admitted he worked a lot harder there than he did in his classes. He enjoyed dorm life and making a lot of new friends. He went on a few dates, but he dated no one seriously or for long. He attended classes and studied enough to get by. "But," Ernie confessed many times over the years, "you might say I majored in ping-pong most of my freshman year."

Ernie landed a summer job working for his Uncle Dan's construction company, building silos for farmers all over Indiana and Illinois. Ernie's agility and small stature (at 5' 8" and 130 pounds) were well suited to the more dangerous work high in the air. He never minded heights, and the added danger was compensated for by extra pay. So he spent most of his summer scrambling up and down ladders, balancing on narrow perches, and often dangling sixty to eighty feet in the air on the side of a silo as he fastened sections of the structure together. The work proved physically taxing as well as dangerous. But over the course of three months, he earned what he needed to go back to Asbury for a second year.

Then one October Saturday that fall of 1950, Ernie received a shocking phone call from home telling him his father had died. Back in Indiana again for the funeral, Ernie weighed the prospect of staying in

Berne to help his mother. But she really wanted Ernie to finish college and answer his calling to the mission field. Several of his siblings who lived nearby assured Ernie that they would look after their mother, and he should go back to school.

"So I really buckled down and studied my sophomore year," Ernie said. Perhaps that was due to the sobering and maturing experience of having lost his father. But another factor probably was that his goal of becoming a missionary to Africa seemed closer and clearer than ever.

One evening during the second quarter of his sophomore year, Ernie had a talk with his roommate, Mark Flynn, when the discussion turned to their future plans. Mark, a premed major, said, "Ernie, if you became a medical doctor, you could reach more people for the Lord than you ever could as an evangelist or a pastor. Why don't you study to become a doctor and go to Africa as a medical missionary?"

The idea seemed so preposterous to Ernie that he looked at his roommate and said, "Mark, the last thing I'd ever do in my life would be medicine! I don't like science! I don't want to be a doctor! I couldn't be a doctor! No thanks!"

Mark refused to be put off by Ernie's adamant response. "Well," he replied, "you could at least think and pray about it."

It was such a foreign idea that Ernie didn't bother to even consider it for quite some time. Mark eventually brought the idea up again, and Ernie brushed it off once more. But that still didn't stop Mark. Ernie knew his roommate had never wanted to be anything but a doctor since he was a little boy, but that was his dream, never Ernie's.

Finally, mostly so he could silence his roommate by telling him he'd done so, Ernie did begin to pray about the possibility. And once he did that, it seemed harder rather than easier to discount the notion. It still didn't make sense to Ernie, but he felt led to raise the subject with his faculty advisor, Dr. Cecil Hamann.

He told Dr. Hamann about his roommate's suggestion. He explained how he'd been praying about it lately and how he'd not been able to stop thinking about the idea. But Ernie also listed ten good, logical reasons it just didn't make sense for him to pursue the possibility of medicine—everything from his lack of interest in science to the fact that he was halfway through college majoring in religious studies. He had barely scraped together the money to pay for college, so there was no way he could ever afford medical school.

Dr. Hamann, who taught biology and headed up the premed program at Asbury, patiently heard Ernie out. Then he told Ernie he agreed with his roommate, Mark; there would be tremendous potential for ministry in medical missions.

"But . . ." Ernie began to reiterate the ten barriers he'd already noted.

Nodding and smiling, Dr. Hamann cut him off. "Ernie," he said, "if God wants you to become a doctor, He can take care of all those problems. Why don't you switch to a biology major and see how you like it?"

So at the end of his sophomore year, despite some lingering doubts, Ernie switched his major. He went home to work with his uncle again for the summer, uncertain what his decision would mean in the coming school year.

Finding a Helpmeet

Other questions were raised that summer as Ernie entered into the first truly serious dating relationship of his life. Lois's parents were missionaries in Gabon, and the whole family was on furlough, living in Berne and attending the First Missionary Church. Ernie's family had known Lois's family over the years. So from the time they began dating that summer, their families and friends thought it was a match made in heaven. Literally.

Everyone knew Ernie felt called to Africa as a missionary. Since Lois had grown up in Africa, she would make a fine missionary herself. In no time at all, this assumption and the accompanying endorsement of everyone who knew them seemed to fan a spark of interest and attraction into roaring flames of serious romance.

Throughout their summer together, Ernie and Lois both sensed God at work in their lives. Though they hadn't been dating long at all, they began to talk seriously about the future—their future—together. Then, just two weeks before heading back to Asbury College, something changed. Ernie tried to explain: "I'd been so excited about my relationship with Lois. I never had that kind of feeling for any other girl before. We really did have a wonderful summer together. Then, right at the end, I suddenly felt no more attraction to her. It was as if God had taken any desire to be with my girlfriend right out of my heart. I didn't understand it. We had been so sure . . . Everyone had."

Ernie may have been confused about what had changed. But he knew without a doubt what needed to happen next. "I felt horrible about it, even guilty," he said. When he asked God why, he didn't get an explanation. "But I knew what the Lord wanted me to do. I had to break off our relationship."

Telling Lois was one of the hardest things Ernie had ever done. She took the news hard, and he thought it would break her heart. What made the whole thing even worse was the fact that once again, Ernie had made what seemed like a sudden direction-changing decision about his future without being able to explain why—not to family and friends, not to Lois, and not even to himself.

Once again he found himself demanding of God, "Why?"

Shortly after returning to school, Ernie took a job in the cafeteria. One day on his way to work, his college classmate Jack Groce hailed him. Ernie stopped and walked over to say hello. The boys inquired about each other's summer, then Jack turned toward a girl standing beside him and said, "I'd like to introduce my little sister, Jennie Sue." With those simple words the answer to Ernie's "why" began be answered.

This wasn't the first time Jennie Sue (eventually shortened to Sue) had seen Ernie's face. She would have recognized him anywhere. In preparation for her freshman year at Asbury, Sue had taken a special interest in her brother's yearbook.

Trying to imagine what college life would be like for her over the next four years, Jennie Sue began thumbing through the book. Stopping at the section containing student pictures, she asked her brother Jack to point out all the "eligible" guys. So Jack sat down beside his sister, began scanning the pages of photos, pointing out friends and acquaintances, and giving a brief verbal sketch of their particulars.

"He's a nice guy . . . That boy lives on my hall . . . You'd like this one . . . That one's engaged though . . . Seen him around but don't really know him . . ."

Suddenly Jack stopped, pointed at one of the pictures, and looked up at his sister. "Sis, this is the one for you! That's Ernie Steury. He's a friend of mine, a real nice boy. And he's had a call to Africa, too."

"This is the one for you!" She knew her brother was half-teasing when he said those words—but only half. There was something about the way he said it that made her look at the photo again. "Tell me about Ernie," she said to her brother.

To say that Jennie Sue Groce took a definite interest in Ernie Steury that day would not be an exaggeration. She turned to that page in the yearbook countless times over the next few weeks. And after grilling her brother a couple more times to tell her everything he could remember about his friend, Jack teased her about Ernie the rest of the summer.

She usually played off the teasing with some kind of light-hearted response. When her mother decided to take the dress she had worn at an older brother's wedding and refashion it into a formal suitable to wear on dates to Artist Series programs at Asbury, Jennie Sue instructed her, "Make it nice, Mother, so Ernie will like it."

If anyone would have pressed her, she would have admitted this infatuation with a boy she had never met was a little silly. But it was also a little serious. The main reason Jack had first stopped at Ernie's picture to tell his sister, "He's had a call to Africa, too," was that Jennie Sue's plans also included missionary service in Africa. So even though she had initially asked Jack to point out the pictures of *all* the "eligible" boys in the yearbook, she knew the field of realistic prospects would be considerably narrower for her.

Jennie Sue Groce's commitment to missions had been almost a fact of life for her since early childhood. One of her favorite people in the world was Miss Alice Day, a family friend and a missionary teacher in Kenya. When Jennie Sue was just eight years old, after a missionary to India had spoken in the church her father pastored, she informed her parents, "God wants me to be a missionary." Some family and friends assumed that declaration was just some sort of emotional stir in the naive heart of an impressionable young girl. But her parents, who had always been big supporters and believers in missions, took her seriously. So did Miss Day and a Sunday school teacher who both encouraged her dream and then regularly prayed for her and about her future for years.

In the beginning Jennie Sue felt only a general sense of calling to missions. But that changed when she was thirteen, again after a special missionary service. This time it was during the annual ten-day summer meeting at John Wesley Camp at High Point, North Carolina, a holiness campground her own father had played a role in founding years before. A visiting woman missionary spoke and challenged the young people in the congregation to make a personal commitment to carrying out Jesus' Great Commission to take the gospel to the entire world. Then the missionary asked anyone who had felt God's calling into some kind of Christian service to come down to the altar. Those who knew the specifics of their call were to come around and stand between the altar and the platform. Several young people did.

Those who had felt a call but didn't know where God wanted them to serve were instructed to kneel on the outside of the altar, where someone would pray with them and for them. So that's what thirteen-year-old Jennie Sue Groce had done.

As she prayed, a traveling companion of the missionary speaker knelt with Jennie Sue, asked her name, and began praying for her, thanking God for her spiritual commitment and her willingness to serve and then praying that God would make His will clear. And as she prayed there at the altar, it became, in her own words, "clear as day" in her mind, or maybe just in her heart, that God was calling her to Africa.

That experience had proved convincing enough for Jennie Sue Groce to cling to that calling and make plans accordingly for the rest of her teenage years. Unlike Ernie, she had heard about Asbury College all her life. Alice Day and several other missionaries who came to speak at John Wesley Camp had gone there, as had her brother Jack. So Jennie Sue never seriously considered attending anywhere else.

After meeting Ernie, Sue watched for him and made a point of saying hello whenever she encountered him around campus. Once she signed up to work the supper shift in the cafeteria, Sue could count on seeing him every evening.

As frequently as she encountered and spoke to Ernie, Sue had no assurance that he ever really saw her—at least in the sense that she wanted him to see her. But that changed one evening several weeks into the fall quarter when she finished unloading her tray of dirty dishes and turned away from the service window to walk back out into the dining room.

From inside the window, someone called her name. "Sue!"

She turned, and there was Ernie approaching the service opening from the other side. "I was wondering," he paused, "if you had plans . . . if you had a date to the Artist Series next weekend."

Her heart suddenly raced. But Sue cautioned herself to stay calm as she slowly shook her head. "No, I don't have a date."

"Then I'd like to take you," Ernie told her. "That is . . . if you'd like to go with me."

She calmly told him she would.

Though Sue knew Ernie had dated some before they met, she found him to be a little backward—in her words, "a basically shy farm boy" fresh from the cornfields of Indiana. But she also appreciated his reserved nature, which is one reason she decided it would be some time before she told Ernie about studying his picture in the yearbook before going to Asbury and asking her mother to fix her formal "so Ernie will like it."

When he finally did hear those stories, Ernie laughed and admitted, "Good thing I didn't know that or I might have run the other way." But by the time he learned how and when Sue first set her sights on him, it didn't matter. He was already hooked—and happily so.

As it turned out, Ernie Steury discovered two loves his junior year in college. While Sue may have been the first, his studies were the second. When taking mostly general education classes his freshman year (the year he claimed to have majored in ping-pong), Ernie's grade point average had hovered between B- and C+. Buckling down the second year, he managed a B average. But his third year, despite a course load heavy in sciences, despite the time required of his new relationship with Sue—Ernie's grades continued to climb to a B+ average.

The Route to Medical School

The summer between his junior and senior years, Ernie worked construction for his Uncle Dan's company. Sue, who was looking ahead and realizing Ernie was on schedule to graduate two years before she would, decided to pick up another quarter's worth of classes in summer school. They wrote each other regularly during those summer months, and if Ernie had any additional time or energy left at the end of the day, he spent it studying for his upcoming MCATs (the annual standardized tests given each fall to determine which premed students qualified for acceptance to medical schools around the country.)

Ernie expected the tests would be hard—perhaps harder for him than a lot of premed students because he had changed his major so late in college that he hadn't been able to fit in all the required courses. With a declared major of biology, he would not be able to complete the full premed track.

So he could hardly wait for summer to end so he could return to school in Kentucky and be with Sue again. But MCATs were also scheduled for fall, and the closer the exam loomed, the more concerned Ernie became that he might not be adequately prepared.

September finally arrived. The long-awaited reunion with Sue seemed to confirm again their love and their budding dreams of a future together. But the long-dreaded MCATs seemed to confirm all his fears. For some reason that Ernie couldn't fathom, there were numerous questions on the exam about economics, and he had never even had a course in the subject. He returned to the Asbury College campus after the exams feeling discouraged about the whole experience. Sue helped bolster his spirits. And Ernie was reminded of what Dr. Hamann had told him when they had first discussed his change of majors: If God called him to be a medical missionary, He would enable Ernie to overcome any and all obstacles.

There were other hurdles to overcome even as he awaited word about his test scores—such as finances. If he did qualify and if some medical school accepted him, Ernie knew there was no way he could afford to pay for a medical education himself. He had worked his way through college; between his summer job building silos with his uncle and working in the college cafeteria, he had managed to earn more than 90 percent of his expenses. But he knew medical school was going to be a lot more expensive and probably too demanding for him to hold down a job during the school year. Borrowing money wasn't a good option because he could never leave for the mission field while saddled with heavy debt.

Ernie wondered if the denomination of his home church (First Missionary) might have funds for training a missionary doctor. He talked to his pastor, who put him in touch with denominational officials. They regretfully informed him they had no such funds available but added, "For years we've needed a medical missionary for our work in Sierra Leone. Let's pray you are that doctor."

Ernie promised to pray with them. But he couldn't help feeling disappointed. When Ernie shared his discouragement with Sue, she suggested he contact World Gospel Mission (WGM). The longtime dear friend of the Groce family, one of Sue's own spiritual role models, Alice Day, served in Kenya with this interdenominational mission agency. Even though they were based in Marion, Indiana (just forty-five miles from Berne), Ernie had never heard of WGM. When Sue learned the organization's president, Dr. George Warner, was scheduled to come to Asbury College that fall, Ernie agreed to talk to him.

One evening after Dr. Warner addressed a meeting of the Foreign Missions Fellowship, Ernie hung around for a chance to speak with him. He explained that he felt called to go to Africa as a medical missionary, that he had taken his MCATs, and while he was waiting for the results he was already applying to medical schools. He also told Dr. Warner he had been able to earn just enough money to get by in college, but he knew he could never afford medical school on his own. Would Dr. Warner's organization have any funds available to help a prospective missionary get the required medical training?

Dr. Warner listened with a genuine interest that encouraged Ernie, and then he sadly informed him that World Gospel Mission had no such fund. "But for many years now we've been longing for a missionary doctor to go to Kenya and take over the hospital work at Tenwek. Let's pray that you are the one we've been waiting for."

Perhaps sensing the young man's disappointment, Dr. Warner attempted to offer what encouragement he could. He asked Ernie to keep him informed about his medical school prospects, and he promised to pray about raising the subject of training funds at the next board meeting.

Ernie needed all the encouragement he could get. Fortunately, Dr. Hamann kept reminding Ernie that the Lord would help him overcome all the obstacles. Ernie valued the wise spiritual counsel of his biology professor, who had become something of a father figure for him in the wake of his own dad's death. But the greatest encouragement and inspiration of all was Sue, who prayed with him and believed with him that God would indeed work out all the details for his future in medical missions. They celebrated together when he finally received word that despite his reservations about the MCATs, Ernie had passed with flying colors. He acknowledged, "The Lord really must have been with me!"

While Ernie was learning to trust that God would be with him whatever happened in the future, he had known for some time that he wanted Sue to be part of that future too. And Ernie was convinced the Lord wanted that as well. So he decided it was high time to make their commitment official.

Between the time of Ernie's proposal and the end of that fall quarter, he received another wonderful surprise in the form of a letter from his sister Clara and a generous check for a hundred dollars, which she suggested he use to buy himself some nice new clothes before he went for his medical school interview. But instead of purchasing a new suit, Ernie went to a jeweler in nearby Lexington, and the next-to-last day of final exams, he surprised Sue with a genuine diamond engagement ring.

Sue had assured Ernie a diamond wouldn't matter, and she had meant what she said. But her excited reaction to the ring certainly mattered to Ernie. He was so thrilled that for a long time he didn't tell her how he had been able to afford it because he didn't want to take anything away from her happiness.

Ernie applied to three medical schools: the University of Cincinnati; Bowman Gray Medical School in Winston-Salem, North Carolina; and Indiana University (IU). Figuring IU's School of Medicine might be cheaper for a lifelong resident of Indiana, Ernie made that his first choice. But he kept praying, *Wherever You want to me to go, Lord; whatever doors You open.*

On December 17, 1952, when he walked into the interview on the Bloomington campus of IU, he didn't know what to expect. Six doctors sat on the other side of a table at the front of the room. They asked him to be seated in a chair before them.

Their first question was, "Why do you want to become a medical doctor?" So he told the panel about his plan to go as a missionary to Africa.

"Aren't you afraid some natives will put you in a pot of boiling oil and eat you?" one of the doctors asked.

Ernie chuckled and replied, "No, I'm not really afraid of that."

Yet another panelist asked, "Do you expect to see any tigers in Africa?"

Ernie tried not to insult anyone's intelligence while explaining that he was far more likely to encounter lions, which are native to Africa (tigers are not). Then he waited for the next question. None came.

When the chairman of the committee thanked him and said, "You can go," Ernie walked out of the room completely disgusted and thinking, *There is no chance I'm ever getting into this med school. What a pointless process!* He was angry with God. *All that hard work to prepare for such a silly interview. Why did you have me go through that, Lord?*

Knowing that Sue had been praying about the interview, he called to report that he thought the whole thing was a fiasco. He was clearly discouraged, so again she tried to encourage him.

Five days later a letter postmarked from Bloomington, Indiana, arrived. Ernie ripped it open to learn he had been accepted into Indiana University School of Medicine starting the following fall of 1953. "What joy!" he remembered. "It had to be the Lord!"

Ultimately Ernie was accepted at all three medical schools where he applied. But Indiana remained his first choice, if the finances could be arranged, which was his motive for following up with Dr. Warner once school started again after the holidays. In a letter dated January 2, 1953, he told the mission society president: "You asked me to keep in touch with you concerning my plans for the mission field. I had inquired concerning help for financing my way through medical school in preparation . . ."

He reported on his interview and its results and then went on to say:

> I am definitely planning to go on to medical school now . . . and I know the Lord will provide in some way even though your board would be unable to help me.
>
> I feel the Lord has definitely answered prayer concerning my admission . . . and I am going to continue to trust Him to lead me and supply my needs. I will be waiting to hear if any other decisions are made by your board concerning financial help for medical students.

Almost three weeks later, Dr. Warner answered Ernie's letter to say that a family who wished to remain anonymous had just contacted him to say they wanted to donate ten thousand dollars, which could be used to start a loan fund for medical school students preparing for a career in missions. "I've not talked to these people," Dr. Warner told Ernie, "so it's obvious God has answered our prayers!"

Again, the Lord had proven Dr. Hamann right by overcoming another obstacle. So once more Ernie and Sue celebrated God's provision.

Once Ernie's place in medical school was confirmed, he and Sue began to think about their future together. As soon as he graduated from Asbury in May of 1953, Ernie planned to work another summer for his Uncle Dan to earn as much as he could toward his first year's expenses. Sue decided if she also went to summer school after her sophomore and junior years, she could graduate from college in early August of 1954, and they could be married just before Ernie started his second year in medical school. So that's what they set out to do.

In the spring of 1953, both Sue and Ernie filled out the paperwork to apply as candidates for service with World Gospel Mission. They were both accepted as official missionary candidates to serve in Kenya, pending completion of the necessary training.

Ernie also made application for a medical missionary scholarship from WGM. His itemized expenses for the school year, including a $241 microscope, were projected to be $1,371.20. But with $475 in earnings and gifts, he estimated he would need $896 in loans. When WGM gave the okay, Ernie signed a promissory note, agreeing to "repay the amount of the scholarship loan with 4% interest, with the provision that this note will be canceled at the rate of $300 per year for each year of service as a medical missionary in the foreign field under the auspices of World Gospel Mission."

Ernie finished his first year of medical school ranked in the top ten of his class. And as Sue worked to complete her final classes during that summer of 1954, they planned the final details of their wedding, to be held on August 20 at her home church in North Carolina.

Ernie spent considerable time over the summer searching for housing in Indianapolis. Apartments near campus cost an exorbitant sixty to seventy-five dollars a month. So he decided a more economical solution would be to find something on the outskirts of the city. He used a chunk of the money earned doing construction over the summer to purchase a used, twenty-two-foot, blue and gray house trailer. Then he paid the first month's rent for a lot at a small trailer park just before he left for the wedding in North Carolina. To a couple of newlyweds, the trailer—which was to be their home for the next three years—felt cozy rather than cramped. Ernie and Sue enjoyed finally being together. And the future never looked brighter.

They weren't so naive as to think there would be no more obstacles to confront before they fulfilled their calling to Africa. Indeed, they would encounter hurdles they couldn't yet imagine. But experience had already taught them that the God who had called them to serve Him was bigger than any obstacle they might encounter. As Ernie had written on his application for missionary service, whatever the future was to hold, he believed the biblical promise given to him (and all God's people), "For I, the Lord your God, will hold your right hand, saying to you, 'Fear not, I will help you'" (Isaiah 41:13).

Chapter 4

MEDICAL TRAINING

As Ernie approached his second year at Indiana University School of Medicine, he applied again for his medical missionary scholarship from World Gospel Mission. He itemized his projected school expenses: $150—travel; $350—tuition; $125—books; $500—board; $75—clothes and laundry; and $50—incidentals, for a grand total of $1,250. He expected to earn $300 and receive gifts of $100. That left a balance of $850, so he asked for a loan amount the same as he had received his first year—$900.

Sue found a job teaching a first-grade class of forty-six students at an inner-city school in downtown Indianapolis. The newlyweds soon settled into the routine of their respective school years.

Fortunately they both enjoyed the challenges they faced. Sue soon got a feel for her first year of teaching. Ernie quickly realized that the second year of medical school required even more work than his first. What kept them from feeling overwhelmed was the fact they were finally married, and they could face all the hardships—the tight quarters, the demands of their work, an extremely limited budget, and the incredibly exhausting long hours—together, even if their togetherness times seemed too few and too far between.

Study partners, other classmates, and professors who got to know Ernie recognized his spiritual commitment and sometimes even expressed admiration for him and his plans to become a medical missionary. Ernie joined the Christian Medical Society and found encouragement and fellowship among that group of students and graduate doctors who shared his faith and values. There were, of course, other professional colleagues who didn't comprehend his calling and did not understand why anyone would go through all the time and work required to become a doctor only to "waste" all that knowledge, skill, and earning potential in the "jungles" of Africa.

But that goal and his sense of divine calling were what motivated both Ernie and Sue to work hard and make the sacrifices they were making. They kept that goal in sight for each other by talking about their dreams, their plans, and their calling to Africa on a regular basis.

In June 1955, out of modesty, Ernie did not inform the mission that he had finished in the top ten of his class for the second year in a row. But he did offer this report on his progress in school: "I finished my sophomore year one week ago, June 11, and started my junior year here in med school this past Wednesday, June 15. I am now working with patients in the hospital every day, and it is much more enjoyable than listening to lectures all day long, six days a week as [we have been doing for two years] . . . This summer I am going through my first quarter of the junior year and am taking my clerkship in surgery. The med school has had to divide the class so that 75 percent of the class is in school all the time and 25 percent of the class is on vacation. My three months [off] won't come until December 15—March 15. During [that time] I plan to work at the Methodist Hospital in surgery as an extern, the Lord willing."

By the midpoint of his medical school training, Ernie had gotten a vision of his future role as a spiritual, as well as physical, healer. He longed for the day he could begin to do that for the mission's medical work in Kenya. Sue tried to encourage him by assuring him the time would come, and soon. Many of the folks who worshipped with them every week at Hope Church, a Christian Missionary and Alliance congregation in Indianapolis, prayed for them regularly and encouraged them both in their preparations for Christian ministry. "We made so many wonderful friends there whose love and support really helped us get through," Sue said.

Toward the end of Ernie's junior year of medical school, he had to decide where he would take his internship. And with the end of medical school in sight, there were other concerns that needed to be addressed. With the goal of practicing medicine in Tenwek, Kenya, Ernie wrote to WGM headquarters, seeking information about what the requirements for a U.S. physician practicing medicine in a British colony would be. Would his U.S. license be accepted, or would he also have to take British Board examinations? Would the British have any special requirements for how long and where his internship should be conducted? Another concern involved Ernie's selective service status. Would WGM be able to obtain an exemption from the draft for Ernie so his work in Africa would not be delayed for two more years while he completed his otherwise required military service?

In Dr. Warner's letter of response, he advised Ernie to do his internship in a place where he could get some experience in tropical medicine, such as Tulane University's school of tropical medicine or at a government hospital in Panama. He also suggested that Ernie consider and pray about becoming an ordained minister, since medical doctors who went through ordination were exempt from the draft "just like other ministers." He also told Ernie that he would check with the superintendent of the mission's work in Kenya about any special requirements the colonial government might have for medical doctors.

But before any questions about the future could be answered, a new and exciting development occurred in 1956 that would affect the Steury family's present and future. Sue thought she was pregnant. Ernie, who had a part-time job in a medical lab, decided to run his own test to be certain. He called Sue from the lab one mid-May day; when she answered the phone, he exclaimed, "Happy Mother's Day, Mother-to-Be."

As excited as they both were by the news, they agreed to wait a while before announcing the pregnancy to friends and families. Sue, who was teaching summer school to help pay the bills, planned a trip home to North Carolina in August. She and Ernie agreed she would tell her folks then.

However, one day early in the summer, Sue experienced an irresistible urge to call and tell her mother, who had been in poor health for years. Mrs. Groce was thrilled at the news from her only daughter. They rejoiced together and talked much longer than usual. By the time they said goodbye and hung up, Sue felt glad that she had called, even though Ernie teased her about not being able to keep their secret.

A few weeks later Sue's father called her and her brother Jack, who was attending graduate school at Purdue in nearby Lafayette, Indiana. Reverend Groce told them if they wanted to see their mother one last time, they needed to come home right away. Her health was failing.

Sue's mother died two weeks after going to the hospital.

There was little let-up in Ernie's final year of medical school. He and Sue didn't want to borrow any more from the mission's medical school training fund, so she planned to teach right up to the baby's birth. Even as she grieved the loss of her mother, Sue joyfully anticipated the birth of her first child. And almost simultaneously, other plans for the future began to fall into place.

The government reclassified and exempted Ernie from the draft after he was ordained that fall, which meant their arrival on the mission field would not have to be delayed further by military service. The Steurys also received word that Ernie had been accepted to and would begin a year of internship in tropical medicine at the U.S. government's Gorgas Hospital in Panama upon completion and graduation from medical school the following spring. For Ernie and Sue, just knowing that he would have this opportunity seemed like they were one giant step closer to the mission field. First Panama, then Africa. After all the years of planning and preparation, it wouldn't be long now.

But another much-anticipated event came next, when Sue gave birth to their first child, Cynthia Ruth, on January 7, 1957. The proud father, just beginning his final quarter of medical school training, took his daughter in his arms for the first time and rendered his professional diagnosis for the new mother (and anyone else who would listen): "She's perfect!"

Ernie's last quarter ended in March. But while he waited to graduate with the rest of his class in June, he did another externship at a hospital in Lafayette. Sue and Ernie's families couldn't have been prouder at his graduation. But there wasn't much time to celebrate or even let the accomplishment soak in before it was time to pack up and head for Panama. Since Ernie would be working in a government hospital, he and Sue, along with their baby daughter and all their earthly possessions, were provided passage on board a naval ship sailing out of the New York harbor bound for the Panama Canal Zone.

Ernie found the year of internship in Panama everything he had hoped for and more. "At the hospital I received valuable experience treating malaria and many other tropical diseases I never would have seen back in the States," Ernie said. "Then on a lot of weekends I got a real taste of mission work when I and some other Christian interns who also were preparing for service overseas would ride mules up into the interior of Panama to conduct medical clinics for people in some of the poorest mountain villages. We'd sleep in hammocks at night and spend all day treating patients who'd hiked for miles just to see a doctor," Ernie recalled. "For the first time in my life I felt like a real missionary because I was able to witness and share my faith as I treated my patients. It was such a rewarding time. And more than ever it made me long for the time when I could fulfill my calling to Africa."

While his internship turned out to be a worthwhile indoctrination in the practice of tropical medicine, it also revealed what Ernie felt was a major shortcoming in his training. Both in the hospital work and through his experience with patients in the remote clinics, Ernie saw just how valuable it could be to have more extensive surgical skills. He would be able to help so many more people if he could complete a surgical residency before he headed overseas.

But the medical needs in Kenya were already so great that the mission didn't want to extend his training any longer. So the Gorgas Hospital one-year internship experience in Panama would be the last of Ernie's formal training.

As anxious as Sue and Ernie were to get to Africa, and as great as the need was for a doctor at Tenwek, the mission still planned for them to spend the better part of the next year doing deputation work—traveling mostly around the Midwest and the Carolinas visiting churches and individuals to raise enough financial support to cover their first four-year term. Like many beginning missionaries, the Steurys could only tell people what ministry they hoped to do in Africa, since they had never actually been there. They had basic information on the history of World Gospel Mission's work in Kenya. But they had no slide show or any personal anecdotes from Tenwek to share. And toward the end of the summer of 1958, when Sue found out she was pregnant again, Ernie found himself coping with the challenge of traveling alone while his young family stayed in a temporary missionary apartment at WGM headquarters so that Sue and Cindy could have the rest and routine they both needed.

Raising support was hardly the only challenge the Steurys faced over those next few months. In answer to Ernie's earlier queries regarding the licensing and credential requirements of the British colonial government, the superintendent of WGM's work in Kenya consulted with an American physician already serving there with another missionary agency (Africa Inland Mission). Dr. Jim Probst was not only familiar with the government requirements, he knew well what conditions Ernie would encounter because he visited Tenwek once a month to consult with nurses, sign orders, and provide the minimal medical oversight required for WGM to operate a legally recognized clinic.

Dr. Probst recommended Ernie take additional medical exams in England so that he could be licensed to practice anywhere in the British Commonwealth. But further research revealed that taking and passing the Canadian Boards would serve the same purpose. So along with traveling and speaking in churches every week, Ernie spent much of that fall studying British medical practices and reviewing his previous training.

When Ernie arrived in Toronto in December 1958 and checked in at the exam site on the McGill University campus, he almost changed his mind and headed right back home. Recounting the experience years later, Ernie said, "When I met several med school graduates who had been studying full-time for months and were taking their boards for the second and third time, I became terribly discouraged. I figured, why waste the time and money? Even the weather was cold, dark, and dreary, so I felt miserable. On top of that I remained very worried about my [pregnant] wife. I kept asking myself, *Why are you even here? What's the point?* And I came oh-so-close to getting right back in the car and heading home."

That was when Ernie recalled the assurance of his college professor, whose wisdom had proven true so many times already. *If God wants me to be a missionary doctor in Africa* (and Ernie believed He did), *then God will enable me to overcome all the obstacles.* So he prayed for the best and stayed for the tests.

Later Ernie received the official notification. He had passed his Canadian Boards and was now licensed to practice anywhere in the Commonwealth. Which meant he would be, along with Jim Probst, only the second American missionary doctor so qualified in all of Kenya.

"It had to be the Lord," Ernie told everyone who rejoiced with him. "Because I was just smart enough to know I wasn't smart enough to do it on my own. By the time I finished the exams, I realized I hadn't been nearly as prepared as I wished I had been."

Someone from the Indiana University Medical Center contacted Ernie early that February of 1959 to tell him the hospital was going through a major upgrading in medical technology and equipment. Would he be interested in taking any of the older, but still serviceable, medical equipment to Africa? He told them he would, of course. They said all he needed to do was come and haul it away.

Ernie had borrowed a truck and was scheduled to drive to Indianapolis to pick up the equipment on the morning of February 18. When Sue awakened that morning feeling abdominal discomfort, Ernie considered canceling his plans. She didn't think it was anything serious. "Just a case of stomach gas," she assured him.

Yet Ernie remained concerned enough to call another missionary couple before he left town to ask the wife if she would check in on Sue a couple times during the course of the day. Then he headed off to Indianapolis to pick up the promised equipment for Tenwek Hospital.

By the time the missionary friend dropped by to see Sue later in the morning, the "gas pains" felt suspiciously like labor pains and had become a lot more regular. But how could that be? The due date was still two months away. By late afternoon Sue's water had broken, the contractions intensified, and there had been no choice but to call her doctor and head for the hospital just as Ernie arrived back home. His first look at Sue made him think she was about to hemorrhage to death. She looked so pale!

While Ernie waited anxiously outside the delivery room, Sue gave birth to a 3 lbs. 12 oz. baby boy named Richard Lee. But she barely had time to see just how fragile and blue he looked before the doctors and nurses whisked him away. Richard died a couple hours later of respiratory failure before Ernie ever saw or held his son.

Both Sue and Ernie were devastated. The following few weeks for Ernie were consumed with consoling and caring for his grieving wife while simultaneously wrapping up the details of their packing and final preparations for their departure for Africa. A couple of his uncles came to Marion to help build wooden crates to contain and protect all the donated medical equipment—including one big, old X-ray machine that would fill a small room all by itself.

As Sue struggled through the beginning of what was to be a long, slow process of physical and emotional healing, Ernie dealt with his own grief by working and focusing on all that needed to happen before their journey. Both he and Sue found relief from their pain by sharing their heartache and trying to imagine what their new life and ministry soon would be like when they got to Tenwek.

Chapter 5

Coming to Tenwek

With mixed feelings, Ernie and Sue and little Cindy bid tearful goodbyes to the Steury and Groce clans in the spring of 1959. Grateful for their families' support in their mission, their minds were on Africa even before their plane lifted off American soil. Though their years of preparation paled in comparison with the decades people had been praying for a doctor for Tenwek, Sue and Ernie were every bit as anxious to get to Kenya as their World Gospel Mission colleagues and the Kipsigis people were to greet them.

After a two-day layover in Switzerland, they landed in Nairobi on May 3, 1959. Their welcoming party included the WGM Kenya field director Jerry Fish and his wife, Bunny, an Africa Inland Mission couple from Ernie's hometown (the Martel Fennigs), and veteran missionary Alice Day, longtime friend of Sue and her family. Everyone was excited that the Steurys had finally arrived.

The Steurys spent a couple days in Nairobi going through the necessary red tape required for proper registration with immigration and the medical licensing boards. Once again Ernie thanked God for His help with the medical exams in Canada, which enabled him to be immediately and fully credentialed by the government of Kenya.

The Majesty of Africa

From Nairobi the Fishes took the Steurys on a fascinating cross-country journey toward their ultimate destination. The view from the rim of the Great Rift Valley reminded Ernie of the psalmist's declaration, "The heavens declare the glory of God; and the firmament shows His handiwork" (Psalm 19:1).

There was much of that handiwork to admire along the way: majestic vistas, curious people, and a seemingly endless procession of African animal life everywhere they looked. After an arduous day of travel over rough and rutted roads, they reached Kericho and the grounds of Kenya Highlands Bible College, a WGM school where the Steurys would live and study the Kipsigis language for their first six months in the country.

On Friday, May 8, after only a couple days in Kericho, even before they could really begin to settle in, the Steurys eagerly made their first-ever visit to Tenwek to finally see where they had felt called to spend the rest of their lives. They had seen pictures, of course, but Ernie and Sue didn't know what to expect as the ribbon of tarmac wound out of Kericho, cut through eucalyptus groves, and climbed up and down over steep, rolling hillsides covered by thousands and thousands of acres of close-cropped tea bushes. Most of East Africa's tea crop was grown in those lush green fields the Steurys could see from the road as it ran mile after mile through vast tea estates, past processing factories, managers' homes, offices, and company-owned workers' villages. Eventually the tarmac gave way to dirt as it meandered up and down, into and through the more rural highlands divided into a patchwork landscape of tiny family farms and the occasional roadside village comprised of mud huts and thatched grass roofs.

At the top of a hill five miles short of Bomet, they turned from the dirt road onto an even smaller dirt track and continued another mile or so to a small cluster of hillside buildings. As the car coasted to a stop, Ernie and Sue got their first look at Tenwek.

Tenwek's History

Missionary Willis Hotchkiss acquired the site on which Tenwek was located in the 1930s. Hotchkiss had poured out his life for the Kipsigis people, preaching and teaching among them for over thirty years. He taught the Kipsigis to use the water mill to grind their grain and to use oxen for plowing. Later he introduced maize (corn), which was scorned at first by the masses. But what really intrigued and attracted the Kipsigis was the introduction of reading and writing by *Kipng'alaldaet* (meaning "The Conversationalist"), a tribal nickname for Hotchkiss.

Originally Tenwek was an undeveloped spot that seemed ideal to Hotchkiss for a major mission station. Located 30 miles south of the equator and 120 miles east of Lake Victoria, the altitude was nearly seven thousand feet, almost high enough to be above the malaria line. The countryside was grass-covered rolling hills with spots of remaining woodland. And just down the hill, in a deep little valley, ran the Nyangores River with its beautiful falls.

Tenwek was located near the center of the Sotik District, which at that time was home to more than thirty-five thousand Kipsigis. The government estimated the total population of the tribe to be about eighty thousand, and of those, only a tiny minority was Christian. Hotchkiss explained to his younger colleague, Robert K. Smith, that good land was precious in Kenya because the soil in most of the country was not good for growing crops. Yet even though Tenwek was a particularly fertile location, no one lived there because it had been a traditional female circumcision site. Many years before, during annual circumcision rites, two young girls bled to death on the spot, and the tribe considered the ground cursed ever since.

Willis Hotchkiss applied for the site on behalf of his mission. None of the Kipsigis objected. Their basic feeling seemed to be, *That place has been cursed. If the white people want it, let them have it.* So the local government council granted Hotchkiss a thirty-three-year lease on ten acres of land for a nominal rental fee of five shillings a year. Willis Hotchkiss then turned over Tenwek and all of his other independent mission work to World Gospel Mission and left Kenya for America during the summer of 1935. Robert and Catherine Smith and their family, who had arrived in 1932, would continue with the ministry there.

Construction work began at Tenwek almost immediately. By October the Smith family moved into a sixteen-by-thirty-two-foot building designed to eventually become a garage. Foundations were poured and work begun on two permanent missionary residences before the rainy season began. The mission hired local laborers with picks, hoes, shovels, and *karais* (metal basins) to begin transforming the steep hillside terrain into a series of four-level terraces.

In March 1936 two new WGM missionaries arrived at Tenwek. Mildred Ferneau and Alice Day (the Groce family friend who had influenced Sue's decision to become a missionary) set up housekeeping. Alice immediately put her secretarial skills to good use handling correspondence for the mission and helping type the manuscript for the New Testament in Kipsigis. Mildred was assigned to run the mission's crude clinic/dispensary. And both women spent every other minute they could spare studying the language. After just two months in country, Alice took over supervision of the new day school at Tenwek.

From the moment of their arrival in Kenya, the WGM missionaries, like Willis Hotchkiss and his colleagues before them, had been bombarded with the medical needs of the African people.

As soon as the Smiths settled at Tenwek, Catherine, though never trained as a nurse, started providing very basic medical services to the local people. Most of what she and the mission offered was elementary first aid. Simple medications were given out in the open. Yet this was more medical care than the Kipsigis people could get short of a government hospital several days' walk away.

Because she did have some nurse's training, Mildred Ferneau was given full responsibility for Tenwek Station's rudimentary clinic when she arrived. The end-of-the-year report for 1936 (the year Ernie Steury started school) indicated just how busy Mildred Ferneau and her little clinic were. "There have been seven hundred clinic patients, eleven maternity cases without one casualty, fourteen inpatients . . ." plus twenty-one calls to minister to sick people in their own homes. While much of the dispensing was still done outside, weather permitting, all this work was conducted from a six-by-eight-foot corrugated iron shed like the one where the women missionaries slept.

Late one night in January of 1937, Gertrude Shryock, WGM's first fully qualified registered nurse, arrived at Tenwek. As thrilled as everyone was to have a registered nurse on hand, the need for additional expertise remained obvious. So it was that when the Field Council, made up of

Tenwek's missionary staff, held their regular business session at the end of January 1937, they sent a report back to their American headquarters. First they expressed their gratitude for Trudy's arrival. Then they unanimously requested a doctor be sent as soon as possible.

By 1939 the mission's medical report showed that 2,070 patients had been treated at the clinic and 165 inpatients had been cared for. But it was never so much the number of patients as their response to the medical treatment they received at Tenwek that encouraged the missionaries. Countless patients voluntarily gave up their charms and fetishes to put their trust in the Christian God rather than the traditional tribal witch doctors. Many who came for physical healing also found lasting spiritual healing in a personal relationship with Jesus Christ.

Tenwek's reputation spread.

In 1946 the mission finally built a bigger dispensary—sixteen by thirty-four feet—with a shingle roof. But more space to work only seemed to mean more medical work to do. On March 2, 1947, another nurse, Edna Boroff, arrived and helped lighten Trudy's load for a time. Trained also as a lab technician, Edna set up a small medical laboratory where the nurses, and eventually their trained assistants, could run simple tests, which aided greatly in diagnosis. But what had been happening for years continued to happen: Each improvement made for the effectiveness of Tenwek's ministry increased the workload for the staff because of the greater number of people who came seeking medical services.

But still no doctor came.

As the years passed, the medical needs grew in proportion to the mushrooming population of the Kipsigis people. The tribe's multiple birth rate—one out of twenty-eight pregnancies resulted in twins or triplets, compared with one out of one hundred in the United States—was as high or higher than any people group in the world. WGM began building permanent medical buildings on the new land given to the mission at Tenwek. A hospital chapel was the first structure raised on the plot. Other permanent buildings followed—two concrete wards and two small four-family units. All the beds in the new wards were soon full, and the overflow slept on the floor of the chapel.

Still no doctor came to live and work at Tenwek.

Several additional WGM nurses arrived in Kenya during the 1950s. Some helped manage the workload at Tenwek. But two of them began additional dispensaries in other parts of Kipsigis territory. The medical reputation of the missionaries at Tenwek had spread throughout the tribe.

If only there were a doctor, so much more could be done.

And yet in 1957, the year Ernie Steury completed his studies at Indiana University School of Medicine in Indianapolis, the annual report of the mission indicated that the handful of nurses stationed at Tenwek, along with their sixteen dispensary workers, treated approximately one thousand inpatients and four thousand outpatients.

As Trudy Shryock had asked more than ten years earlier, *Where was the doctor God was calling to this great ministry?* What excitement all the WGM missionaries in Kenya felt when they finally heard the great news: "He's on the way!"

And now he was here. The long-prayed-for doctor had finally arrived.

The Steurys looked around at the large welcoming party who had quickly gathered round for their first look at the doctor and his family.

Ernie later wrote, "It was a great joy to see the hospital for the first time. We enjoyed meeting each of the missionaries and renewing acquaintances with several we knew before coming to Africa."[1]

The actual tour of the medical facilities didn't take long. While the work had grown considerably since it began in a tiny utility shed almost thirty years before, Tenwek remained more of a dispensary than a hospital. But everyone involved, missionaries and Kipsigis people alike, anticipated that was going to change with Ernie's arrival.

No sooner had the nurses walked him through the wards and shown him their maternity room than they began to talk with Ernie about the need for additional facilities. In anticipation of his arrival, the staff had already begun to dream about the future. Ernie was still feeling overwhelmed with questions about the present. How would he best utilize his training and skills in such a primitive and limited setting? Where

1 *Call to Prayer,* August 1959, World Gospel Mission.

could they set up an operating room? When could he get started? What needed to be done first?

The Tenwek staff showed Ernie and Sue the house where they would live when they finished their language training in Kericho. The dwelling, with poured concrete walls and a painted stucco exterior, was located on the hillside a stone's throw below the medical buildings. Named "The Old Time Religion House" in honor of the group of folks who had donated the funds for its construction, it had been used as a missionary residence for years. But in preparation for the doctor's family, it was newly remodeled to include an indoor bathroom complete with sink, toilet, and bathtub; however, the old stucco outhouse still stood like a sentinel in the small yard behind the house.

Ernie and Sue spent most of those first days at Tenwek meeting people, struggling to remember strange new names, and trying to imagine what life would be like once they moved to Tenwek for good. Ernie also took several hours out of his day to visit a remote clinic one of the nurses manned out at Kaboson.

The Steurys' introduction to the Kipsigis people included an invitation for Ernie to preach on Sunday, May 10, in the Willis Hotchkiss Memorial Church there at Tenwek for a special prayer day service. All day long people congregated in from the countryside and many nearby Africa Gospel churches for this special time of worship and to meet the new daktari for whom they had prayed for so long. Ernie and Sue were thrilled to see more than twelve hundred people crowd in and around the church that afternoon. Even more exciting was the response to Ernie's first sermon, which was translated into Kipsigis by a veteran missionary. Dozens of nationals came forward to pray at the altar when the invitation was given at the close of the service. The congregation was uplifted. Not only did the new doctor bring promise of better medical care for the Kipsigis people, he could preach the gospel as well.

That initial trip to Tenwek gave the Steurys their first up-close-and-personal sense of the Kipsigis people—both in terms of their wonderful, welcoming spirit and their tremendous physical needs. Plus, it gave them a glimpse into their future—a small taste of what real missionary life could be like in the years ahead.

The primary struggle both Ernie and Sue faced in the next few months was with their Kipsigis language study; yet they understood the reasons for an intensive and sometimes frustrating period of language concentration. They both needed a grasp of basic Kipsigis vocabulary and grammar in order to effectively minister in that culture.

Staying in Kericho to study also made sense, because it removed any temptation for the Tenwek staff to interrupt Ernie's language lessons every time there was a medical emergency they thought a doctor should handle. So it was a toss-up whether it was the new doctor or the veteran nurses who were the most impatient for those six long months of language study to end so the Steurys could finally move to Tenwek for good. In the meantime, Ernie, Sue, and Cindy made a number of short visits to Tenwek about every other weekend to familiarize themselves with the people and to allow Ernie to consult with the nurses on the treatment of some of their most serious cases.

The First Surgery

During one of Ernie's weekend visits to Tenwek, Edna Boroff summoned him to examine a pregnant woman who had been carried into the hospital by some very concerned relatives.

"She needs to see a doctor," the family said.

Edna quickly determined they were right. She briefed Ernie about the patient's medical condition while they rushed into the maternity ward: The woman had begun labor two or three days earlier. Her water had broken, and everything had seemed fine at first. But as the hours passed, nothing more seemed to be happening. Despite steady and strong contractions, the baby was not progressing through the birth canal.

The Kipsigis women tending the young mother saw how she became weaker and weaker as time passed. They knew the baby had to be born or the mother and child would probably both die. In desperation they had taken sharp sticks and tried to dig the baby out—unsuccessfully. But in the process they had done significant internal damage to the woman, and her wounds had quickly become infected.

Recalling the case later, Ernie said, "Previously any maternity patients requiring caesarian section would be transported from Tenwek to the district hospital in Kericho. But my initial exam convinced me the woman's uterus was about to rupture. If that happened she would bleed to death in a matter of minutes—if not seconds. No way would she survive the long drive to the nearest government hospital. Which meant I had to do something quickly or both mother and baby would die."

Ernie had never before performed a caesarian section by himself. His original plans to take a year of surgical residency were canceled because the WGM board had felt they could wait no longer to get a doctor to Tenwek. So Ernie had received very little surgical training. Now there was no time to dwell on that fact. There was no one else to perform surgery. He was the only doctor within fifty miles.

The first thing Ernie had to do was find and uncrate the operating table and the surgical instruments he had shipped from the States. Then he set up Tenwek's first surgical unit in a cramped eight-by-ten-foot corner room partitioned off inside a twenty-by-twenty-foot block building (originally built as a medical ward for patients needing to stay overnight). After he assembled the operating table and the nurses sterilized his instruments in a pressure cooker Sue had brought with her other kitchen supplies, Ernie quickly thumbed through a medical text to review the procedure.

Ernie administered a local anesthesia and prayed with the woman. "I knew unless God intervened, she and the baby would die," Ernie said. "So all I could do was pray and trust the Lord. Then, believing He would undertake, I began to make an incision. Once I got inside I discovered the uterus was so close to rupturing that I didn't even need a knife to cut it open. I simply separated the muscle with my fingers and pulled the baby out.

"While the nurses worked to resuscitate the infant, I began sewing that semi-necrotic uterus back together. It was such a mess I wondered for a while if I'd ever get the bleeding under control. But God did help me. Both the mother and her baby recovered. And the woman actually prayed to accept Jesus Christ as her personal Savior before she went home.

"I was so grateful—because I realized if she and the baby had died, it could have been a very long time before people would have trusted me to operate on anyone else."

As it was, there were other real hurdles the Kipsigis people would have to overcome before they ever became comfortable with this strange new concept of surgery. It probably didn't help that the only Kipsigis word they had for surgery was the same one they used for butchery. Their lack of understanding of the basics of modern medicine further complicated things. Even Ernie's early surgical successes raised new fears and confusion among the local people. When he anesthetized patients, many of the relatives believed he had killed them before cutting them open, sewing them up, and then bringing them back to life.

While such beliefs no doubt added an aura of mystery and special power to the reputation of the new doctor at Tenwek, they also played into a long cultural heritage of fear and superstition. Where the Kipsigis Christians welcomed and very quickly accepted the mission's new doctor, Ernie soon realized it could take some time to win the trust of most people. He made many house calls and accepted every invitation he could to be with the people in their own homes to try to build their trust. But the level of acceptance he hoped for was slow in coming.

Pincher Ants in the Nursery

One day, not long after the Steurys had completed their language study at Kericho and finally settled into their new life and full-time work at Tenwek, Ernie and Sue were awakened by the cries of three-year-old Cindy. Thinking she probably needed to go to the bathroom. Ernie grabbed a flashlight and hurried into her room. As he picked up his whimpering daughter, she laid her head against him, and he felt something crawling on his face. Shifting his daughter and redirecting the beam of his flashlight, he spotted a pincher ant scurrying down his arm. Turning the light on Cindy, Ernie saw movement in her hair. More ants!

Calling for Sue, Ernie rushed his daughter back into their bedroom. The two of them removed more than a dozen pincher ants from Cindy's head. After Sue put their daughter down in their bed, Ernie went back into the child's bedroom and found more pincher ants on the bed. When he turned the light onto the wall, he was horrified—an entire army of pincher ants swarmed down the wall, heading for his daughter's bed.

Ernie thoroughly sprayed the bed, the floor, and the wall with insecticide to be sure the ants were gone. By the time he got back to bed, Cindy was vomiting. The toxin from the handful of ant bites she had received had made her sick. Ernie began to realize what could have happened if he hadn't gotten to his daughter when he did. A few minutes longer, and that swarm of ants could have killed her. Long after Cindy had gone back to sleep, Ernie laid awake in the dark, listening to the sweet sound of his daughter breathing peacefully and thanking God for His protection.

An Unusual Patient

Early in Ernie's time at Tenwek, a Kipsigis woman from a nearby village came running up to him shouting, "Daktari! Daktari! Come quickly!" He understood enough of the language that he grasped her sense of urgency. She was also saying something about dying. He slowed her down with a couple of questions. Then he realized she was talking about a cow that had just given birth.

Ernie tried to explain that he was not an animal doctor, but a doctor for people. If she understood the distinction, she obviously didn't care. She kept begging, "Please, Daktari! Come help! She will die!"

Ernie quickly asked the Lord to help him know what to say to this woman or what to do. He had no idea if or how he could help this woman, whose pleadings had become almost hysterical. Yet he realized how important this cow was to her and her family. For most Kipsigis farmers, the milk from one cow (many farmers owned only one) could mean the difference between that family's economic health and abject poverty. Ernie knew he couldn't send this farmer's wife away without trying to help.

"Take me to your cow," he told her. He grabbed a bag of assorted instruments, and they set off on a brisk walk across the countryside. During the thirty-minute hike to the farm, Ernie asked questions and tried to determine the problem.

The family's cow had gone into labor. But the calf had been breech and had become lodged in the birth canal. Fearing more for the life of the mother cow than the calf, the woman's husband had finally gotten a rope around one or two of the calf's legs and literally dragged the young animal out of its mother by sheer force. Amazingly, by the time Ernie approached the farm, the tiny calf already stood wobbly-legged beside its mother and appeared to be fine. The mother cow, however, was lying motionless on her side with a big shiny glob of something right behind her. From a distance it looked like a pile of afterbirth. But as Ernie drew closer, he saw what it was. When the farmer had pulled the calf out, the cow's entire uterus had come along with it. It had not been detached but rather was merely turned inside out and now lay outside the cow on the ground. Ernie had never seen an inverted uterus before. So the doctor/scientist part of him wanted to study the fascinating phenomenon even as the practical farm-boy side of him tried to decide how to save the poor animal.

Ernie asked the Kipsigis woman to fetch him a large container of water. When she brought it, he knelt behind the cow, lifted the uterus off the ground, and gently began to wash it free of all the dirt and grass that coated it. Finally, seeing no alternative, he began to slowly push the uterus back up into the cow with his bare hands. When he was finished, the cow pushed herself up on her feet, and her hungry, bawling newborn calf began to nurse.

Years later, when Ernie recounted his cow story to a veterinarian friend in the States, the vet confirmed that Ernie had done the right thing. The vet told Ernie, though, "It's absolutely impossible to get an inverted uterus back in a cow without first anesthetizing the animal."

"Fortunately," Ernie laughed, "I didn't know that."

Walking back to Tenwek with a satisfied smile on his face, Ernie thanked God for helping him know what to do. He couldn't help thinking, *Maybe when they start telling people what I did for that cow, more men will be willing to trust me to treat their women and their children.* Indeed, that's what seemed to happen. And as the doctor's reputation spread far and wide, more people began coming to Tenwek for help.

Blood Transfusion

A young man, Tue Seram, was brought to Tenwek on the verge of death. The diagnosis was simple: He was dying from a gastrointestinal hemorrhage caused by a perforated typhoid ulcer. But the treatment was far more difficult: Tue Seram was too weak to survive any operation without a blood transfusion—a procedure never before performed at Tenwek.

Ernie, however, knew it was possible to do the procedure. He had brought to Tenwek some blood-typing serum and a couple of bottles in which to collect and store blood. So he tested the patient to see what type of blood he needed, then explained to some of the Kipsigis staff what he wanted to do. None of them had ever given blood before, so they refused. The patient's family members took one look at the size of the bottle Ernie said he wanted to collect blood in and refused, believing that giving that much blood would kill anyone.

Fellow WGM missionary Gene Lewton, a universal donor with O negative blood, volunteered to give a unit. But Ernie needed more. An Asian businessman living in the nearby town of Bomet showed up to donate a second unit. After watching those two volunteers step forward, one of the hospital's Kipsigis staff came to Ernie and said, "If you people can give blood for our people, surely we can too!" So he gave a third unit of blood.

When Ernie set up the equipment to give Tue Seram the transfusion of blood taken from one American, one Asian, and one African, the man's family watched with fascination. Ernie chuckled, "I think they fully expected their loved one to change colors as the blood flowed into his veins."

The transfusion worked. The patient regained enough strength that Ernie decided to operate immediately. Unfortunately none of the nurses were available right then, so Ernie drafted his first donor, Gene Lewton, to assist him in surgery. For this fellow missionary, who had come to Kenya with WGM as a builder to oversee the mission's construction projects and industrial operations, this was his first opportunity (though not his last) to participate in surgery. Ernie showed Gene how to scrub.

Together they prayed with the patient before administering anesthesia and starting surgery.

"That first OR was so tiny," Gene recalled, "Ernie actually had me crawl under the operating table to stand on the other side of the patient and hand him the instruments as he called for them." This veteran missionary builder watched in amazement as the doctor did some human plumbing—cutting out the ulcerated section of the patient's intestines, reconnecting the healthy tissue, checking carefully for additional leaks, then quickly and efficiently closing the patient back up. "What a memorable experience!" Gene Lewton exclaimed.

It turned out to be an even more significant experience for the first Tenwek patient ever to receive a blood transfusion. Tue Seram not only quickly regained his strength and his health, but he accepted Christ as his Savior during his recovery. "It was wonderful to see the difference in him," Ernie said. "He was healed not only physically but spiritually as well. What was now in his heart showed through on his face."

After two months of convalescence, Tue regained most of the sixty pounds he had lost during his illness. On Tue's last day at Tenwek, Ernie gathered the nurses and some of the other staff in Tue's room for a time of prayer and praise. The grateful patient first thanked the medical staff and then those who gave blood. Finally, he thanked God for making him well again. Afterwards, he went back to his family and his village—"the same color on the outside but a changed man on the inside."

There were many "firsts" during the Steurys' early days of service at Tenwek—not just for the Kipsigis people but also for the new doctor. Countless times Ernie executed what he laughingly called "cookbook surgery." When a patient required an operation Ernie had never before performed (and sometimes had never even witnessed), he faced a terrible dilemma. "I knew if I operated and failed, my patient might die, but I also knew if I didn't operate they would certainly die. I was the only doctor there. So I had no choice but to pray, prop a medical textbook open beside me, and pray constantly for the Lord to give me wisdom and steady hands."

"Many were the times Ernie brought medical books home to study the night before a new and difficult surgery," Sue said. "He'd finish reading by lantern light, and then he'd get down on his knees and pray for the patient and ask the Lord's help with the next day's operation."

More often than not those patients made remarkable recoveries, indicative of Ernie's innate gifts as a surgeon and his amazing aptitude for quick learning, or, as Ernie modestly explained, "God was so gracious to help."

During his first year at Tenwek, Ernie performed nearly two hundred surgeries. It was on-the-job training for a doctor who had no formal surgical training. The Steurys later reported, "The Lord has given us unusual opportunities the past few months, especially in the field of surgery . . . a man gored by a buffalo, a woman stabbed through the abdomen with a spear, and several cases requiring removal of parts of the large or small intestine. Many of these have been brought back to good health and to a saving knowledge of Jesus Christ. The Lord has richly blessed the work, and we praise HIM for it!"[2]

For many years the Kipsigis people had relied on the missionary nurses at Tenwek for medical care; thousands had found help there in the past. Before Ernie's arrival, surgery patients might have been transported and treated at the nearest government hospital, but most could not have found or afforded necessary treatment and almost certainly would have died. As the new doctor at Tenwek, Ernie was making an immediate and significant impact. He sensed it, and so did the Kipsigis people. More and more of them heard stories of the powerful new doctor at Tenwek who treated people in ways they had never heard of before. Many people who were dying went to Tenwek to be seen and treated by this doctor and came home to their families and their villages—happy, alive, and well again.

2 Steury letter to American supporters, July 1960.

Chapter 6

Challenges of Life in Africa

Cultural Differences

Despite the spreading reputation of Tenwek and its new doctor, and despite the increasing numbers of Kipsigis streaming into the hospital for treatment, Ernie continued to encounter significant cultural obstacles to the growth of his medical ministry in that part of Kenya.

One WGM nurse, Edna Goff (who arrived at Tenwek along with Eldema Kemper in 1960), told of the time a local pastor ran to the Tenwek mission station to tell Gene Lewton, "Come! Down by the river there is a woman who has been beaten." Gene heard enough to know the situation called for a doctor, so he summoned Ernie and they hurried to the spot. But the woman was no longer there. She had been carried home, so Ernie had to hike another quarter of a mile to reach her.

Ernie and his team found the woman lying on the ground, writhing and moaning in pain. Tears coursed down her cheeks. Standing at one side and grinning mockingly was her husband, who had beaten her because she had refused to take his clothes to the river and wash them at ten o'clock at night.

While examining the woman, Ernie found a large, open, lacerated head wound evidently inflicted with a *panga* (a long, sharp, machete-like weapon also used as a tool to cut shrubs and chop brush). Blood from the wound ran down the woman's neck and back. Her hand had been broken and mangled until it hardly resembled a hand, and her elbow was badly swollen.

When Ernie proposed taking her to the hospital, the husband laughed, saying he had no money to pay for treatment. Though Ernie offered to take her anyway, the man stubbornly refused. When Ernie continued to press, an old woman dressed in animal skins and standing just beyond a nearby fence began shouting: "Let her alone! There is nothing wrong with her! Can't you see there is nothing wrong with her!" It was a local witch doctor, come to practice her own brand of medicine. There was nothing Ernie and his staff could do except return to the hospital with a heavy heart—never to see that woman again.

Witch doctors often saw the growing acceptance of the hospital and modern medicine as a threat to their traditional power and influence in the tribe's culture. But their opposition was usually indirect—attempting to apply persuasion and pressure on patients through older, tradition-bound friends and relatives—rather than posing any serious physical menace for the missionaries or the hospital staff.

"The majority of the Kipsigis people accepted and welcomed us from the start," Sue recalled. "They are naturally a warm, outgoing, and loving people. And we soon found they felt special empathy and compassion for us when they learned our arrival had been delayed due to my pregnancy and the subsequent loss of our baby son, Richard. Sons play such an important role in their family culture that the Kipsigis Christians in particular identified deeply with our loss; they prayed for us regularly before we arrived and then went out of their way to demonstrate caring kindness and genuine concern once we got there."

Even so, there was some initial skepticism about the transformation of Tenwek from a clinic/dispensary to a fully functioning hospital. But one day within months of Ernie's arrival, the assistant chief of the area was carried to the hospital by some of his friends. He complained of severe pain in his hip.

When Ernie saw the man, he prayed for wisdom to know what to do. "I'd heard stories about his angry, active opposition to anything having to do with God, the church, or the mission." Now here was this Kipsigis leader, who had been very public about his enmity toward the hospital, coming to Tenwek for treatment. "God was certainly giving us a great opportunity to witness. We found the cause of his severe pain was a hip abscess, so we put him in bed and started antibiotic treatment. We were thrilled to see him walking again by the third day; the Lord had worked a miracle. The man left the hospital well in body and with the Holy Spirit working in his heart. We have since heard reports of his friendship toward the mission, and we are praying that the Lord will bring this man to Himself. Please pray with us."[1]

The Kipsigis culture itself presented real obstacles. From the beginning of their dispensary work in the 1930s, the Tenwek nurses had a hard time recruiting and training national helpers because Kipsigis custom called for a very careful, almost religious, avoidance of blood and other bodily fluids for fear of contamination. Call it superstition or taboo, the belief that physical or spiritual danger or death could result from such exposure reduced the number of Kipsigis willing to assist the missionaries in patient care. For years, only a handful of eager helpers stepped forward. Most of them, through the example of the dedicated missionaries and as a result of their own experience, came to accept and understand their calling as a form of sacrificial Christian service for their own people. Even so, a great percentage of the Kipsigis looked down at them and questioned their wisdom in defying the old cultural attitudes and taboos regarding bodies, body fluids, and bodily functions.

Though the Kipsigis spoke in awe of the new doctor's surgical skills, and even though many of the most curious tribes people would stand on boxes in the yard outside the surgery room window to catch a glimpse of an operation in progress, the thought of working with the doctor and actually caring for the personal physical needs of the patient, even if that patient were a relative or friend, was culturally abhorrent to most of them.

Ernie soon found that the most effective way of combating the customs was by example. He figured that by taking on those jobs the Kipsigis considered most unpleasant and unacceptable, he would prove their superstitions baseless. So it was that the new American doctor, in addition to examining and admitting new patients, making daily rounds to see everyone in the hospital, and performing one or more surgeries almost

1 *Call to Prayer,* February 1960, World Gospel Mission.

every day, also personally made certain the hospital's latrines were cleaned before he went home each night.

More primitive than American-style outhouses, these latrines provided no seating; rather, there was just footing in the form of a couple short lengths of two-foot-by-four-foot boards flanking a small hole in the floor with a long drop to a pit below. But even a set-up as rudimentary as that often required instruction for many people whose traditional sanitation practice consisted of digging shallow holes in the bush out behind their huts.

Many of Tenwek's patients were extremely sick. For them and for the family members and friends who accompanied them to the hospital, proper usage of the facilities was a trial-and-error learning experience. Consequently, latrine cleanup was always an unpleasant job, yet Ernie accepted it with no complaints.

Ernie further demonstrated a servant's heart in his bold and determined response to another taboo—dealing with the bodies of patients who died.

For centuries Kipsigis burial practices reflected their culturally conditioned fears regarding death and bodies. When a Kipsigis man died, his eldest son would come for the body in the middle of the night. To avoid contamination, he would strip off all of his own clothing before hoisting his father's naked body over his shoulder for a lonely trek to the traditional burial ground outside his village. There he would place the body in a shallow grave he himself had dug. The whole thing was a sad and solitary ritual—the most unpleasant of duties conducted in darkness and dread. When an elderly woman died, burial duty fell to the second son. If a child died, it usually fell to the mother to scrape out a grave and bury her own.

The death of hospital patients at Tenwek sometimes complicated the traditional tribal system. On some occasions the family member whose designated duty it was to dispose of the body was not there. Other terminal patients came or were carried to Tenwek for treatment from such a distance that it was impractical or impossible to transport their bodies all the way back to their home villages. So the mission allowed burials on a plot of wooded hillside land not far from the hospital grounds. The bleak and woeful burial rituals conducted there never failed to touch

Ernie's heart, even though he had accepted the realization that not all of his patients would recover, no matter how expert his treatment nor how earnest his prayers. It particularly pained him to watch a weeping and wailing young mother trudge along the trail between the morgue and the cemetery, carrying her dead child in her arms.

So it was that Ernie frequently helped a mourning family member carry the body of a loved one to the Tenwek cemetery or to one of the local villages for burial. Though he usually performed these selfless acts of service with relatives under cover of darkness, the local people soon heard the stories and retold them throughout the tribe.

Ernie considered his actions merely a simple, natural expression of Christian compassion and servanthood. Years later he understood the powerful symbolic message that his acts of kindness communicated. In the view of the local culture, he was identifying himself as a loving family member who so cared about his patients that he took on and shared the most unpleasant responsibility—burial duty—ever required of a Kipsigis son or parent.

The local people were so impressed with Ernie's compassion that before long some of the hospital's national Christian staff broke custom and voluntarily began helping relatives deal with the bodies of patients who died. "I was one of the first to do that," recalled one of Tenwek's African staff and an active church leader in a local congregation. "Dr. Steury was a humble man whose example said more than his words. He didn't preach and tell us our old tribal customs and attitudes about bodies were wrong and needed to change; he simply taught the Kipsigis people a whole new way of demonstrating Christian love and compassion to one another. We no longer have the same problem finding people who want to work in a hospital; in our culture today it is one of the most desired and respected jobs anyone can have."

Staffing Shortage

With a busy surgical schedule, an overflowing inpatient population, and more outpatients lining up than could be seen in a day, the professional nursing staff was spread thinner than ever before. World Gospel Mission immediately began to recruit additional nurses for Tenwek. But it proved impossible to keep pace with the demand. The only way to bridge the gap was with national staff, which presented an incredible challenge—and not just in terms of numbers.

For many years almost all of Tenwek's national hospital staff were Kipsigis Christians recruited from local congregations of the Africa Gospel Church. "Not only were they warm and loving Christian people," Ernie said, "but they were some of the brightest and most capable people from the Kipsigis tribe. They learned quickly. And they learned well."

And yet bringing modern medical care to a remote African hillside using limited financial, technological, educational, and human resources presented some unique challenges for Ernie, for the professional nursing staff, and for their mission agency.

"How do you get across the importance of establishing and maintaining a sterile field in the operating room," Ernie asked, "when you're instructing a surgical assistant who has lived her entire life in a mud hut with a dirt floor? For that matter, where do you find prospective X-ray technicians among a people who have never had an electric light in their own homes? Or where do you begin lab-assistant training for someone who has never before looked through a microscope?"

The people were willing and able to learn. But working in the realm of modern medical science demanded an instinctual as well as intellectual leap for anyone growing up in a world and a way of life no more than a generation or two removed from the Stone Age. With no inherent cultural technology or even any significant indigenous mechanical experience, it's not surprising most Kipsigis had little basis for faith in, or understanding of, modern medicine or the underlying science on which it was based.

It was an uncommon luxury for one of the missionary nurses to assist Ernie in surgery—their skills, time, and energy were better used screening and treating patients who didn't require a doctor's attention. Occasionally Ernie drafted one of the other missionaries to assist him, but he soon came to depend on bright young Kipsigis staff members like Ezekiel Kerich. Ezekiel had received formal training in Nairobi as a lab technician but quickly learned how to dispense medications, administer shots, prep patients for surgery, and assist Ernie in the operating room.

Equipment and Technology

By no means were all the challenges facing Tenwek Hospital related to cultural and staff issues. Providing modern medical treatment at such a remote location posed serious technological obstacles.

The hospital generated its own electricity. But with the high cost of diesel fuel, the mission could afford to operate the power plant only a few hours every day, which was why electrical equipment such as the maternity ward's incubators required a low-tech back-up plan—hot water bottles and blankets—to keep premature babies warm. Evening rounds had to be conducted by lamplight. And Ernie cranked up a small back-up generator to power operating room lights for any after-dark emergency surgery. If it broke, he had to fix it.

The facilities and the equipment itself often dictated how and what services could be provided. The number of lab tests the hospital conducted was limited not just by the level of the staff's expertise but also by the lack of available laboratory space. For years Tenwek's medical library consisted of a couple shelves of books over a desk crammed in a space originally designed as a supply closet. And Ernie's original operating room truly was so small that the only way for a nurse or the surgeon to get from one side of the patient to the other was to duck under the operating table.

The supplies, instruments, and medical equipment, much of which had been donated, were old though serviceable and better than anything to be found anywhere in Kenya outside the capital city of Nairobi. A prime example was the bulky but venerable X-ray machine transported to Africa along with the Steurys' other original freight shipment.

Challenge number one was finding a place where the X-ray would even fit. There was no room for such a monstrosity in any of the current medical buildings. Gene Lewton remembered, "Ernie and I finally decided the only place for it was in the old garage building [originally built as a residence for the first missionaries living at Tenwek in the 1930s] a couple terrace levels down the hill below the hospital. That was the best we could do at the time. And it was a whole lot less inconvenient than transporting patients all the way into Kericho every time we suspected a broken bone—which is what we had to do all those years before Ernie came.

"I helped install the machine in the building. Then I built a safety wall and attached a lead shield for Ernie to stand behind when he cranked that thing up. But many were the times I saw him peek over that shield or step out from behind the wall while the X-ray was running to make certain his patient remained still and positioned just right.

"I never seriously considered the dangers of that until we realized the old machine was scattering enough X-rays that a twenty-five-foot grevillea tree outside the building eventually withered and died from radiation exposure. After that, even though he knew brief discharges posed little or no threat to individuals needing just one or two X-rays, Ernie took special care to warn patients where to line up outside the building in order to keep out of the X-ray's line of fire while they waited their turn. And with that tree as an object lesson, the people listened. Yet Ernie himself stayed and stood in that X-ray room for shot after shot after shot—using the same big, durable X-ray machine for years because it was the only one we had."

Necessity dictated a lot of Ernie's medical ministry during those early years at Tenwek. There always seemed to be more demands than he could meet. And one of the needs that always appeared at the top of any checklist was more space.

From the day Ernie arrived in Kenya, Tenwek Hospital was operating at capacity and beyond. But then that was nothing new. Years of overcrowding in the wards had long since convinced the mission of the need for a new medical building. Since the nurses couldn't keep up with the demand, WGM didn't dare add to the hospital until they had a resident doctor in place to shoulder the increased caseload. Plus they wanted their new doctor's professional input before they proceeded with any hospital expansion plans. So it didn't take long for Ernie to recognize and begin talking to headquarters back in Marion, Indiana, about the pressing necessity for a new building with space to house the X-ray department, a larger laboratory, an outpatient examining room, business and staff offices, sterilizing facilities, and a standard-sized operating room. "This building will be called the Shryock Medical Building in honor of Mrs. Gertrude Shryock Root who faithfully labored among the Kipsigis for so many years. The cost of the new building will be approximately $13,500."

Construction of the building had just begun the following year, 1961, when Ernie wrote, "The number of patients and the scope of work here at Tenwek Hospital has been steadily increasing, and the need for additional space has become more acute. Many have been turned away for lack of space and time unless the condition required immediate surgery. Our present operating room, office, dispensary and laboratory are in a small four-room building originally built as four two-bed wards. The rooms are very crowded, but much has been accomplished in the tight quarters . . . The past two months we have experienced an epidemic of whooping cough in the area. Because of the lack of space the children were put to bed on the floor of the chapel. On one occasion we had fourteen patients in the chapel, and on average we have eight or ten. We are trusting the epidemic will soon end."[2]

It did. But other epidemics followed. Malaria. Measles. And more. And as each subsequent crisis waned, patient numbers continued to climb. Tenwek's hospital ministry and its impact among the Kipsigis people were greater than ever.

The growing demands energized Ernie and the hospital staff in those early years. In 1960 and again in 1961, Tenwek provided for the physical and spiritual needs of a record number of patients. Those needs, like the never-ending lines of patients who lined up outside the hospital doors every morning, might have overwhelmed some people. After all, the reason Ernie needed a bigger waiting room was that he was the only doctor at the only hospital serving—by this time—almost three hundred thousand members of the Kipsigis tribe.

No matter how many patients Ernie and his staff could treat at Tenwek, there were many more they couldn't. No sooner was the Shryock building dedicated—freeing up enough space to nearly double the number of available hospital beds to more than sixty—than those beds filled and the staff began plans to add yet another ward.

"On the one hand, such growth in our hospital ministry was very exciting," Ernie acknowledged. "Not only were we better able to treat the

2 *Call to Prayer*, July 1961, World Gospel Mission.

physical needs of more people, it also meant an increase in our spiritual impact."

From the time his college roommate had talked him into switching majors by arguing that medicine could be a more effective evangelism tool than preaching, Ernie had recognized the dual role of a Christian missionary doctor. Then when he arrived at Tenwek and saw the incredible and unending physical needs of the people, he quickly faced the realization that all the medical treatment Tenwek could offer, as important as it might be, was merely temporary. Every one of his patients would die—sooner or later. Therefore he obviously needed to be as concerned about their spiritual health as he was about their physical condition.

"Which is why, from that very first emergency caesarian section, my staff and I stopped and prayed with (or at least for) every patient before every surgery. And we had an understanding that everyone who came to Tenwek for medical care—outpatients and inpatients alike—would be presented with the gospel message while they were with us."

That spiritual emphasis began paying dividends immediately. Dozens of patients made decisions for Christ the first year or two. And that encouraging number continued to grow to 163 people who became Christians during 1962.

Yet what continued to trouble Ernie were the sheer multitudes of people who weren't being reached and helped either spiritually or physically. "One of the things that bothered me most," he admitted, "was the number of patients I saw with preventable conditions. Little children dying from common childhood diseases for lack of a basic vaccination program. Patients dying of worms or amoebic dysentery contracted from contaminated drinking water and unsanitary conditions in their homes. I would treat their condition and often save their lives, our staff would nurse them back to health, and then we'd send them home where they'd encounter the same causal factor again and the whole cycle would repeat itself."

Ernie and the rest of the Tenwek staff were stretched to the limit just trying to cope with the very sickest segment of the population who came through the hospital doors. They simply didn't have the personnel or the financial resources to even think about the sort of broader, preventative measures Ernie knew could have an even bigger impact for many more people. Maybe someday. In the meantime, Ernie had to content himself with what physical and spiritual healing he could provide his patients.

Healing Bodies, Renewing Lives

The staff commonly saw broken bones at Tenwek Hospital. Those who climbed trees, played football (soccer), drank beer, and encountered wild animals often sustained serious injuries. One boy, however, broke his thighbone while running. Thirteen-year-old Arap Ruto was brought to the hospital in severe pain with his left thigh badly deformed. X-rays showed a cyst on the femur six inches above the knee. Ernie took the boy to surgery, removed the entire cyst, and sent it to Nairobi for diagnosis. The days in bed seemed long to Arap Ruto, as he was unable to move much with his left leg in a Thomas splint. However, several days after surgery, he gave his heart to the Lord when he heard the gospel and realized that Jesus died for him. The change in his heart and life was a blessing to everyone.

Arap Ruto seemed to be singing or reading his Bible most of his waking hours. He also shared his new faith and volunteered to read the Bible to every patient who occupied the bed next to his. In the evenings when Ernie walked up to the hospital to check on patients, he could hear the boy's voice for some distance—singing songs of praise and devotion to the Lord.

Three weeks after surgery, the staff received the pathology report from the Nairobi lab—the cyst was benign. So a few days later, they took Arap Ruto back to surgery to put in a large bone graft from the tibia and iliac crest so that his thighbone might begin to fill in the large gap where the cyst had been removed. That operation was successful, and the following three months of bed rest resulted in good healing of his thighbone.

"Arap Ruto has gone home now, but his radiant spirit made a lasting impression here at Tenwek. Please pray that this young man [will remain strong in his faith] as he goes back to live in his [non-Christian home environment. And that] God is able to finish the work that He has started in this young life!"[3]

3 *Call to Prayer,* November 1962, World Gospel Mission.

Another early and memorable case led to what was the first neurosurgical procedure ever performed at Tenwek, perhaps the first such operation ever done in that part of Kenya. Yet Ernie recalled the whole episode in matter-of-fact terms: "The man was brought in semi-conscious. He had been hit on the head with a stick topped with a steel ball. We took X-rays which showed a very severe fracture with a large piece of bone depressed on the brain. We operated the same day to elevate the bone. And the man completely recovered and is going home [soon]. The Lord has wonderfully answered prayer."

Stories such as these further enhanced the reputation of Tenwek and of the young missionary the Kipsigis had given the name *Mosonik,* or "Left-Handed One." Like the majority of individuals in most populations, including the Kipsigis, Ernie's dominant hand was his right. However, necessity had taught him to be almost ambidextrous in the operating room, so anyone observing him in surgery was impressed by how much he used his left hand. And whenever he conducted pelvic exams, he always did so left-handed, so his maternity patients were the first to begin referring to him as Mosonik. The nickname not only stuck but spread quickly throughout all of Kipsigis land.

But the doctor's busy hands, along with the rest of his body and spirit, needed a little rest. So as their first four-year term came to an end, the Steurys began making plans for their scheduled yearlong furlough back in the States, to begin in 1963. Ernie and Sue looked forward to reconnecting with family and friends, reporting on their work to supporters, and representing WGM in a speaking ministry throughout the country. There would be a brand-new Steury returning to the States as well: Jonathan David had been born on December 12, 1961. WGM felt fortunate and excited to have found a young doctor and her teacher-husband to fill in at Tenwek while the Steurys were stateside, with long-range plans for this new doctor to continue in ministry at the hospital alongside Ernie after that.

Chapter 7

So Many Need Our Help

For Ernie and Sue, time with family and friends passed quickly and ended on a disappointing and unexpected note. The doctor who had begun working at Tenwek just before the Steurys left on furlough decided rather suddenly not to stay. And because the hospital needed a qualified physician on site to insure adequate medical care, WGM had no choice but to ask Ernie and Sue to cut short their time in the States and hurry back to take over the hospital work in Kenya again in March 1964. The abrupt change of plans was complicated by the fact that Sue was pregnant again and due to deliver the end of April. Sue was surprised that the airline let her on the plane because her due date was only a few weeks away. The Steurys took off from New York on March 27, stayed in London one day to rest, and arrived in Nairobi not long after dawn on Easter Sunday.

When they realized they would be back in Kenya before the baby's birth, Ernie had suggested they utilize the Nairobi hospital where Jonathan had been born. But Sue knew that Ernie's hectic hospital schedule would not allow him the time to stay with her in Nairobi to await the birth. Plus, she didn't want to be away from home and her other children, Cindy and Jon, so she argued for having the baby at Tenwek. Ernie reluctantly agreed. Thus it was that Nathan Edward, weighing in at 9 lbs. 8 oz., finally arrived two weeks late on May 30, 1964.

"We didn't anticipate the response of the people to the first white baby ever born at Tenwek Hospital," Sue said. "The Kipsigis women in particular were thrilled. It was as if they were saying to me, 'You had your baby at our hospital; now you are one of us.'"

The excitement and joy the Steurys shared over Nathan's arrival was tempered by the anticipated departure of Cindy for boarding school at

Rift Valley Academy (RVA) in Kijabe, a good half-day's drive away. "Most missionary families sent their kids off to school starting in second grade. And I'd dreaded that day for years," Sue said. "We'd managed to put that off for Cindy by being on furlough during most of the 1963–64 school year. But now the time had come, and I just wasn't ready."

RVA was an excellent school with a great reputation for its high academic standards, its committed Christian staff, and a loving family atmosphere that became home away from home not just for children of other WGM missionaries in Kenya but for MKs (missionary kids) representing several mission agencies working in many different African nations.

"I just wasn't sure that any third grader was ready to leave home to go to school. I definitely wasn't ready to let mine go," Sue said.

Cindy's absence left a big hole in the home life of the entire Steury family. Three-year-old Jonathan regularly reminded everyone of their loss every time he asked how long it would be before his big sister came home and whenever he displayed a normal preschooler's frustration that his baby brother could not go outside and play with him. Sue or Ernie wrote their daughter every week. And every month or so, they tried to find the time and an excuse to at least pass through Kijabe; however, the many other demands on their personal and professional lives made it impossible to visit the school nearly as often as they would have liked.

As happy as Ernie was to be back serving the Lord among the Kipsigis people at Tenwek, the thought of another four long years being Tenwek's only physician—on call twenty-four hours a day, seven days a week—was a serious emotional letdown. To make matters worse, the workload at the hospital was even heavier than it had been when he left.

One late afternoon just before Christmas, Ernie heard the Kaboson Land Rover enter the hospital grounds. When he saw Ramona Thomas (the WGM nurse who ran the outlying Kaboson clinic near the border of the Maasai territory) driving, he knew his work for the day was not yet finished.

Ramona brought with her a Kipsigis man who had been injured the previous night in a fight when a number of Maasai warriors had attempted to steal his cattle. On this occasion the victim of the attack had suffered a serious chest wound. But when Ernie asked if an arrow had hit him, the man assured Ernie that one of the Maasai had stabbed him with a knife. Though he couldn't see or feel anything in the wound, Ernie took an X-ray as a precaution He put in a tube connected to a water-seal bottle to allow the collapsed lung to re-expand and the blood in the chest cavity to drain. Then he closed the wound.

"The staff had already settled this patient in a ward when the X-ray was ready for viewing," Ernie said. "What a shock to see the outline of a barbed arrow with a four-inch metal shaft, inside his chest, embedded in the collapsed lung. When the arrow struck the man and entered his chest, he never noticed the hollow wooden shaft that had become dislodged and fallen to the ground. When he felt the blow, he'd looked up and seen a Maasai warrior close by and just assumed a knife had struck him.

"We rushed the patient back to surgery, and there, with God's help and the chest opened, we did get the arrow removed and the lung clamped and sutured to control the bleeding. Two weeks later that patient rode with me to the Kaboson dispensary on his way home."

But it wasn't the unusual nature of such work as much as the sheer amount of that work that put a strain on the entire Tenwek Hospital staff. The Steurys' early January 1965 prayer letter summed up the busyness of the first few months of their second term by saying: "Christmas holidays are usually quiet at the hospital with not as many patients as usual. But there is always the exception. Tuesday morning after Christmas, at 3:00 a.m., Ernie was called to the hospital for surgery. He returned home at 7:00 a.m. for breakfast, then back to the hospital [for rounds]. 10:00 a.m. to 1:00 p.m. he was in a hospital board meeting, then home for lunch. Then while showing a couple visiting government doctors around the hospital he was called to see an emergency patient with a bowel obstruction. By 3:00 p.m. things were being prepared for surgery. During that surgery, two more emergency surgical cases were admitted—another bowel obstruction and a C-section. By the time he had finished the third one, the night had passed. The doctor came dragging into the house about 6:30 a.m. (after more than twenty-six hours on the go), had breakfast, and napped for a couple hours before returning to the hospital to see the many other sick ones waiting for his attention. We are thankful to report that all four of those surgical patients are well on the road to recovery."

On the back of one copy of that prayer letter, which went to former Kenya missionary colleagues then working at mission headquarters back in the States, Sue addressed a personal note. She apologized for responding on Ernie's behalf, saying he had been too busy to even look at the pile of mail on his desk. By way of explanation she wrote: "This is a typical Saturday afternoon for Ernie—you know—his afternoon off!? He's up at the hospital—had one minor surgery this morning, a major surgery this afternoon, and a broken leg yet to set or put in traction. When it rains it pours! He had two emergency surgeries yesterday." Sue underlined the next two sentences for emphasis: "What's the possibility on another doctor for Kenya? They are about to wear the first one out!"

A couple months later Ernie finally wrote his own report to the same friends back at headquarters. "First of all, I want to give you a few facts about the hospital. Number of beds—50; number of outpatients in 1964—6,526; number of inpatients—1,698; major operations (April through December)—60; minor operations—91; X-ray examinations—318. This past year 55 people found the Lord at the hospital, and so far in 1965 we have seen a wonderful response. This morning after church a former patient we operated on for a bowel obstruction last year came up to speak to me. He found the Lord while in the hospital and he wanted me to know he was still living a Christian life. This morning he was especially happy because his two young sons have also become believers now. He really is such an enthusiastic Christian; it's thrilling for us to see former patients like this."

In his letter Ernie also gave a progress report on the construction of Tenwek's newest building—a kitchen/laundry unit to service the hospital. Up until this time inpatients who came to the hospital had to bring along a friend or relative with them to prepare their meals, which only contributed to the crowded conditions, with clusters of people huddled over cook fires scattered all over the Tenwek grounds. And that had presented another challenge to quality care when traditional tribal dishes were prepared for patients whose medical condition called for dietary limitations.

Ernie went on to say he hoped they could soon get a grant from the Kenyan government to build an inpatient ward at the dispensary in Kaboson. "The needs are tremendous there. Ramona Thomas [the RN who lived on site] is seeing as many as 90 outpatients a day. We are also being asked to open up more dispensaries in other locations, but we just don't have the staff. Pray that the Lord will send some nurses and doctors and hospital administrators out to help us."

The Need for Power

Ernie's dreams were not limited to plans for new buildings or the acquisition of additional staff. In his relatively short tenure in Kenya, he had already caught one of the visions first held by Willis Hotchkiss and the WGM missionaries he led to Tenwek more than thirty years before. Ernie wrote headquarters that in considering the equipment needed to furnish the new kitchen/laundry facility ("a proper washer, extractor to spin the clothes, a set of cookers, dishes, trolleys, etc. for the unit"), he had been consulting with his medical colleague with Africa Inland Mission. "Dr. Probst insists that we should investigate the falls again with the idea of putting in all electrical equipment in the new unit. The hydroelectric scheme would be adequate for that . . . and the savings in fuel [used by the generators] for the next four or five years would pay for the hydroelectric equipment. There is a unit available in Koru, but we do not know if it would fit our situation."

Other missionaries had told Ernie about earlier explorations into the hydroelectric option for the mission. In the mid-fifties someone had donated a used turbine generator set to WGM. They shipped it all the way to Kenya at great expense and even sent an engineer out to install it. But the local people had opposed the idea. They had been afraid that when the water went into the machine, the turbine would eat it, and their cows would have no water to drink. Demonstrations had been held to show tribal leaders where the water went in and the same water came out. But they couldn't understand how you could make power without consuming something. So the whole plan had fallen apart.

But Ernie wanted to bring up the idea again and maybe have the mission apply once more to use the falls as a power source. He indicated he had spoken with some local officials "who told us they were sorry the falls were denied [earlier], and if we ever want them [again], we can have them. It remains to be seen whether they really meant that. All of this will need much prayer and the leading of the Holy Spirit. Whatever we do [about an added source of power] will involve a lot of money, but we need to expand to take care of the needs."

As a doctor, it was that great *need* Ernie saw all around him that not only directed and drove his daily work; it fueled his future dreams as well. Whether those dreams involved improved nutrition, additional space, more trained medical assistance, or added electrical power, just imagining how each of those things could affect Tenwek's ability to meet more people's needs in the future gave Ernie an added measure of hope to press on with the many and varied needs of the present.

Ernie's faith, while tested by ongoing demands and challenges, somehow remained strong and determined, as reflected in a prayer support letter written in the summer of 1965 that began: "Dear Friends, Progress is the key note today, whether it is in the work of WGM in Kenya, the outreach of our Africa Gospel Church, or the development of new African countries." He told of recent reports from four Kipsigis church workers "who have been taking the good news of Jesus Christ to their own people and other tribes living outside the Kipsigis Reserve. This is the strength of the Church—to look beyond its own needs and reach others who have not yet heard [about Jesus]. This is progress!

"Sue helped organize a VBS teachers course. The interest and response was thrilling. Many children found the Lord as teachers applied what they learned. Other opportunities are presenting themselves. We have been invited to a completely new area [in nearby Maasai territory] where there is no Christian witness or work whatsoever . . . The people want a dispensary, school and church. Is this where the Lord wants us to step out and progress? Pray that He might lead us in this matter.

"Tenwek Hospital is also making progress. More patients, more work, more buildings, and more opportunities are a constant challenge. Here [pictured in the letter] you see our new kitchen/laundry unit which is urgently needed. We still lack $3,500 to finish the building. Can you help?"

Unexpected Encouragement

Ernie found encouragement from an unexpected source when a young medical student from Tufts University Medical School in Boston opted to spend several weeks doing a summer internship at Tenwek Hospital. Richard Morse had responded to the invitation to accept Christ during an altar call at a recent Billy Graham evangelistic crusade in Boston. In the aftermath of that experience, he had somehow learned about Tenwek and Ernie and thought it might be a worthwhile part of his medical education (not to mention his Christian discipleship) to spend a little time at a mission hospital with a missionary doctor.

Though Ernie had no idea what might come of Dick's initial inquiry, he invited him to come ahead—the first young medical student to visit and serve at Tenwek. For weeks Dick Morse followed Ernie around the hospital, observing, asking questions, and assisting in an incredible variety of cases he would never have seen at home. "At the end of his time with us," Ernie recalled more than thirty years later, "Dick stood up during our Sunday evening church service and told us he felt God was calling him to Tenwek. What a thrill and what an encouragement that was for me—to finally hear that another doctor was coming to help. Even if it couldn't be until after Dick finished his residency in another few years."

In June 1966 the Steurys' prayer letter highlighted "answers to prayer so that you may rejoice with us." They began by mentioning the many spiritual decisions made among hospital staff, students at WGM's secondary school there at Tenwek, and many nearby village people, who came for a special series of meetings featuring a visiting American evangelist.

"Another cause for rejoicing is the 'go-ahead' from government officials to start monthly dispensary visits to the new and needy Naikarra area in Maasai—where we feel the Lord is leading us.

"The patient load at Tenwek Hospital has increased very much over last year. We are glad to report an increase in those finding spiritual help as well as physical healing . . . Forty-six patients have accepted the Lord in the first four months of 1966 compared to fifty-six for the whole year of 1965. For this we rejoice! As you see, due to the increase in patients, there are also increased opportunities to witness to many who would never hear the gospel otherwise. For many come to the hospital who would never go to church.

"We are rejoicing too in the number of children being reached in our Vacation Bible School programs.

"Politically speaking we can rejoice in our capable leader, President Kenyatta, who, in the face of great problems, has stood for the right and maintained peace in his country. Pray that the Lord will give him wisdom as he continues to oversee the affairs of Kenya."

Crowded

The insistent knocking on the front door awakened Ernie out of a deep sleep. One of the hospital staff had come to ask him to see a patient who had just arrived. The night was dark and the wind uncomfortably cold as he walked up to the hospital at one o'clock in the morning.

When he entered the emergency room, Ernie saw a middle-aged Kipsigis woman lying on the examining table moaning with severe abdominal pain. She had been vomiting. Her abdominal distension was severe enough to indicate she probably had a bowel obstruction. So preparation was made immediately to take her to surgery, and within minutes the nurses and the African staff had everything ready for the operation to begin.

They bowed their heads in prayer, knowing that God would help them in performing the surgery and trusting that the patient would find Jesus

Christ as her personal Savior before leaving the hospital. The operation went well, and the patient was in good condition when they took her down the ramp to the ward.

Ernie tried to open the ward door, but it would not budge. That was nothing unusual—he knew there must be a patient lying on the floor against the door. So he pushed gently while calling out and asking whoever was there to roll over so they could bring in a new patient. Then as they moved down the aisle between two rows of beds, they had to stop several more times to wait for various patients to get up and move their beds of blankets so the staff could get their surgery patient to her bed. Of course, prior to her admission, that bed had not been empty. Another patient had to be taken out of it and assigned to the floor to make room for her.

Tenwek Hospital had been crowded like that for months. They had fifty beds, but the inpatient count varied between 75 and 125. Many times they had more patients on the floors than in the beds. The staff knew the concrete floor was not comfortable, especially for sick people, but now they were about to run out of floor space. There were plans for a new nineteen-bed ward. Even that would not be enough beds for everyone, but it would relieve the crowded conditions and free up more floor space for the patients who wouldn't have a bed.

People were coming to Tenwek with physical needs and with hungry hearts that were responsive to the gospel. During the first six months of 1966, fifty-six patients made definite decisions for Christ.

Ernie tried *not* to sensationalize the situation. If anything, he downplayed personal hardship and the headaches the conditions caused him—figuratively or literally. "Ernie regularly bumped his head on the iron frame of those old hospital beds as he tried to get to those patients lying beneath them," Sue recalled. "But what was worse were the times he rushed home in the middle of the day to clean up and change clothes because some very sick person in a bed had vomited down on him while he examined one of the patients on the floor below."

Yet Ernie never blamed his patients. He realized they suffered more from the adverse conditions than he ever would. So whenever he spoke or wrote about the work, he tried to emphasize the needs of the people over the sacrifices he had made or the challenges he faced practicing medicine in such a primitive setting. And though Ernie recognized that the setting and conditions he worked in imposed certain limitations on the medical care Tenwek Hospital could provide, his emphasis on people's needs may explain why he refused to let those conditions dictate the quality of care Tenwek provided for patients. There was never an attitude of "this is good enough for Africa."

According to Sue, "He let his staff know they would not settle for second-best work. They couldn't do everything they might have done with more resources. But he was determined to set the highest possible standards for everything they did at Tenwek Hospital" because the people deserved, and God expected, no less.

They Come in Search of Help

Ernie's hospital staff shared that same sense of mission that enabled them to look past the difficult circumstances to focus on the ultimate needs of the people who came to Tenwek in search of help. Edna Boroff, who had been nursing in Kenya more than ten years when Ernie arrived, told this story.

"One day a nine-year-old boy named Kiplangat fell out of a tree and suffered a compound fracture of the leg. With the bone protruding from the skin, his parents knew they needed to get him to Tenwek Hospital, but there was no ambulance to call, so the family improvised a stretcher. Branches were cut from a nearby tree and tied together to form a frame, and an old burlap bag that had been used to carry charcoal was sewed across the frame to make a swinging bed.

"Suffering severe pain, the child was placed gently on the bed, [the family working] patiently to find a position for the fractured limb that would ease the pain as much as possible for the journey. Then four young men took up the stretcher and carried it for fifteen miles [up and down over rugged hilly trails] to our hospital.

"When Kiplangat arrived at Tenwek, he was in such a state of intense suffering that medication had to be given before he could even be lifted off the stretcher. Then as soon as possible the leg had to be straightened from its bent position, x-rayed, and put into traction.

"During those first few days, Kiplangat was very unhappy. The pain was so severe, and he was lonely for his family. But as he soon began to improve, we found him to be a very happy child. It was a joy to go to his bedside and talk with him. Every few days he was thrilled to receive some new picture card we gave him—or a little empty medicine bottle or some other small thing that he could hold in his hand and claim for his very own.

"His parents loved Kiplangat and had worked hard and tenderly to get him onto that crude stretcher and into the hospital. When I saw how patiently the father cared for his son, I was reminded of our heavenly Father who, with great patience and tenderness, deals with a soul that is spiritually ill, trying to bring healing to each wounded and broken heart. Here at Tenwek Hospital, we minister to many children who are afflicted with sickness of soul because they do not yet know Jesus."[4]

On the one hand, the work was so rewarding that it provided Ernie all the incentive he needed to keep going. But at the same time, after being on call night and day for week after week and month after month, the task seemed so endless that it could get very discouraging. When he had to wade through the sea of humanity huddled on the floor just to make his rounds or when the line of outpatients still waiting to be examined was as long at suppertime as it had been at breakfast, Ernie admitted, "I couldn't help wondering if God was speaking to anyone else about the devastating need I saw all around me. I remember one time being so exhausted and discouraged that I told Sue, 'I just don't understand why God isn't calling other doctors to come and help us.'

"'I'm sure he is,' Sue assured me. 'It's just that they aren't listening.'"

Ernie later recalled one of the most discouraging low points: "I had just gone to bed late one night when I noticed a glow outside my window. Then I heard the sound of tapping on the glass and a voice calling, 'Dr. Steury? Dr. Steury—come quickly!' I pulled on my clothes and rushed up to the hospital, following in the wake of Tenwek's night watchman and his lantern. When I reached the hospital I found a patient with an

4 *Call to Prayer,* October 1966, World Gospel Mission.

obstructed bowel who obviously required immediate, emergency surgery. Without it he would have died."

Ernie cranked up the hospital's back-up generators to power the operating room lights as his staff prepped the man for surgery. They prayed with the patient, administered anesthesia, and began the operation, which went slowly but was a complete success.

"Just as I finished closing the wound," Ernie said, "one of our hospital aides rushed into the OR to tell me there was yet another very serious case over in outpatient. And it went that way all night long, with one surgical case after another coming into our emergency room. I was still operating when the sun came up the next morning. I made it home a few minutes for breakfast before coming right back up the hill to work the day shift. By the time I stumbled home that evening I told Sue, 'There is just no way I can go back up to the hospital for anything tonight; I'm just dead tired. I managed a few bites of supper and headed right for bed. Not an hour passed before there was another knock on my bedroom window. It was the night watchman again, 'Dr. Steury! Dr. Steury!'

"By the time I got dressed and started up the hill this time, I was really having a personal pity party. 'I can't do this!' I told God it was just too much. 'WHY?' I demanded to know, 'Why in the world can't you find someone else to come and help me? I can't keep this up by myself!'"

But even as he hiked up the hill toward the darkened shape of the hospital buildings, verbally assaulting God with those thoughts as he walked, Ernie suddenly realized he had subconsciously begun humming the notes of a song. "I couldn't believe it," Ernie often told people later. "I said to myself, 'You've got to be crazy! There is nothing to sing about here tonight!' Then it hit me what the tune was, and God assured me with the words from that song—*The joy of the Lord is my strength.* I knew in that instant, *I can do this. Because the Lord will help me!*

"And you know what? He did give me the strength I needed as I operated that night. The surgery went quickly—and well. And I walked back home, climbed into bed, and slept peacefully until morning."

But that was by no means the last time God would need to give Ernie Steury an extra measure of encouragement and strength to do what He had called him to do at Tenwek Hospital.

The 'Cross-the-Valley Neighbor

As a teenager at the turn of the twentieth century, Mongesoi Arap Ng'etich served as a gun bearer for the famous elephant hunter, W. D. M. "Karamoja" Bell. Mongesoi converted to Christianity under the preaching of Willis Hotchkiss himself. Then, after being baptized and given a new name, Reverend Johana A. Ng'etich became the first Kipsigis missionary to his own people in Sot, the tribal division that included the territory around Tenwek. Despite violent opposition and even threats of stoning from some of his own tribesmen, he persevered to start a number of congregations throughout the area. He served as one of the original twelve elders of the Africa Gospel Church (AGC). After the AGC became a self-governing denomination in the early 1960s, Reverend Johana headed up that government as the church's moderator (the equivalent of a bishop in some denominations). Many hundreds, if not thousands, of Kipsigis came to Christ under his ministry over the years.

Reverend Johana had a way of showing up at Tenwek on mornings after Ernie had performed middle-of-the night surgery. "When I was up in the night and looked across the Nyangores Valley, I saw the operating room lights on. So I stayed awake, praying and asking the Lord to help you until I saw the lights go out again," he would tell Ernie. "How did it go? How is your patient?"

Over time Ernie learned why Reverend Johana took such an interest in the medical work at the hospital. It was because he had prayed for more than twenty years that a missionary doctor would come to Tenwek. He saw Ernie as God's wonderful answer to those prayers.

Knowing that many of those late-night operations were emergency C-sections, Reverend Johana also felt a special empathy for everyone involved. He had lost his first wife and their baby during childbirth, and he was grateful to God that the presence of a missionary doctor at Tenwek meant other families would be saved from such a heartbreaking experience.

This sainted old prayer warrior was a constant encouragement to all the missionaries at Tenwek, but especially to Mosonik. "The two of them became great friends," Sue said. "Reverend Johana was like a spiritual father to Ernie." So whenever Ernie turned on the back-up generator to provide power for some late-night emergency surgery, he knew the operating room lights would also signal his old 'cross-the-valley neighbor to connect with a Higher Power on his behalf. Some nights the young surgeon sensed neither he nor his patient would survive until morning without the auxiliary energy and strength drawn through that old man's powerful back-up prayers.

Ernie wanted the Kipsigis people to recognize the spiritual power of prayer and the even greater love of God. He not only shared the good news of Jesus with each of his patients, but he also required that all fetishes and charms given out by local witch doctors be removed before anyone could be admitted and treated at the hospital. "We wanted them to know without a doubt," explained Ernie, "that the God we prayed to was more powerful than the spirits and superstitious notions their witch doctors relied on."

Ernie knew his theory was working when he saw a cardboard sign at the entrance door to the hospital. Eliud, one of the national staff, had written in crude lettering: "We treat. God heals." But before long, the wording changed after Ernie received feedback that some of the hospital's Hindu patients, mostly Indian shopkeepers from the nearby village of Bomet, had expressed their agreement with the sign. "We want to make sure our Hindu friends understood what God we were talking about," Ernie said. So they painted a big sign saying in English,

Welcome to
Tenwek Hospital
We treat; Jesus heals.

Then they planted that sign with its simple statement of faith on the hillside above the hospital grounds. Those same words are now painted on a concrete sign that still stands on that spot today, greeting patients and visitors and everyone who enters or even passes by. Those four little words powerfully summed up what the hospital did and why, making clear Tenwek's mission and beliefs: *We treat; Jesus heals.*

Chapter 8

Dealing with Kipsigis Traditions

Of course, many situations required the Tenwek staff to stand up and pit their Christian beliefs directly against cultural superstitions. Ernie did that whenever he defied tradition by helping Kipsigis families bury their dead. One time a family came back to Tenwek to collect the old clothes of their loved one who had died in the hospital six months earlier. Many Kipsigis families used such belongings to perform a traditional ritual honoring the spirit of the dead.

The staff usually held on to the clothes of deceased patients for some time since their family members later returned to collect them. Staff members would mark and store the clothes and other belongings in little cubbyholes on a shelf designated for that purpose. "But much of what was left was so old, tattered, and dirty," Sue said, "that it was almost ready to crawl off on its own after a few months down in the morgue. So we'd recently cleared the shelves and dispensed with the grubbiest garments just before this family showed up. After one of the nurses explained to the oldest son that we didn't have his father's clothing any more, the whole clan stormed into the hospital to find the doctor."

Ernie tried to apologize, but the grieving family members were too upset to listen. The son shouted at Ernie and complained that they could not have their ceremony to appease the spirit without the dead man's clothing. He insisted Ernie produce the clothing at once. Ernie told the angry son that he was sorry, but it would not be possible for him to produce the deceased man's clothing. At this the man interrupted him and said if they didn't get the clothing back, he would find out where the doctor lived, and they would all march around the house chanting and cursing his home and his entire family.

The threat of a curse was a serious thing among the Kipsigis—at least for the non-Christian people. One time a sick patient came into Tenwek braying like a donkey after an angry neighbor had cursed him. Their belief in the horrifying power of a curse was so strong that they could make each other do almost anything just by threatening one.

So the angry family members were taken aback by Ernie's relatively calm reaction: "If you must curse my house, go ahead." He explained that he and his family were not afraid because his God was more powerful than any curse. "I'm sorry about the clothes," he apologized again. "But we no longer have them. So a curse isn't going to do you any good." With that, he turned and walked away.

Some of the family members were still angry when they left. But as far as Ernie knew, they never bothered to go down and curse the Steury house.

Tale of the Loquat Tree

Occasionally the missionaries would find a benefit to some of the old tribal customs and beliefs—a lesson the Steury children learned from their love of loquats. "We had a nice loquat tree in our yard," Sue said, "but the fruit would no sooner get ripe than it would disappear. It seemed many passersby felt no qualms about shamelessly walking into our yard and picking our fruit. Those who did feel guilty were even more of a problem; instead of gently and carefully plucking a piece of fruit and sauntering away, they would break off a whole limb and run off with all the loquats hanging from its branches. So if anyone stopped and asked if they could have some of our loquats, we always said, 'Yes, but just pick the fruit. Please don't break off any branches.'"

Frustrated by how few loquats they got to enjoy, the Steury children discovered a loquat tree growing right in the middle of the Tenwek cemetery. Because of the Kipsigis' superstitious wariness of the dead, the Steury kids had the fruit of that tree all to themselves—to the consternation of any Kipsigis people who happened to look up in the tree while walking along the road below the graveyard. "Don't you eat that fruit! The spirits and the diseases of those people buried in that ground will finish you!" The Africans were so superstitious about anything that related to death and dying that they refused to speak directly and plainly, using euphemistic terms such as "finish you."

The Steury children shrugged off the warnings and were somewhat amused by the Kipsigis' alarm. But mostly they just enjoyed the supply of their "spirit-protected" fruit.

"No-Name" Wives

Some other traditional Kipsigis beliefs and practices proved to be not only interesting and amusing; they were troublesome as well. Something as simple as taking a patient's family history could be a frustrating experience for the hospital staff. Many times an obviously concerned and caring husband brought a sick or injured wife to the hospital but would answer "I don't know" when an admittance clerk asked the woman's name. In Kipsigis culture, a married man never spoke his wife's name out loud, except to officially announce that he was divorcing her. He might use any number of endearing terms—the Kipsigis equivalent of dear, honey, sweetheart, or old woman—but he would never acknowledge her by name out loud.

No matter how many offspring a husband and wife might have, they would both be reluctant to say the number out loud for fear that jealous spirits would overhear and take one of the children. And that same sort of belief in spirits also explained traditional Kipsigis architecture. For as long as anyone remembered, the Kipsigis people lived in round huts because they believed that spirits hid in corners.

Troubling Tribal Traditions

Some tribal customs and beliefs were not so innocuous and not the least amusing. Tribal superstitions regarding dead bodies, sick people, and blood certainly complicated a doctor's job and made it hard to hire willing hospital workers, but the customs that truly horrified Ernie were those that took a terrible toll in lives and suffering among the Kipsigis people themselves.

The first destructive custom Ernie confronted was the common practice of infanticide in the case of newborn triplets. Edna Boroff and the other missionary nurses had taken their stand on this issue in the 1950s when Tenwek's first set of triplets was born. The positive impact the babies' survival had among the Kipsigis was reinforced by the second set of healthy triplets born at Tenwek in 1961. As friends and neighbors watched those triplets and their families thrive, they realized there was no curse on the second-born child. As a result, within a few years the killing (or allowing the death) of the second triplet born was no longer an accepted practice among the Kipsigis people.

The second tribal tradition Ernie and the other missionaries opposed proved harder to change, because the centuries-old tribal tradition of female circumcision impacted every Kipsigis woman, not just families with triplets. Kipsigis converts to Christianity offered the first real resistance to the practice. Because of the ritual's ties to traditional religious beliefs in spirits and witch doctors, these new Christians refused to participate in the rites. American missionaries working among the Kipsigis people not only opposed female circumcision ceremonies on spiritual grounds, they were horrified by the needless suffering women endured in the course of this terribly brutal practice medically referred to as FGM (female genital mutilation).

Ernie's initial exposure to this custom took place in the emergency room when worried mothers sought treatment for their daughters' infections and appalling wounds inflicted during the procedure. But it became a much more personal issue to Ernie when girls scheduled to be circumcised appealed to him for protection. Sue cited one particularly memorable example.

"There was this young Christian girl who didn't want to go through the ceremony. Her father, who was not a Christian, told her, 'Then no man will have you for a wife!' But she knew he was more concerned about the dowry he might lose than the husband she might not get. So she came and asked Ernie for a job, thinking if she could leave home to work and live on the mission station at Tenwek, her father would let the matter drop. Ernie wasn't so sure it would be that easy. But he found her a job and a place to stay and assured her, 'We'll try to protect you.'

"One day soon after that, I looked out our front window and saw Ernie standing near and talking to a tall Kipsigis man. They seemed to be having a very animated conversation. As the man began to get more and more agitated, I realized he was holding a *panga* in his right hand and I remember thinking, *Ernie Steury, you better watch out!* I never did know exactly what Ernie said to him. Whatever it was, that father finally left—still angry. But at least he walked away.

"Ernie set up a meeting to talk with the daughter. He invited a few of the Kipsigis hospital staff to sit in as witnesses. Ernie explained to the girl that her father had come to see him, demanding to take her home. When Ernie had informed him that she couldn't go because she was working for the hospital, the girl's father had accused him of kidnapping and holding his daughter against her will. He claimed to have come to get his daughter, take her back to their home village, and enroll her in school.

"'So I need to be clear on this,' Ernie told the girl. 'And I want these other people to hear this as well. What is the truth here? Are you here because we won't let you leave or because you don't want to leave?'

"'I don't want to leave!' The girl began to cry. 'I don't care what my father told you—he is not going to put me in school. He and my brothers want to take me home so they can send me away to circumcision camp! Please, Daktari, please let me stay.'

"Ernie promised he would not send her back home. And that was the last we heard from her family for some time—until we went away from Tenwek for a few days on a family vacation. While we were gone, her father and brother came to Tenwek and literally dragged the girl home by the hair, weeping and screaming.

"They had her forcibly circumcised. She hemorrhaged and was critically ill from an infection. A Kipsigis chaplain at the hospital told us the girl had sent word that her family would let her go to Tenwek for treatment if someone from the hospital came for her. So Ernie, the chaplain, and one of our nurses took the hospital's Land Rover out to her village. But when the girl's mother saw them approaching the family's hut, she threatened to call her husband and sons if they didn't turn around and leave. When Ernie walked toward her, explaining that he'd come because he'd heard her daughter was sick, the woman grabbed a *panga* from above the door and gave out an ear-splitting whoop!

"The chaplain rushed in and grabbed the woman before she could do any real harm. And while he restrained her, Ernie and the nurse retrieved the girl. 'We need to take your daughter to the hospital for treatment,' Ernie explained to the mother, who seemed to have calmed down.

"'We better leave now,' the worried chaplain told Ernie, 'before the men get here.'

"'If you are still here when they come, they will kill you,' the woman said.

"Just as Ernie and the others were helping the girl into the vehicle, her father and brothers came running up. While the father loudly threatened Ernie, one of the brothers gently led the girl back into the hut. The confrontation ended. And there was nothing more for Ernie to do but to climb in the vehicle and drive away.

"When he got back to Tenwek that day, Ernie was terribly worried about that girl. He prayed for her at supper that night and before we went to bed. And the very next day she came walking into the hospital on her own for treatment. She survived and in time made a good recovery."

Ernie and Sue realized the most effective way to impact the culture and bring about an end to such cruel customs was to change the hearts of the Kipsigis people—one person at a time. Sue was so excited about her growing ministry with children that she included a picture of the children who attended a vacation Bible school at Tenwek in one of their support letters. "We are happy to report that many of these children, and others from the twenty VBS groups, found the Lord as their personal Savior," she wrote. "Pray that these children will remain true to the Lord and lead others to Him."

Where Is This Man, Jehovah?

Like her husband, Sue never lost sight of the fact that the hospital ministry remained a key to communicating a life-changing (and culture-changing) message to the Kipsigis people, which was what she tried to communicate in an article.

"'Where is this man—Jehovah?' That was the question old Arap Kosge asked one of our staff when he arrived at Tenwek Hospital. His daughter was attending Kenya Highlands Bible College [in Kericho], and she asked if she could bring her father to the hospital. She said, 'He is an old man and he is very sick. Perhaps nothing can be done for him physically, but I want him to hear more about God because I want him to become a Christian before he dies.'

"The family was told to bring him to the hospital. He was probably told often that he would hear about God here, so that is why he wanted to meet *this man Jehovah* immediately upon his arrival. Arap Kosge was indeed very ill. He was dying of cancer, so there was not much medicine could do for him, but he did hear about *this man Jehovah*. Several of the hospital staff witnessed to him and prayed with him and eventually introduced him to the Person he was looking for.

"He grew worse. The family wanted to take him home so he could die there. But I am happy to tell you that before [he left Tenwek] he found *this man Jehovah* and clearly testified to some of our staff that he was going to heaven to live with Him."

Stress Relievers

A growing number of Kipsigis staff caught the vision of Tenwek's hospital ministry. Ezekiel Kerich soon became Mosonik's right-hand man. The medical background he had gained in his lab assistant training gave him a foundation for understanding other areas of hospital work. So Ernie first taught him how to serve as a surgical assistant and then to dispense medicine and administer injections in the wards. He also learned to operate the X-ray equipment and develop the film. "Ernie and Ezekiel became like brothers," Sue said. "Ernie not only loved him, he came to trust and depend on Ezekiel."

Ernie depended on others to do more and more as the work continued to grow. The fifty-bed hospital averaged 186-percent inpatient occupancy during 1966, which meant for every fifty patients in beds, there were forty-three patients under the beds.

A bit of a respite came when two physicians from Chicago arrived in Kenya on a short-term missions trip early in 1967. They helped share Ernie's load at the hospital for a few weeks and even made it possible for him to get away for a conference in Nairobi without having to worry. The camaraderie with the visiting doctors meant as much to Ernie as the help, but it also added to his longing for the day when Tenwek would have more than one resident doctor.

The Steurys had hoped that day would come before they took their next furlough, which was scheduled to begin in the summer of 1968. It did indeed look like a new WGM missionary candidate, Dr. Robert Wesche and his family, might get to Tenwek just in time. And Dick Morse still planned to begin raising his support as soon as he finished his residency program. Ernie tried to imagine, *What could be accomplished at Tenwek with three full-time doctors?* He could hardly wait to find out.

In the meantime the everyday challenges seemed relentless. Sue tried to do what she could to ease the burden. In addition to the time-consuming demands on any wife and mother, working in the Sunday school and VBS ministries, and helping part time in the school library, Sue accepted a bigger role in the business side of the hospital. She had been overseeing the payment of the hospital staff; now she assumed responsibility for all of the hospital bookkeeping. That added exposure to the medical ministry at Tenwek made Sue even more aware of the ceaseless stress her husband was under.

To ease the stress Sue provided breaks from the routine whenever and however she could. Family trips, if only to Kijabe to visit Cindy for the weekend, got Ernie out from under the pressure for a day or two. Overnight camping trips in Maasai to hunt game, though infrequent, also helped. One time Ernie even talked Gene Lewton into going after cape buffalo "in revenge for all the emergency patients" the creatures had provided him since he had come to Africa. Cape buffalo are the most cantankerous and deadliest creatures on the continent, but Ernie bagged one with a shot through the heart and happily took home one massive set of horns.

Mechanical Mastermind

Not all the pressures Ernie faced were people problems. Not all the demands he dealt with were medical. Many were purely mechanical.

If he wasn't patching up patients, he was repairing the hospital's finicky infrastructure. "We would be in the middle of an operation when the lights would go out," Ezekiel Kerich recalled. "Dr. Steury would be the first one to ask, 'What happened? What's wrong?' Then he would say to whoever was assisting him, 'Okay, you take care of this patient. I'll be back as soon as I can.' He would go down to the power plant and work on the generator until it was running again. Then he'd return to the hospital, scrub in again, and continue the surgery.

"Electricity was something he grew up with. He understood it. We didn't. So many things were new to us. But not to him. So he was the only one who could fix them."

Even after WGM added qualified staff to oversee an industrial department that supported the growing needs and work of the hospital, Ernie often had to answer questions about diesel generators, water pumps, and other systems that kept the hospital running. Many times in those early years the other missionaries could call him to solve their plumbing problems or fix one of the kerosene-powered refrigerators used in the staff residences.

"Sometimes when I went to his house to tell him we needed him up at the hospital," Ezekiel reported, "I would find him wearing a suit of overalls, under his car, changing the oil. Dr. Steury was a man who could do anything!"

That mechanical aptitude paid off for the hospital in countless ways—big and small—including Ernie's reassembling of Tenwek's very first sterilization unit for surgical instruments. One of Ernie's brothers-in-law (an architect by trade) designed a new building with completely new furnishings for a medical practice back in the States. When he was offered the old equipment, the Steurys' brother-in-law accepted and shipped to Tenwek a variety of used medical instruments and equipment, including a small, old, but very functional autoclave that Ernie could use to steam-sterilize his surgical instruments.

The problem was that the autoclave had been completely disassembled when it was taken out of service. "Ernie was so excited when the box arrived safely at Tenwek," Sue recalled. "But when he opened it, the machine was in pieces. And there were no instructions."

Undaunted, Ernie spread out all the parts and set about rebuilding the contraption. He remembered seeing a similar machine somewhere—maybe at Indiana University Hospital—during his training. Drawing on that memory, his innate mechanical skills, and a large measure of common sense, the reassembly proceeded slowly but surely. Whenever he could spare a minute, between patients, while the staff prepped a surgical case, or just before he left the hospital to go home for the night, Ernie tinkered a little more with that apparatus.

"It took him a week to get it all back together in working order," Sue recalled. "But it would have taken a lot of people a year . . . and then they would have had a dozen parts left over." But that sterilization equipment not only worked, it continued to work for decades. The only real downside: It was one more piece of machinery for which Ernie assumed ultimate responsibility. Whenever the nurses or other staff had trouble getting it to function properly, the only logical person to call was the "mechanical mastermind" who put the thing back together piece by piece.

That Yankee ingenuity and independent can-do attitude—no doubt rooted and fostered by his upbringing on a farm in America's heartland—served Ernie, the hospital, and his patients well during those challenging early days in Kenya. For years he made crutches for patients who couldn't walk. Ernie created his own traction systems using tin cans filled with sand or cement for the weights that he hung on frames constructed out of spare pieces of metal. Because he treated so many small children who rolled or fell into the open cook fires in the middle of every Kipsigis hut, he designed and built a wire crib frame to be used in the pediatric ward to hold the sheet up off the babies' burned and blistered skin.

You Killed My Son

Of course, all of that innovation took time and energy, but what may have been even harder for Ernie to deal with was the emotional toll extracted by the expectations so many people had of him as he recalled in this story in WGM's magazine, *Call to Prayer.*

"'You killed my son! You killed my son! Why did I ever bring my son to the hospital for this white man to kill him?' The bereaved mother repeated this again and again after I told her that her son had died.

"Arap Siwon came to the hospital after having been sick for two weeks. When he arrived he was too weak to stand alone. I examined him and found that he needed emergency surgery as there was evidence of a perforated bowel. I started intravenous fluids and took him to surgery as soon as the operating room and instruments were ready. Before we put a patient under anesthesia, we always pray with him. When I asked Arap Siwon to close his eyes, he was very willing to cooperate. I asked the Lord to bless the patient and to give us strength and wisdom as we operated on him. Following the short prayer, I spoke to Arap Siwon and asked him if he had heard about Jesus Christ.

"'Yes, I have heard,' he answered.

"'Have you ever repented and and asked Jesus into your heart?' I asked.

"'No, but I want to,' he replied.

"As I spoke about Christ's great love and told him of Jesus' death on the cross for him, there seemed to be great eagerness to accept Christ. So I asked him to pray, and my heart was thrilled to hear his spontaneous words—asking God to forgive his sins and make him His child. He needed no help in his prayer, as it was coming from a hungry and repentant heart.

"Following the prayer he quietly drifted to sleep as we administered the anesthetic. Surgery revealed his bowel was indeed perforated due to typhoid fever, so I repaired the bowel. However, Arap Siwon never regained consciousness before he slipped away to be with Christ, his newfound Savior.

"Our hearts were saddened at the loss of this patient, but we grieved even more for the mother as she wailed and beat her head against the sidewalk because of the death of her son. Because she grieved as those who have no hope. She did not comprehend that her son had found peace and eternal life before he died. So our attempts to comfort her were useless. She obviously didn't understand anything we said. All she knew was that this white man had killed her son."

Yet We Hope

Despite the painful losses he experienced, despite the overwhelming need confronting him every day, despite the tremendous emotional and physical demands that wore on his body and spirit, Ernie Steury still found reasons of his own for encouragement and hope. Ironically, he saw the continued growth of the hospital and its ministry (with all that contributed to his prodigious workload) as a basis for optimism. The completion in 1967 of both the Naikarra Dispensary out in Maasai and the hospital's new twenty-bed men's ward greatly heartened Ernie because he recognized the promise of improved ministry.

He was even more excited with the arrival of Deborah Marie Steury on Saturday, July 22, 1967. "We came out to Kenya with one child and went back with two after one term. Now we'd come out with two and were going back with four after our second term," Sue laughed. That obviously wasn't a pattern she expected to continue.

Another cause for hope came with the addition of another doctor. Dr. Robert Wesche, his wife, Dora, and their little girl, Dawn, arrived in Kenya. While en route to Africa by ship, the Wesches were forced to make an unscheduled stop for emergency surgery in South Africa after Dora suffered a near-fatal ectopic pregnancy. At long last, Ernie would have a fellow physician who could share the responsibilities of WGM's medical work. After the mandatory six months of language training at Kericho, Bob would move to Tenwek. For Ernie, knowing that a full-time doctor could continue his ministry at Tenwek while he was in the States was reason enough for rejoicing.

The news that Dr. Richard Morse had completed his pediatric residency and was planning now to be in Kenya before Ernie's furlough ended was a double blessing. The thought of having three doctors working at Tenwek seemed almost too good to be true. That alone might have been reason enough for Ernie to be not merely optimistic, but downright excited, about the future.

The greatest source of all encouragement for Ernie, however, was his faith in the trustworthiness of his God, the theme he told about in this story he wrote for WGM's magazine, *Call to Prayer*.

"It was raining slowly and the night was very dark as we struggled through the mud. No matter how hard we tried, we could not get the 4-wheel-drive vehicle to climb out of the rut. We couldn't go straight ahead because of a big mound of rocks and dirt piled right in front of us waiting to be spread out to make the road passable. They weren't doing any good now, however, for instead of making the road better they created an obstacle which we could not get around. Finally, after backing up for almost a quarter of a mile, we found a place where we could get out of the rut. The road had become a sea of mud from many days of rain, and, as we continued on our way, we began to wonder if it was really worthwhile trying to go to the women's meeting. But Sue had promised to speak to these women during special services, so we drove on.

"When we finally arrived at our destination we were happy to see that, in spite of the rain, many women were already there. As the house in which we were meeting began to fill up, we realized God was working in the hearts of these women. They had come for a blessing and for spiritual food and the Lord was not disappointing them. I was thrilled to hear the testimonies of these Kenyan women! Many of them had faced difficult trials, but the Lord had given them strength and victory. As Sue spoke, their hearts and minds were eager to receive every word. We were glad we had not turned back.

"Many times we feel as if we are *stuck in a rut* in our work. There is always more than we can do. At times there are many obstacles to block progress and it seems difficult to go ahead. But we always find that there is a way out of the rut with God's help, and as we move ahead, we find that He has prepared a blessing for us."

For Ernie Steury, whose greatest motivation was to "make Christ known to the people of Kenya," his stuck-in-a-rut article probably felt like a very poignant personal parable representing his own feelings after ten long and strenuous years at Tenwek. However, what Ernie may have been too close, or perhaps just too tired, to see was just how effective he had already been at making Christ known to the people of Kenya by his own example of service and sacrifice.

Where Ernie identified with that stuck-in-a-rut image, Ezekiel Kerich said the Kipsigis people saw the image of Christ in Daktari Steury. And not just in how he served them—cleaning their latrines, burying their dead, dropping everything to meet their medical needs—but in his relationships, his interactions, and his character. "In everything he did, everything he said, everything he was—his way of life was to manifest God's love," Ezekiel said, "by showing and practicing that love with everyone he met.

"People recognized his concern even in the loving way he spoke to them when he took their medical history: 'How are you? Where did you come from? What can I do for you? Why did you come to the hospital today? Can you show me where the pain is? When did this begin?' The way he listened to them convinced the people he cared. That impressed people.

"When Dr. Steury first came to Tenwek, most of the Kipsigis people did not know what to think. They had no experience with a medical doctor. They were so amazed by his operations and his powerful medicines that before long people would come and want a shot to make them better. After we got the X-ray, many people would come and ask him to take a picture of their insides to help them feel better. But before long, everyone had heard stories about Dr. Steury and all the amazing things he did at Tenwek. Most people still didn't understand what he did, but they trusted him. In fact, they trusted him so much that sometimes when sick patients arrived at the hospital and learned that Dr. Steury was not there, that he'd gone to Nairobi or he was out at one of the clinics, they would begin to wail, 'Daktari Steury is not here? Oh, oh, I am going to die!' But whatever their disease or injury, if they learned that Mosonik was there, they would happily declare, 'If I can see Mosonik, I know I will be well!'"

Chapter 9

MEETING NEEDS AND EMBRACING OPPORTUNITIES

For their second furlough beginning in July 1968, the Steurys again settled in Ernie's hometown of Berne, Indiana, where they lived in a furnished apartment provided by the Missionary Church. Ernie spent three months of that year in the States working at the nearby Bluffton Clinic, doing surgery to brush up on his skills and keeping up to date on progress and changes in modern medical practice since he had been out of the country.

Ernie and Sue shared much positive news with family, friends, and supporters about how the Lord was blessing the work in Kenya. During their four-year, four-month second term, Tenwek Hospital's facilities had nearly doubled from forty-two to seventy-two beds, while the inpatient numbers had tripled. More than 550 spiritual decisions had been reported at the hospital over the six-month period prior to their coming home. Yet the Steurys wanted desperately to let people know how much remained to be done.

As Sue told supporters: "It's harvest time in Kenya, and the opportunities for medical services are truly unlimited. But we have stretched our reapers to the limit and beyond."

Wherever Ernie spoke and to anyone who would listen, he would say, "The needs and opportunities are tremendous, but we are so limited. The number of inpatients at our hospital is so great that more have to sleep on the floor than we can put in beds. And right now there is just one doctor, one nurse, and our African staff to care for them. Pray with us that God will supply nurses and the necessary finances to expand our medical work—that we might take advantage of these God-given opportunities to minister to body and soul."

Everywhere the Steurys went on deputation, people responded to the personal stories and the slides they showed to illustrate the medical needs of the Kipsigis people and the work going on at Tenwek. But in a very real sense, Ernie and Sue faced a doubly difficult challenge in their fundraising efforts. They spent so much time and effort talking about the needs of the hospital ministry that by April of 1969 they still weren't certain where they stood in terms of their personal financial support for the next term. But response to their appeal was encouraging enough for the Steurys to finalize their plans for heading back to Africa.

For the second furlough in a row, Ernie received discouraging staffing news from Tenwek. Dora Wesche had never fully recovered her health, so she and Bob needed to return to the States for her follow-up care. For a short time the hospital was again without a full-time doctor. Dick Morse was still finishing up his language training in Kericho and would move to Tenwek only weeks before Ernie and Sue returned.

Though Ernie's dream of three career doctors working together at Tenwek hadn't come to fruition, he was thrilled to finally have Dick Morse on hand to share the hospital load. Another medical person, Marilyn Van Kuiken, joined the Tenwek staff during the time of the Steurys' furlough. Though new to Kenya, she was a veteran missionary nurse who had served for eight years in the Ethiopian province of Eritrea.

"In my first six months at Tenwek I heard so many stories about Dr. Steury from the patients and staff that I was more than a little awed to finally meet him when he got back from furlough," Marilyn recalled. "But it didn't take long to realize just how humble—how human—both Ernie and Sue were. They eventually became my best friends."

Far from Home

Over the next few months after their return from furlough, the Steurys came to appreciate and rely on Marilyn's friendship, as well as her professional skills, in some very significant ways as Sue and Ernie were both tested as never before. Early in 1970 two personal crises confronted Sue.

Sue had not felt well for a week and couldn't eat. Since she followed the pattern of many patients in the hospital at the time, Ernie initially thought it was a virus that would soon blow over. But it didn't. While they were all eating breakfast one morning, Cindy looked at her mom and said, "Mommy, your eyes are yellow."

Ernie said, "They had better not be!" But when he checked, they were. So the "virus" took a new name—hepatitis. And in a few days it wasn't just Sue's eyes that were yellow; she was yellow all over! There wasn't much medicine Sue could take for it; she just needed to rest and let her liver get built back up. And she felt so rotten that rest was about all she felt like doing.

All the Steury children, who were home on spring break, did more caring for their mother than Sue did for them over the next few weeks. Ernie and their new "Aunt Marilyn" came down from the hospital several times a day to check on Sue and find out from Cindy if her mom was staying in bed and following medical orders.

A little more than two weeks into her physical ordeal, Sue received some shocking family news from back in the States. Her father had died of a sudden heart aneurysm. That devastating emotional blow, on top of her illness, was made worse by the realization that she didn't have any of the necessary resources—not enough time, finances, or even strength—to get to America for her dad's funeral so she could grieve with her brothers, her stepmother, and the extended Groce family.

Ernie, their children, Marilyn Van Kuiken, and the rest of the Tenwek missionary family did all they could to surround Sue with loving concern and attention. But never had Tenwek seemed so far from North Carolina as it did those next few weeks, as Sue could only rest and thank God for John Walter Groce's love and influence on her life. She took great comfort in the sweet memory of the one visit he and her stepmother had made to Tenwek soon after Jonathan was born and in knowing of her father's pride and approval of her and Ernie's commitment to missions.

Sue had not completely regained her strength before Ernie began having severe headaches. Those went on for two weeks before he became sick with a fever. A blood test soon revealed he had a full-blown case of malaria. While he had treated enough malaria cases and certainly knew all the symptoms in others, he hadn't considered that possibility for himself. No one in the family had ever been infected in all their years in Africa; mosquitoes weren't a serious problem due to the cool nights at Tenwek's high elevation (over 6,500 feet). He finally figured that he had probably been exposed to this serious case of malaria during a recent trip to Nakuru with the family.

His fever, chills, and headaches got so severe that Ernie became delirious, prompting fears that what he had was cerebral malaria. Afterwards Ernie expressed doubts about that, but then he was not exactly in the best shape to make a self-diagnosis. Dick Morse hadn't been in Africa long enough at that point to have a lot of experience treating the disease.

With Sue still feeling fairly weak, a lot of Ernie's care fell on Marilyn Van Kuiken, who hiked down the hill from the hospital several times a day to check on him. According to Marilyn, Ernie made a better doctor than patient. "For four days in a row, the pain kept him from getting any sleep at all. That, plus the fact that Ernie went out of his head from time to time, made me think it was cerebral malaria. Finally I said to him, 'Why don't you take a course of quinine—it's what we give the malaria patients at the hospital.'"

"That will just depress me!" Ernie replied in a most uncharacteristically weepy and pitiful voice.

Marilyn might have laughed if he hadn't sounded so pathetic. "You're already depressed," she told him. "Let me talk to Dick and get you started on the quinine."

Ernie tried to argue.

"You need to sleep," Marilyn insisted. And she started the regimen of medicine that did indeed allow him to rest and begin a slow recovery, which wasn't nearly complete when Tenwek experienced one of its most unusual and dramatic crises.

Distress Call

On September 25, 1970, Dick Morse had gone to the Kaboson Dispensary for clinic day. Ernie was making his morning rounds when a runner reached the hospital calling for Tenwek's Land Rover ambulance to be sent to the other side of Bomet. There had been a motor accident, and several people were injured.

Ernie went with the ambulance to the scene. A tour group from the Inner Wheels Club of England, traveling in six Volkswagen Microbuses, had been returning from a sightseeing safari in the Maasai Reserve when one of the buses overturned. After the vehicle rolled several times, only one of its seven passengers remained inside. Three women had been fatally injured. Another who sustained a broken neck and head injuries required emergency surgery. The other passenger (the husband of one of the women who was killed) and the driver suffered extensive cuts and bruises.

Ernie sent a message to Kaboson for Dick to hurry back to help care for the injured. All the hospital staff, whether they were on duty or not, turned out to handle the emergency.

The man who had lost his wife was taken to Nairobi after being treated. From there he flew back to England with her body. But the other two passengers and the driver were kept at Tenwek for a time because their condition was too critical for them to be moved. One woman accepted Christ while recovering in Marilyn Van Kuiken's home.

As relatives back in England learned of the accident, they became concerned about their loved ones being cared for in a "small mission hospital" somewhere out in the African bush. So the general manager of the touring company personally journeyed to Tenwek to see about the survivors. He acted surprised and very grateful for the quality of treatment they were receiving and assured their families by phone that they were all being properly cared for. The story made headlines in British papers and in Kenya's *Nation*, a national newspaper.

While the staff at Tenwek would never know the ongoing spiritual impact resulting from that tragedy, they soon experienced one more welcome "victory." The Inner Wheel Clubs were the women's auxiliaries of the Rotary Clubs in England. So when the surviving members of the tour group returned home, they organized a financial campaign to purchase and ship a much-needed state-of-the-art portable X-ray unit to Tenwek Hospital.

Though a difficult year, 1970 was also an encouraging one for the missionaries at Tenwek Hospital. There were 674 decisions for Christ in the hospital alone. And Ernie received word that his home congregation, First Missionary Church, Berne, Indiana, was sending a ten-thousand-dollar donation to make possible the construction of yet another building to relieve the continuous overcrowding. By the time that isolation ward was completed the following year, construction began on a new maternity ward, which increased the hospital's capacity to one hundred beds.

But as always seemed the case at Tenwek, no sooner did the new wards open than they too filled to overflowing. The increased patient load rendered the lab and other service facilities inadequate, which led to yet another building project—an addition to the Shryock Medical Building to greatly expand lab space while also providing an administration office and a physiotherapy room. And when he wasn't busy overseeing construction and tending to more patients than ever in the hospital, Ernie, together with Dick Morse, performed 230 major operations and 550 minor surgical procedures at Tenwek in 1971.

Just Another Day at Tenwek

For most of the night, Edna Boroff had been in and out of maternity monitoring the labor of a woman she knew was going to need a C-section. But she was waiting as long as she could before sending for Ernie since she knew he had gotten almost no sleep the night before. Finally, about four in the morning, she decided the time had come. But as she walked out of maternity to find someone to send down the hill to get Ernie, she saw the outpatient area all lit up. She wondered, *What's going on in there?* She hurried over to check.

There she found Ernie, who had already been called to deal with a much bigger emergency. Robbers armed with *pangas* had broken into a shop down in Bomet and viciously attacked two night watchmen they had encountered inside.

As Ernie hurriedly examined the bloody and unconscious victims, he asked Edna what she needed. She said she had an emergency C-section waiting.

"You'll have to help me here first," he told her. "These men need surgery immediately." Both victims suffered so many wounds to the head, neck, and shoulders that it looked like their attackers had tried to behead them. They had come so close with one man that Edna could hardly believe he was still alive.

Ernie had already sent for Dick Morse, so when he arrived it was decided Ernie and Edna would take the most critical man while Dick and Marilyn started on the second victim in the smaller OR. Edna gave instructions to one of the Kipsigis aides to continue monitoring the woman in labor and to get her if the baby's heart rate began falling.

Ernie had just gotten all the bleeders closed up in the patient's neck and Edna was sewing up a terrible gash in his leg when the maternity assistant stuck her head in the OR to tell Edna the baby's heart rate had suddenly dropped to eighty.

With both operating rooms in use, Ernie and Edna grabbed what instruments and supplies they needed, left an assistant watching their patient, and raced for maternity. "We'd never done a C-section right in maternity before, but we didn't have any choice," Edna said. "We scrubbed in, Ernie opened the woman up, and saved both mother and baby." The entire procedure took only minutes to complete before they headed back to the operating room and a patient who remained in very critical condition. The wounds to his face, neck, and skull would take hours to repair.

A few minutes later Edna heard a screaming woman being carried past the OR toward the maternity ward. She left to investigate. Within minutes she returned to tell Ernie she had another patient for him—she suspected a ruptured uterus. So they rushed to the maternity ward again for another C-section; this time the baby had already died, but they managed to save the mother.

Not long after that Edna had to drop out of surgery again to check out more commotion she heard coming from the maternity ward. Sure enough, another patient in labor had been carried to the hospital for miles through the dark of night over narrow, rough trails. She and the baby were both in distress.

There was nothing to do but fetch Ernie once more. For the third time between 4:00 a.m. and 7:00 a.m., Edna and Ernie had to stop in the middle of life-or-death surgery to perform another emergency C-section. They saved that mother and her baby, and things finally settled down after the sun came up. Around mid-morning Ernie sent Edna off to try to get a little rest. He finished working on his surgery patient about noon, but Dick's operation went on a while longer. Both of their patients survived. But for the doctors there were still the usual rounds, the long line of outpatients outside the hospital doors, and even some previously scheduled surgeries to be done. It was just another day at Tenwek.

Chapter 10

The Servant Leader

No one working at Tenwek had any real downtime, so everyone on the staff tried to maximize the use of all assets. The outpatients who began queuing up at the hospital door before six every morning were screened into groups based on the level of care needed. Sick people with routine complaints could get basic treatment and the most common medications from one of the African nurses' attendants. Those cases they couldn't handle would be seen by one of the nurses who could provide more difficult diagnoses and treatments. Any patients requiring a doctor's attention would be asked to stay, and then, at the end of the day, if either Ernie or Dick could break free from ward and surgical duties, that doctor would head to outpatient to see all those cases deemed serious enough to require a physician's expertise. Those who couldn't be seen would then leave and come back another day. If they had no transportation or had walked too far to return home for the night, patients often slept in the yard outside so they could be first in line when the hospital doors opened the next morning.

Everyone's resources were stretched to the limits of their talent and training—and often beyond. Nurses were trusted to do more diagnosis and make more decisions than would have ever been expected of them (or allowed) in America. At Tenwek, the staff had no choice. Because there were just too many things that only a physician could do, the entire staff tried to be the most efficient stewards possible of the doctors' time.

The surgical schedule in particular required stamina and adaptability. "I remember many long days in the OR when we didn't even take a break to get something to eat or drink," Marilyn Van Kuiken said. "I'd be constantly wiping the sweat off Ernie's brow, and every few minutes I'd poke a straw in behind his surgical mask so he could sip from a bottle of juice or a soft drink to keep from getting dehydrated.

"A lot of days when he couldn't leave the OR for lunch, Sue would come up to the hospital with sandwiches for us. She would feed Ernie his, a bite at a time, at the corner of his mouth while he continued to operate."

Even maternity patients needed to take a number. "The doctors used to call me 'Good-news Edna,'" Edna Boroff laughed. "I'd wait until I knew they were just about to finish a surgery before I'd stick my head in the OR door and tell them I had a C-section waiting outside. Sometimes I'd have two or three women lined up and waiting as soon as they finished. I'd try to save up my cases for efficiency's sake."

Yet no matter how urgent the surgery or how pressing the schedule, Ernie always took time to minister to the spiritual needs of his patients. Since most of the education in the area took place at mission schools, the majority of Tenwek's younger patients had some religious instruction. At the very least, they knew who God was and had been told that Jesus was His Son, so it didn't take long to explain the basics. But even the patients, old or young, who lived so far out in the bush that they had never had any previous exposure to the gospel message, were often very receptive.

Some experts in the history and methodology of Christian missions around the world have theorized that God has provided some underlying sense of truth in the practice and tradition of every culture that prepares the people to understand the gospel message. This sense of truth may be what the apostle Paul referred to when he wrote about Gentiles who never had any instruction in Scripture, yet already understood some measure of God's truth because the law had been "written in their hearts, their conscience also bearing witness" (Romans 2:14–15).

Indeed, traditional Kipsigis beliefs could support this theory. These people have an ancient legend in their tribal culture—an often-told story about a great being who lived in the sky behind the sun and once had a son who was killed. Those who practice their traditional religion will often pray, "Old Great Being, please don't hold it against us for the killing of your son!"

So when the Kipsigis people heard the scriptural account of a powerful Creator God who lived up in heaven and loved the world so much

He sent His son to save it, and that Son willingly gave up His own life as a sacrifice to pay for the world's sins, they had a point of reference. The biblical story just seemed to ring so true in their hearts that many Kipsigis seemed anxious and ready to accept it.

Saving the Lost

One day a Kipsigis family brought in an eighteen-year-old boy with a bowel obstruction. When he started complaining of pain four days earlier, they had gone to a witch doctor for bush medicine. He could do nothing. The boy's pain grew worse. He pleaded for help, but it was four days before his family finally brought him to Tenwek. By then immediate surgery was his only chance of survival. As he prepped the boy for surgery, Ernie gave him a spinal to ease the pain.

But before they started surgery on this young man, Ernie asked him, "Do you know the Lord Jesus?" Once Ernie learned the boy wasn't a Christian, he explained to him who Jesus was and why we need Him as our Savior. When he inquired if the boy wanted to ask God's forgiveness, the young man said he did and prayed to invite Jesus into his heart. Then it was time for the surgery to begin.

As soon as Ernie opened him up, he realized there was little he could do. The family had waited so long that the boy's bowels were already full of gangrene. Ernie removed everything he could, but the infection had progressed too far. The boy never made it out of surgery.

There are testimonies about people who came to the Lord at the eleventh hour. This dear boy found his salvation literally at the twelfth hour because his doctor took five minutes to share the gospel message with him. That was always a priority for Ernie, who over the years led hundreds—if not thousands—of his patients to the Lord.

The Pig Project

Ernie's midwestern farm background figured into a couple of practical "hobbies" he engaged in while at Tenwek. Even with the occasional big game hunts, there was never really an abundance of fresh meat for the missionaries to eat. So when Ernie began to notice how much of the food prepared in the hospital kitchen went uneaten and had to be thrown away, he came up with an idea he thought could solve both problems: the "pig project." His brilliant, not to mention mouth-watering, plan made perfect sense; the missionaries could have their own economical source of bacon, sausage, chops, and ham from pigs they raised by feeding them the leftover hospital food that was currently going to waste.

The trouble with this idea was that the Kipsigis people had a very Old Testament perspective on pork. They thought pigs to be loathsome and unclean animals. Not only would they never consider eating the meat, they wouldn't even consider having pigs around; in their culture keeping swine was about as low as a person could get. None of the Kipsigis people wanted to help take care of Ernie's pigs, and they really didn't understand why the Daktari wanted to have anything to do with them himself. The only person willing to feed and care for pigs was a colorful, middle-aged character, Arap Chumo, who was chronically unemployed and considered a little "mentally off" by the local Kipsigis people. Having left Arap Chumo in charge of the pigs while on furlough, Ernie's initial attempt at the "pig project" had pretty much died out while the Steurys were gone.

But Ernie was determined to try again. When he learned of a monastery near Nakuru where the brothers were keeping a herd of swine, he recruited Arap Chumo to go with him in a mission pickup to see if he could purchase some young feeder pigs to raise. The monks happily sold him three pregnant sows. They quickly and expertly grabbed the sows by the ears and tail and ran them up onto the back of the pickup.

Ernie quickly closed the tailgate and opened the windows on the pickup's camper shell so the pigs wouldn't get overheated in the tropical sun. Then he climbed in the cab, started the engine, and set off back to Tenwek.

One of the sows kept trying to stick her head out the window right behind Ernie. So as he drove, he kept reaching back with his left hand and shoving her snout back inside. He worried that if they really tried, the pigs could leap out of the truck, and he would never see them again.

As they bounced along the rough dirt roads, Ernie said, "Arap Chumo, you need to watch those pigs. If one of them looks like she's going to try to jump out, you tell me. I'll stop, and we'll make sure she stays in."

Arap Chumo promised to keep an eye on the animals. But he was fascinated by the passing countryside. It was the first time in his life that Ernie's addled assistant had ever been away from Tenwek, and certainly the farthest he had traveled. He was so busy gawking at the people they passed and enjoying the beautiful scenery that he completely forgot about his assignment. At what point he had quit watching, Ernie didn't know, but when the pickup bounced over a particularly deep rut, Ernie heard a loud squeal. He glanced back and counted only two sows.

"Arap Chumo!" he exclaimed. "Where is the other pig?"

"Oh-Oh-Oh-Oh!" the flustered man replied. "What happened?"

Ernie pulled to the side of the road, braked to a stop, and jumped out. In the distance behind them he could make out two men walking and driving a pig along the road toward them. Arap Chumo began running back up the road, waving his arms and shouting to get the men's attention. Ernie quickly yelled for him to stop and motioned him back to the truck to wait. He was afraid the spectacle of a noisy, arm-waving Arap Chumo might spook the pig and cause it to run into the heavy brush lining both sides of the road. They might never find it again.

"Let's just wait," Ernie said. So they did. And when the men arrived with the pig, Ernie showed them the two in the pickup and explained that this third one had jumped out. He thanked the men for returning it and got them to help get the pig back in the truck, which involved much maneuvering. He backed the truck into the ditch and up against a small embankment so Arap Chumo and the two men could herd the escaped pig up the rise, over the lowered tailgate, and into the truck.

Ernie closed a couple of the camper windows to reduce the chances of another escape, but then the temperature began to rise very quickly. Knowing that pigs don't have any sweat glands, Ernie worried that his three-not-so-little-pigs story might have a very sad ending unless he found a way to cool them off.

In the next town Ernie stopped and went into a shop to buy a bucket. Then he drove the pickup down to the edge of a nearby stream, scooped up several buckets of cool water, and poured it on his overheated pigs. By the time he finished this chore, he had three happy pigs and a crowd of curious children pressed in around the pickup for a closer look at these strange creatures that they had never seen before. On the five-hour drive home, Ernie stopped a few more times to water down his cargo.

When they reached Tenwek, Ernie drove directly to the pigpen, thinking this particular adventure was finally over. Unfortunately the three balky pigs refused to get off the truck. No amount of prodding with sticks could get them down the steep incline of the sturdy wooden ramp he had constructed to offload his livestock.

While Arap Chumo continued poking the protesting pigs and a large crowd of students from Tenwek's secondary school gathered round to investigate all the squealing, Ernie pondered his next course of action. There seemed no alternative but to climb into the back of the truck and somehow drag the pigs out. But once he got inside, the low roof of the camper forced him to bend over. At such an awkward angle, he simply couldn't get enough leverage to budge the stubborn animals.

Then Ernie remembered the monks' strategy and decided to give it a try. When he grabbed an ear of the nearest sow in one hand and yanked on her tail with his other hand, she squealed like crazy, but she did start moving. As she picked up a little momentum, Ernie held on tight to try to guide her. But he was shuffling along, bent over at such an awkward angle that he stumbled and fell across the sow's broad back. The startled pig leaped off the tailgate and plunged down the steep ramp with Ernie holding on for dear life. When they hit the ground, Ernie lost his grip and splashed down in the middle of a big sloppy mud wallow. The school children burst into raucous laughter at the Daktari's plight. But not one of them ever offered to help.

By the time Ernie got all three sows into the pen, both he and his pigs were covered from head to toe in mud and manure. The pigs, however, were more content with their predicament than Ernie was and a whole lot happier than Sue was when Ernie entered the back door.

"What happened to you?" she wanted to know.

"I'll tell you as soon as I get a bath," he told her, obviously anxious to clean up. But she insisted he strip off his filthy clothes right there at the door before she would even let him in the house.

Sue immediately grabbed the smelly garments and deposited them out in the yard. When she got back inside the house, she walked down the hall past the bathroom. She could hear water running. Then suddenly Ernie began to laugh so hard and so loud that Sue became alarmed.

"Are you all right in there?" she called to him. He said he would explain as soon as he got washed up. But he kept right on laughing.

By the time he finished and came out, Sue's curiosity just about got the better of her. She had to hear his explanation. But Ernie was still laughing so hard it took forever for him to relate the whole story.

Despite such an inauspicious start, Ernie's pig project eventually proved a major success. The sows delivered three healthy litters of piglets that soon consumed much of the hospital's kitchen garbage; they especially loved all the leftover *gimyet* (cornmeal mush the Kipsigis ate with every meal).

The first few times Ernie butchered one of his pigs and divided the meat among the missionaries, none of the African staff wanted any. However, after a few of them eventually sampled some of the pork the missionaries cooked, Ernie had to butcher two pigs at a time to meet the demand—another small way in which he began to influence Kipsigis culture.

A Chicken Revival

Chickens, unlike pigs, were such a familiar part of traditional local custom that the family flock usually wandered in and out of the Kipsigis' dirt-floor huts right along with the barefoot children. The chickens often roosted inside.

Any free-range birds sold in local markets, however, were often so scrawny and tough that the missionaries had to pressure-cook them for hours before their meat was tender enough to chew. Once again Ernie's farm background convinced him he could do better. He decided to purchase a crate of newly hatched chicks from Nairobi and raise his own finer flock.

When Ernie got his first batch of baby birds, he kept them safe and sheltered for a time in the cellar beneath the house. He fashioned a small chicken-wire enclosure and kept it bright and cozy with a small kerosene lantern reflecting off a shiny piece of sheet metal he had shaped and placed especially for providing light and warmth. A couple times a day Ernie would go down into the cellar to feed, water, and check on the chicks.

One day he came home for lunch and smelled something hot. He hurried down the cellar stairs to find his baby birds sprawled motionless all over the floor. For some reason the kerosene lantern had flared up, overheated the pen, and filled the basement with smoke. Ernie was sure all his chicks were dead. But when he picked one up, he realized its little heart was still beating. It had evidently just passed out.

He quickly plunged the tiny creature's head in and out of the water bowl to try to revive it, and then he started alternating one-finger chest compressions and blowing soft puffs of air into its beak until the little bird began to squirm in his hand. He quickly set that one down and picked up another to repeat the process. Within minutes he had the entire batch of birdies back on their feet.

The following day when Marilyn Van Kuiken joined the Steurys for dinner, Ernie chuckled as he told her about performing CPR on his little flock. "You mean to tell me you actually performed mouth-to-mouth on those birds?" she asked.

"Oh, Ernie didn't mind," Sue piped in. "They were really cute chicks."

As Marilyn and Ernie began laughing, Sue added, "In fact, I'm thinking of growing a few feathers of my own, just to get a little more attention around here."

"The Lord Is Helping You"

One day a World Gospel Mission missionary, David Lee, fell off a thirty-foot-tall water tower at the mission's remote clinic out in Kaboson. He could have broken his neck, but instead he completely mangled the hand he used to break his fall. When other missionaries drove him to Tenwek, Ernie took one look at David's swollen hand and wondered if he would ever be able to use it again. The X-rays confirmed the severity of the damage; nearly every bone in the hand itself was not only shattered, but displaced.

"We are going to send you to Nairobi right away," Ernie told him. "If you don't get an expert to put you back together, you may never be able to use that hand again."

David replied, "I don't want to go to Nairobi. I want you to operate, Ernie."

"But I've never done any hand surgery like this," Ernie told him. "You need an expert."

"But I trust you, Ernie," his colleague told him. "I know God will help you."

Ernie finally agreed. But it was with more than a little fear and trepidation that he began the operation to put a steel pin through David's hand and wire all the pieces of bone back together.

After the surgery and a lot of physical therapy, it became evident that God's hands were guiding Ernie's; David regained full use of his hand.

That was hardly the only time a missionary colleague had to convince Ernie to do surgery on him or her. When Marion Lewton needed a hysterectomy, she came to Tenwek from her home in Maasai and insisted she wanted Ernie to do it. "And I told him I didn't want a spinal," she explained later. "I wanted to be completely asleep."

Most of the time Ernie used spinals because the hospital's supply of other anesthesia was often limited. Tenwek didn't have an anesthesiologist, so Ernie had to operate, administer, and monitor the anesthesia all at the same time.

"So for Marion's surgery," Marilyn Van Kuiken recalled, "Ernie drafted me as his assistant and anesthesiologist. He told me he wanted her lightly sedated, so that's what I tried to do. However, we were still in the middle of the operation when Marion's eyes flickered open. Her eyes seemed to focus on me and then shift to Ernie. Then she startled us by announcing loudly, with conviction and expression: "Ernie, I know the Lord is helping you!"

Marion sank back into a deep sleep when Marilyn immediately upped the dosage. "I remember thinking, *That was lightly sedated, all right!"* Both she and Ernie had to chuckle because what Marion had said and how she had said it sounded just like she would have talked if she had been wide awake and alert. Even though Ernie occasionally got encouragement from his patients *before* surgery and quite often heard words of gratitude and praise from patients *after* surgery, that was the first and probably only time he ever had a patient wake up during a major operation just to cheer her surgeon on.

Marion was even more positive in comments about her postoperative experience. "Where in the world could I have ever received better care? Not only did I have an excellent surgeon who prayed with me and for me before my operation, but afterwards he took me into his own home so he could carefully monitor my recovery. If I got restless in the middle of the night, he would get out of bed to give me something for the pain. I hated to be such a bother because I knew how little sleep he got most nights anyway. He insisted I was no bother at all, that he was glad to do it. And I knew he meant it. That kind of sacrificial love was not just part of his ministry; it was part of who he was."

Ernie Steury's skills and character obviously earned the respect and appreciation of fellow missionaries stationed throughout Kenya. But how did their judgments compare with those of the people who saw him up close and personal on a daily basis?

According to Dick Morse, there was only one explanation as to how a perpetually understaffed mission hospital on a remote hillside in an undeveloped corner of Kenya could provide quality health care to so many people. "We were all part of a team," he said. "And we worked together so well. That's why we grew. And it's the only way we survived."

Tenwek still didn't have a very big team in the early 1970s. The professional nursing staff of five women served staggered four-year terms so that only one of them went on furlough at a time each year. That little group of women accomplished far more than anyone had the right to expect. Eldema Kemper, Ramona Thomas, and Eddie Goff continued the work at the clinic in Kaboson and Naikarra, seeing over twenty-eight thousand patients and 276 Christian conversions at the Kaboson dispensary alone. Those numbers kept climbing each year.

The nursing contingent at the hospital itself did increase by 50 percent from two registered nurses to three when Jeannine Spratt, a young career nurse, joined Marilyn and Edna at Tenwek in 1972. The three of them not only cared for five thousand inpatients the following year, but they assisted the doctors in surgery, trained national staff, and took care of over fifty thousand outpatients (an average of 150–200 per day). Two young medical technologist missionaries, Carol Trachsel and Sara Hill, ran the hospital's lab and assisted the rest of the medical team in more ways than they were formally trained for.

Ernie Steury was definitely the team leader of WGM's medical mission in Kenya. He directed the hospital's daily work, oversaw its historic growth, and envisioned its future. But he accepted no more credit for it than anyone else did. "We all gave God the praise for any success," Marilyn Van Kuiken said, "whether that achievement involved an excellent outcome to a difficult surgery, the completion of a new facility expanding the ministry, or the widening of the hospital's positive reputation. We just knew any credit was more the Lord's than ours."

Even so, as uneasy as it made Ernie feel, in the minds of many WGM supporters back in the States, as well as most of the people the hospital served, Dr. Ernie Steury *was* Tenwek Hospital. His was the face of WGM's medical mission in Kenya. While he reluctantly recognized and eventually accepted the inevitability of that role, he always considered himself just one of the members of a team. "From his earliest years at Tenwek," Edna Boroff observed, "Ernie was always very much a *servant* leader. I'd been in charge of the medical work at Tenwek for so long that when Ernie came, our field director decided to reassign me to the dispensary out in Kaboson, in order to give Ernie a chance to establish his authority and set up the hospital the way he wanted it. It quickly became obvious that strategy really wasn't necessary, so I came back to the maternity work at Tenwek. The two of us never had a bit of trouble getting along. Because Ernie wasn't just an excellent doctor, he was a true Christian gentleman who was always thinking more about the needs of others than about what he wanted them to do for him.

"I remember one night we had a maternity patient so sick with malaria that she had a hemoglobin of two. Most people die if their blood count falls that low. I volunteered as a donor because I had the right blood type. But Ernie wouldn't let me do it because he knew I would be on duty all night and wouldn't have a chance to rest and build my own reserves back up. Anyway, the patient's condition grew worse overnight, so I went ahead and gave her a unit of blood without telling Ernie. Early the next morning I think we were doing an emergency C-section when I suddenly became very woozy and had to find a place to sit down. The next thing I knew I started having convulsions. Naturally Ernie wanted to examine me, so I had to confess what I'd done. He didn't say 'I told you so' or scold me at all. He simply instructed me to go home, eat some breakfast, and get some rest.

"When I insisted that I couldn't do that yet, he wanted to know why. I informed him I had to get that day's supply of milk ready for the babies in the nursery. He told me, 'Don't worry about that; I'll do it for you. Go home and get some rest.'"

Other staff reported the same selfless, serving attitude. In fact, they all vividly recalled one consistent reaction to the constant interruptions Ernie faced. Whether he was running someone's bowel through his fingers (literally) in search of lesions during an operation, hurrying across the compound in response to some urgent summons, or sitting at the supper table with Sue and the children—who had already waited an extra hour for him to come home so they could eat together as a family—his standard response was to stop what he was doing, look up at the person needing his refocused attention, and ask, "What can I do for you?"

Staff Training and Leadership

Ernie demonstrated the same servant attitude toward his national staff. From the beginning of his work at Tenwek, Ernie realized there was more work to be done than the missionary staff could ever do on its own. If the hospital ministry were to grow, he would have to depend more and more on African helpers.

For its first few years, Tenwek Hospital relied only on a few Kipsigis, primarily Christian women, who were willing to defy tribal mores to work with sick and dying people. Those few who were willing to take that risk had no professional instruction and only minimal education of any kind. Their training had to start from scratch, like learning the difference between teaspoons and tablespoons in order to dispense prescribed doses of medicine. Since most of the first nurses' assistants read very little and didn't write, all the medicines in the tiny pharmacy were labeled and administered by number. Liquid medicines were assigned numbers

1 through 30; pills started at number 31. Dependable employees who showed any aptitude were taught the additional skills of giving injections, checking blood pressure, and screening outpatients.

Ernie and the nursing staff took a special interest in training their Kipsigis assistants to play an increasing role in both the physical and spiritual sides of the hospital's medical ministry, singling out those bright and committed enough to assume higher and higher levels of responsibility. While the hospital was not large enough to conduct an official government-recognized training program for nursing assistants or other hospital workers, many of those who worked for a time at Tenwek were able to find jobs at government clinics and dispensaries closer to their home village when they chose to do so.

For several years Ezekiel Kerich was a rarity—a man willing to work in health care. Ernie had spotted his potential early on and invested enormous time training him to take on a wide range of tasks. By 1972 the ministry of the hospital had grown so large that Ernie appointed Ezekiel as the first hospital administrator. In his new role, Ezekiel oversaw Tenwek's daily business and the hiring, training, and supervision of the African staff. Ezekiel was uniquely qualified to comment from a Kipsigis perspective on Daktari Steury's leadership style.

"I did my training as a lab assistant at a government hospital with government doctors where I had learned to be obedient or else. The doctors were in charge. And they spoke sharply to the other people working around them. I worked with Dr. Steury for many years, and I never heard impatience or anger in his voice—even when I knew something had upset or bothered him.

"He was a very humble man. He never acted superior. He didn't consider himself a big operating man. He taught me much as I grew from an assistant to hospital administrator. But I don't remember him ever *telling* me what to do or how to do it, he always *showed* me. He led not by ordering people around but by working *with* people. He was the reason why so many of our people began to want to work at Tenwek Hospital. No matter how much the hospital grew, everyone saw Dr. Steury as the leader—the one people looked to—Mosonik."

It wasn't only the people who had worked with Ernie in the more than dozen years he had been in Africa who took note of his personal leadership example. During the 1971–72 school year, a junior premed major at Ernie's alma mater, Asbury College, felt his own call to go into medical missions. David Stevens began talking with his dad, traveling evangelist Maurice Stevens, about the direction he felt God leading.

One day Reverend Stevens said to his son, "You know, Dave, I think it would be great if you could go to Kenya this summer and spend time with Dr. Ernie Steury. I have known Ernie for fifteen years. Your mom and I have supported him since the beginning of his ministry. Of all the mission hospitals I've visited in the world, of all the missionary doctors I've seen, I think Ernie is the best."

Dave Stevens recalled: "This was high praise coming from Dad, who had led short-term mission trips all over the world. So in June of 1972 I excitedly got on a plane and headed to Africa. For much of that summer I lived in Ernie and Sue's home. The Steury house contained maybe twelve hundred square feet, and they had four children. So Ernie asked his two boys to sleep on the living room couch for a few weeks in order for me to have a room to myself.

"I ate breakfast with Ernie every morning and went up to the hospital with him each day. I didn't know a thing about medicine. But he taught me how to scrub, took me into surgery, let me pass him instruments, explained things, and answered questions—naive questions, stupid questions. He answered all of them with infinite patience.

"We would go up to the hospital to do surgery in the morning. Then we would come down the hill and climb under one of the nurses' cars to make some repairs. Suddenly we would get called up to do an emergency C-section, and after that maybe we'd try to repair an old water heater in the house of one of the less mechanically gifted missionaries. Then back to the hospital to see another fifty to seventy-five patients in the afternoon. Sometimes we wouldn't get back to the house for dinner until 8:30 or 9:00 p.m."[1]

---

1 David Stevens, *Jesus, M.D.* (Grand Rapids: Zondervan, 2001).

Dave learned a lot that summer because Ernie Steury was willing to invest his time and energy in a young college student with nothing more than a budding interest in medical missions. He went home from Africa at the end of that summer with a vivid and lasting picture of what it was like to be a missionary doctor. And what had impressed him most wasn't so much the medicine Ernie obviously knew and expertly practiced but the attitude and example of Christian servanthood he lived and the relationship that style created between the doctor and his patients.

Christian Compassion

Marilyn Van Kuiken recalled a patient, a Kipsigis girl who had been an active member among the youth in a nearby congregation of the Africa Gospel Church where her Christian family faithfully attended. As a teenager, she had started running with the wrong crowd of friends and became pregnant. Embarrassed and ashamed of her behavior, she didn't want her family and Christian friends to know, so she decided to abort the baby. Whoever she went to for the abortion botched the job so badly that she became severely infected. And still this young girl didn't tell anyone she was sick until the pain got so bad she couldn't get out of bed. When she finally confessed to her parents and asked them to forgive her, they rushed her to the hospital right away. But by then the girl was in critical condition.

"When we admitted her, she was in such pain she couldn't walk," Marilyn said. "But she insisted on seeing Mosonik. So we called Ernie right away. He came to her bedside and took her hand to ask how he could help her.

"Lying there, doubled up in agony, she confessed to him what she had done. She told him her parents had forgiven her. Then she begged him, 'Oh please, Mosonik, will you forgive me!' As if he could speak for God. Ernie assured her not only that he forgave her, but what was more important for her to realize was that God had already forgiven her, if she had asked him to do so.

"She suffered such horrible pain and had such a high fever, we tried to sedate her. But sometime later she cried once more for Mosonik. He came again right away and held her hand—providing his soothing touch—and he prayed with her until she calmed down.

"Later that night she died. One more patient who made peace with the Lord in her final moments because Ernie was there—caring, sensitive, and concerned about her needs."

Because the Hands Are Kind

"Another time I was in outpatient," Marilyn recalled, "when this ancient, little, shriveled-up man came walking in. He looked like he was at least a hundred. But he was probably only in his eighties—which was still very old for a Kipsigis. So I asked in a very deferential tone, 'What's eating you, old man? (*Old man* or *old woman* is a respectful salutation for an elderly person in Kipsigis.) What village are you from?' I'd never seen him around Tenwek before.

"He named a place I thought I recognized as being way over by Nakuru—more than a hundred miles away. But I wasn't sure I'd heard him correctly, so I repeated the name in the form of a question.

"He nodded his affirmation.

"I couldn't believe it. This man had to have traveled past at least a couple government hospitals and several more clinics where he could have gotten treatment absolutely free. We didn't charge our patients much—just enough to cover our operating expenses, maybe the equivalent of five American dollars for something like an appendectomy. But that was nevertheless a very significant sum of money for most Kipsigis people, so I still had a hard time believing this elderly gentleman had come to Tenwek. 'Why have you journeyed all this way to our hospital?' I asked him.

"And I will never forget his response. He looked at me and smiled as he said, 'Because the hands here are kind.'"

Chapter 11

Family Life in Kenya

The reputation for such quality of caring and service and the demonstrations of servanthood that helped earn that reputation obviously didn't come without tremendous personal sacrifice—and great cost.

Ernie Steury paid much of that price in a currency always in short supply: from his own limited treasure of time. In what was without doubt the greatest regret of his life, he would sadly admit in his later years, "There was just so much to do in those days—so many responsibilities, so many people, so many needs—that Sue pretty much raised our children."

Those same unrelenting demands that made it seem that some days would never end also resulted in Ernie's feeling that years (even entire four-year terms) had passed by in a flash. From time to time a milepost of such significance would pop up so suddenly that Ernie was forced to stop and acknowledge the rate at which life seemed to be accelerating.

Boarding School

The Steurys' third term of service in Kenya (1969–1974) encompassed a number of those milepost "surprises," one of which took place in the fall of 1971 when Nate left home, at the age of seven, to begin school at Rift Valley Academy with Cindy, who was beginning high school, and Jon. Nate was the third to go, leaving "just one of my little chicks still in the nest," as Sue lamented. "You would have thought it would have been easier after Cindy and Jon, but it wasn't. If anything, it got more difficult to let go with each child."

To understand the difficulty, imagine for a moment how it must have felt as a parent to approach your child's first day of second grade knowing from that point in childhood until they graduated from high school and left home for college, your seven- or eight-year-old would never again be living at home with you for more than three months out of every year (except during furloughs).

"Sending our children off to boarding school was the hardest thing I ever had to do in my life," Sue recalled, her voice catching on the words. "And Ernie felt the same way. Looking back, if there was anything about our lives we could change, it would probably be that. But at the time, we just didn't think we had any choice. We were in Africa where God wanted us to be, doing what we knew God called us to do. We believed boarding school for the kids was just part of the cost."

All four Steury children shared a lot of positive memories from their early family life and childhood adventures at Tenwek. They, like their parents, expressed their own regrets about having been sent off to boarding school at such an early age, although they each claim varying degrees of emotional trauma from the experience.

"We might not have understood at the time how hard it was for Mom and Dad as well," Cindy said. "But they certainly let us know they wished we could have stayed home. We always knew they didn't feel they had any choice."

Sue and Ernie worked hard to maintain a sense of connection with the children, even when they were away in school at Kijabe. "Mom always packed what she called chow boxes for us to take with us at the beginning of every term," Jon remembered. For days before the children left, Sue would make candy, bake cookies, and collect all kinds of special little treats to pack in a big square tin box each child carried along to school. If they rationed the goodies and didn't share with too many friends in the dorm, their taste of home lasted a week or two.

In addition to regular cards and letters, Ernie and Sue visited Rift Valley Academy whenever they could. Nate was the only one whose birthday didn't fall during or near a term break, so to keep him from feeling slighted about never getting to celebrate at home, the Steurys usually went to school and celebrated as a family with him there.

Ernie and Sue also tried to make the trip to see the children and their classmates compete in races and other games each year for RVA's annual Titchie Field Days. Cindy laughed about Ernie volunteering to supply the pork for a fancy pig roast the year she was involved in putting on the high school's big annual junior-senior banquet; he and Sue drove halfway across Kenya with a whole butchered pig in the back of their Volkswagen Kombi to make good on that promise.

Big Game Hunting

In their first four-year term, Ernie and Sue got away for only one real vacation—a much-needed week of relaxation on an Indian Ocean beach near the Kenyan port city of Mombasa. Most of the time they made do with a few hours here and there to rest and unwind. They would go for an occasional afternoon drive and look for some picnic spot out in the countryside.The British owners and executives of some nearby tea companies had stocked some of the highland streams with rainbow trout, so every once in a great while Ernie and Gene Lewton (or sometimes the Lewton and Steury families) would get away for a picnic and maybe an hour or two of trout fishing.

But some of the most memorable and enjoyable outings Ernie and Sue and their family ever had were overnight camping and hunting trips out to Maasailand. Not that there weren't wild animals to see at Tenwek: Hyenas occasionally roamed the grounds, and it was common to see small herds of bushbuck (a small antelope) right out on the roads. However, from the time their work was first established among the Kipsigis, Tenwek missionaries would routinely apply for big game permits to hunt particular sections of land in Maasai territory in order to harvest meat for the mission. Other missionaries had regaled Ernie with hunting tales, so his first chance to experience an African safari felt like a dream come true for an Indiana farm boy who had honed his hunting skills on barn birds and rabbits.

Fellow WGM missionary David Kellogg, who accompanied Ernie on his first hunt, recalled setting up camp near a small stream in Maasai. "Then we took a hike down to the water to scout out the terrain and look for tracks. I remember stepping over a log on the trail and watching that log suddenly take off and realizing what it was about the time it disappeared in the tall grass—a really huge python.

"The next morning Ernie and I spotted a bunch of Thompson gazelles. We circled downwind and worked our way in close enough for a good shot. Ernie dropped a nice buck for his first African trophy. We admired the horns, and I flipped the animal onto his back, his legs in the air and ready for field dressing. 'He's all yours,' I told Ernie.

"What happened next really surprised me. Growing up on a farm like he did, I knew Ernie would have seen and probably helped butcher some animals. So I expected him to take his hunting knife and gut that gazelle in a few quick strokes. Instead, he used his knife like a surgical scalpel and made this long, careful incision from the sternum all the way back to the crotch. Then he methodically removed one organ at a time, carefully lifting it out, holding it up, and examining it for a while before setting it aside and bringing out another one. Ernie was so intrigued and curious that it took forever to dress that one gazelle and then divide up the meat so that every missionary family at Tenwek and Kericho could enjoy fresh gazelle for the next few days."

Due to the scarcity and high price of domestic beef or pork in that part of Kenya, the missionaries relied on wild game as a primary source for fresh meat. So in the months and years to come, Ernie had ample opportunity to familiarize himself with the anatomy of many interesting African animals. His own family enjoyed and looked forward to those hunting trips for the camping experience in the wild and the chance to enjoy the beauty and variety of God's remarkable creation up-close and personal. The Steurys often encountered lions on trips to Maasai and occasionally a small herd of elephants. Several times they witnessed the impressive wildebeest migration. As happened with most people who have never seen a giraffe outside the confines of an American zoo, they marveled at the surprising speed and grace of those animals as they watched herds of wild giraffe loping across the African landscape, their long legs churning up the ground and their majestic heads held high above the tops of the acacia trees silhouetted against the African skyline. Most of the game the missionaries brought home came from the gazelle and antelope families. But on occasion Ernie shot warthogs or wildebeest. During one abundantly successful hunt, Ernie bagged an eland—the largest African antelope—which weighed over a thousand pounds. "Since we didn't have a constant supply of electricity, none of the missionaries had deep freezers at the time," Ernie remembered. "Just kerosene refrigerators with only tiny freezing compartments. So that bounty of eland meat ended up feeding all the missionary families at Tenwek and Kericho, plus a great number of our Kipsigis friends."

While those periodic big game hunting trips served as welcome and much-needed diversions and while they definitely made for interesting animal adventures to write home about, the constant, daily focus of the Steurys' lives in Africa was people—and the never-ending needs of the Kipsigis tribe.

Family Vacation

As the children grew older, the only way for Ernie and Sue to guarantee uninterrupted family time was to get away from Tenwek where no one could reach them. They tried to set aside a few getaway vacation days during December, April, and August when the children were home between school terms. Even with reservations and extensive planning, getting Ernie out the doors of the hospital could be a challenge.

The Steury children all recall one particularly memorable Easter holiday. "Everyone was packed and ready to go," Cindy recounted. "All excited about a week at one of our all-time favorite vacation destinations—in a tropical beach cottage just outside Mombasa on the coast of the Indian Ocean. We planned to start the long, two-day drive early in the morning, but by late afternoon we were still frustrated and waiting for Dad to get out of surgery. When he finally came rushing down the hill to the house, we all jumped in the car and took off before some other emergency could arise."

The Steurys' vehicle at the time was a tiny British-made Anglia, a car so cramped that once the family crammed in, there was no room for any luggage, which is why, attached to the top of the little car, was a big wooden box Ernie had constructed to hold everything they needed for a week at the beach. No suitcases, just everyone's belongings—folded ever so neatly in compact stacks, then jammed tightly into that homemade car-top carrier.

Evidently everything was a little too tightly jammed because, according to Cindy, "We had barely passed the security guard's gate, starting up the road on the hill just above Tenwek, still within sight of the hospital, when the top of that box popped loose and all our stuff went flying. Everyone's clothes, plus the linens we took for the beds in the beach cottage, landed on the muddy road. We weren't two minutes from home. But we didn't dare go back for clean things for fear someone would call for Dad and we wouldn't get away until the following day."

Instead they gathered up the muddy stuff and shoved it all back in the box. Ernie lashed the top on with some extra rope. Then they drove off, figuring they would wash their things once they got to Mombasa. They had a great week of swimming, snorkeling, and fishing under the sun in the clear blue waters of the Indian Ocean and relaxing together in their rented cottage playing Scrabble, Monopoly, Risk, or Rook every night.

One of the luxuries of finally having two doctors at Tenwek to cover for each other was that it was now easier to get away from time to time. But that got tougher again when Dick went back to the States on his first furlough in 1973. Ernie managed the load by himself again for a time. Then, when he desperately needed a break, WGM sent Bob Wesche and his family from the States back to Tenwek for a month to help out and make it possible for the Steurys to get away on another weeklong holiday with the family.

However, even after Sue and Ernie determined to make family time a higher priority, it was much easier to get away for a few hours, or maybe a day or two at a time, than it was for a week-long vacation. Whenever Ernie had to drive to Kericho or Nairobi or just out to see patients at a dispensary for a day, he tried to take one or more of the children along for company. Visits to the clinic in Naikarra were combined occasionally with an overnight camping trip for the family or a day of hunting in Maasailand. "The boys were in their element when they could help Ernie skin a wildebeest or a gazelle," Sue said.

Everyday Activities

Since the days and nights of recreation away from Tenwek were too few and far between, Sue looked for creative ways to help Ernie relax and get his mind off work for an hour or two at a time.

One was the Steury family garden. As Sue would laughingly say: "You can take the boy off of the farm, but you can't take the farm out of the boy." Ernie discovered that Tenwek's climate was ideal for growing tomatoes, squash, carrots, lettuce, cauliflower, cabbage, and cucumbers. He planted and raised his own strawberries. And over time an array of trees and bushes and vines in the Steurys' yard produced lemons, loquats, tangerines, oranges, passion fruit, and grapes.

Ernie never had much time to tend his garden. But he did experience such tremendous enjoyment just watching it grow that he would find a few minutes every day to go out and survey his domain. For most of the weeding, watering, and cultivating, the Steurys hired a Kipsigis gardener who also helped Sue with kitchen and household chores. Arap Tue Mising (whose name means "Son of the Very Black One") worked for the Steurys for so long that he became a part of the family. In the beginning, Tue Mising wasn't familiar with all the vegetables the Steurys wanted to grow, but with very little instruction from Farmer Ernie, he became an excellent gardener.

Entertaining was always a good option for relaxation, so despite their cramped living quarters and other limited resources, the Steurys hosted many get-togethers. Sometimes Sue would tell one or more of the other missionary women what she was fixing for supper and invite them to bring a dish or two to share in an informal dinner party.

"I wouldn't give anything for the fellowship we shared and the memories we made with our missionary colleagues in Kenya," Ernie said years later. "Because we were all so far from home, we really did become a family."

Marion Lewton agreed: "Ernie and Sue were like brother and sister to Gene and me." The Lewton children, like the Lister children and others that followed, called the Steurys Uncle Ernie and Aunt Sue. And the Steury children did likewise with the other missionaries. "Most of our MKs grew up feeling closer to the 'aunts and uncles' in our Kenyan family than they did to their extended families back home," Marion said. "A lot of times so did the adults. When we were stationed at Tenwek, before Gene and I began working out in Maasai, Sue and I would pray together for our families and we'd cry together and hold each other up when things got rough.

"I knew Sue's concern for Ernie and the constant pressure he was under. All of us did. We all prayed for him and gladly joined in whenever Sue tried to create a distraction—like Friday night family game nights."

If Ernie hadn't come down from the hospital by the time the party was scheduled to begin, Sue would often go looking for him. He would promise to be done within minutes, and Sue would hurry back home to keep the festivities going.

"Unfortunately," remembered Marion Lewton, "there were too many times when our fellowship would be interrupted by a knock on the door, and the 'daktari' would be needed to take an X-ray or perform emergency surgery. Once when Sue had planned a big birthday party for him, we had to hold most of it without the guest of honor. I never ever heard Ernie complain about those interruptions. Sue wouldn't say much either, but there were many times I could tell she was fighting back the tears when her husband got called away from some celebration or special meal she'd been planning for days. We all realized Ernie's time was not his own. Yet 'Uncle Ernie' was never too busy to squeeze in a house call if one of the missionary kids was sick. God gave him such a tremendous gift of patience that it seemed he always had time for people."

Ezekiel Kerich made much the same observation. "Many times I saw him drop his fork and spoon on the dinner table and go running for the hospital. If he had to make a journey to Nairobi or Kericho or was away from Tenwek on holiday, when he returned, the watchman often would be waiting at the front gate to stop the car and tell Dr. Steury, 'You are needed in the operating room' or 'Miss Boroff asked that you hurry to maternity.' Then without even going home first, Dr. Steury would get out, leave his car at the gate, and go wherever he was needed."

Ezekiel went on to say that in the forty years he knew and worked with Ernie, "I don't remember one time when he didn't stop what he was doing and come to answer a call. Because the Kipsigis people saw that, they knew he cared."

Or as one wizened old Kipsigis gentleman said about Daktari Steury's dependability, "Mosonik was like the river which never stops. He was always there."

Aspects of Tenwek Life

During many of the Steury children's growing-up years, their father's responsibilities and demanding hours kept him from spending as much time as they, or he, would have liked with the family. But since the hospital was just up the hill from their house, they always had the option of spending time with him at work. All four children took advantage of that opportunity.

As a rule, Jon and Nate showed less interest in the medical work than Cindy and Debbie. The boys were usually more interested in chasing stray cats out of the hospital with pellet guns than watching their dad remove an appendix. "They enjoyed spending time with Ernie doing mechanical chores," Sue said. "So when he had to fix a generator or work on one of the cars, he often had the boys with him, showing them what to do." Sue cited the time Jon and Nate (in their teens) were out in Maasai with some mission visitors when the WGM vehicle they were riding in started making a strange sound. The boys quickly jacked up the car, pulled off one of the rear wheels, cleaned some dirt or debris off the brake drum, and had everyone on the way again within minutes—problem solved. According to Sue, "Those visitors were very impressed."

The Steury girls, in contrast to their brothers, translated their exposure to medicine at Tenwek Hospital as a head start toward future careers in nursing.

Cindy said, "From the time I was very small, I would go up to the hospital, get on a stool, and watch Dad operate through the window of that little OR. By my junior high years, we had a bigger facility, and I would often scrub in and assist him. I cherished those times with my father, and I'm sure that's a big part of why I chose nursing as a career."

Marilyn Van Kuiken said, "Cindy also used to spend a lot of time holding and helping take care of the newborn babies in the nursery. And

I remember helping her deliver a baby in maternity when she was fifteen or sixteen.

"But little Debbie was the one with the earliest interest in medicine," Marilyn added. "When she was just a toddler, Sue would carry her up to the hospital to talk to Ernie while he was in surgery. Debbie always wanted to see everything. When she was six, I taught her how to scrub. Jeannine Spratt sewed her a little surgical gown, and we'd pull a box or a stool into the OR so she could watch."

According to Debbie, "Aunt Marilyn also taught me the names of the instruments. So for simple, routine cases Dad let me hand them to him as he called for them.

"Some of my most vivid memories from childhood were being with him in surgery or tagging along wherever Dad went at the hospital, from the OR, to outpatient, to X-ray, out to fix the generator, or wherever. I remember he walked so fast; I always had to run along behind him just to keep up. Especially after Nate started school and I didn't have anyone left at home to play with, I became like Dad's shadow."

For the Steury children, even the more ordinary experiences of childhood often came with a distinctive twist. Sunday school and family worship with the Africa Gospel Church congregation at Tenwek on Sunday mornings always had a lively African flavor, but every Sunday afternoon Aunt Marilyn conducted a special Sunday school class for any and all of the missionary children, residents, and visitors alike who might be on the station for that weekend.

The tiny Steury house was big enough for the family in part because everyone spent so much time outside. Winter, which technically ran from June to September, could get a bit chilly at night, but never too cool to be out and about in shirtsleeves during the days. There were trees to climb and a nearby riverbank to explore, as long as the children were wary of the occasional poisonous snake or "mentally off" stranger. The children's safety was part of the motivation for always having a family dog—both to play with the children and help keep an eye out for danger.

The boys taught Bruno, the Steurys' black Labrador mix, to climb trees in search of doggie treats and toys they hid out up in the branches. Yet he was more Debbie's dog than anyone else's. After Nate started school, Bruno became her constant companion and playmate.

Because of the bond between Debbie and Bruno, no one wanted to break the bad news to Debbie the day poor Bruno went over the falls. It happened one afternoon when two American medical students, who had come to Tenwek on a summer mission work team, took a hike down by the river. Bruno went romping along with them, fetching sticks they threw for him—ahead on the path, then out in the water. Without really thinking, one of the students hurled a stick far out into the river, and Bruno plunged after it. But before he could retrieve the stick, the current caught him, and the visitors watched in horror as he was swept over the precipice of the forty-foot falls and out of sight. They quickly climbed down to the bottom of the falls to search for him—but no Bruno. The powerful force of the cascading water must have dragged his body to the bottom or already carried his body on downstream.

The medical students felt horrible about their role in what had happened to poor Bruno. But they felt worse yet trying to decide how they could tell Debbie. All the way back from the river they discussed what they would say.

But as they approached the Steury house, they couldn't believe their eyes. There in the front yard sat Bruno, waiting and wagging his tail in greeting—still very wet, but none the worse for wear. He was not so fortunate some time later when he encountered a spitting cobra. The snake blinded him, and Bruno had to be put to sleep.

Bruno's place was eventually filled by a German shepherd named Cinder, whose claim to fame was her knack for opening latched doors (most doors on the station had lever-style handles rather than standard round doorknobs). Mastering that skill enabled her to go in and out of other Tenwek missionaries' houses at will. "Consequently," Marilyn Van Kuiken laughed, "I had a steady stream of dogs and children running through my house. But I never minded. In fact I volunteered as designated dog-sitter whenever the Steurys went on furlough."

Difficult Choices

"I don't think any of us ever doubted our parents' love," Debbie said. "But there were times as a child when it was hard not to be a little resentful when their responsibilities interfered with important family times."

Sue cited the following example: Every year on the day after Christmas, the Kenyans, like the British who had governed the colony for so many years, celebrated Boxing Day, the traditional time when the British upper classes boxed up leftover food from their own Christmas feasts, gave it to their servants, and granted them the day off to spend with their own families. In Kenya, that was also the day when all the WGM families in the country gathered together for their annual mission Christmas.

"We were celebrating at the Bible College in Kericho this particular year," Sue said. "I had the food prepared and already loaded in the car when Ernie told me, 'Honey, I just need to check on a couple patients before we take off.'

"A few minutes later he sent word, 'Tell Dick to leave his keys. I'll bring his car later.' We had all been planning on riding together in our Kombi. A woman had just been carried into emergency; her husband had celebrated Christmas by getting drunk and attacking her with a *panga*. Ernie thought it was going to take a while to patch her up, so we went on to Kericho without him.

"It ended up taking from nine that morning to three that afternoon to sew up all the woman's wounds. Ernie missed the entire party—the big annual Christmas program the children always put on for us, the huge traditional Christmas dinner, and all the favorite trimmings each family brought—everything. By the time Ernie finished at the hospital, it was too late to drive to Kericho, so he walked home to an empty house, fixed leftover hot dogs he found in the refrigerator, and tried not to think about the turkey and dressing and gravy the rest of us enjoyed that day.

"Of course, everyone felt terrible for Ernie. And I don't ever remember another time our children fussed like they did that day. They were really angry about the whole thing. Especially at the man who'd attacked his wife. When we got home to Tenwek that evening they were still complaining and demanding to know,' How could that man do that on Christmas? What a mean man! Why did he make Daddy miss our Christmas at Kericho?'

"Ernie sat the kids down and did his best to explain. He told them the man was drunk, which meant he probably didn't even know why he'd done what he did. And then he looked right at the children and assured them, 'I really, really wanted to come and be with you today. But if I had come and left this woman, she would have died. She has little children, and they would never have had a mommy ever again. I had to stay—to help save her for her children. And at least we can do other things together—because you still have me.'"

Ernie and Sue prayed many times that their children would realize their reason for making the sacrifices they made—that sometimes what God called people to do required some very difficult choices. Sometimes what missionaries have to do can even be scary.

The Enemy Is Here!

Late one night one of the maintenance men from the hospital knocked on Ernie's bedroom window and called, "Dr. Steury! Dr. Steury, come! The enemy is here. Come quickly. There are many."

What enemy? Many what? Ernie had no idea what the man was talking about. But it didn't sound good.

As Ernie himself told it later: "I don't know why I did it—I'd never done it before—but as I dressed and hurried out of the bedroom, I went to my closet, unlocked my padlocked gun case, pulled out my shotgun, and grabbed a handful of loose shells with birdshot from a box I also kept there under lock and key.

"By the time I reached the lower gate into the hospital compound, I could hear a ruckus that sounded like it was coming from the hospital business office. As I started up the sidewalk I suddenly noticed a couple of our night watchmen, who had evidently run away to hide when the commotion started, were now walking along behind me carrying bows and arrows.

"We hadn't proceeded very far before someone spotted us and started throwing rocks and empty glass pop bottles. We ducked behind the wall by the chapel as the glass shattered on the sidewalk nearby. The bottles and rocks were raining down from the terrace above us. I shouted, 'I've got a gun, and I'm going to fire it!' I put a shell in the chamber, aimed up into the air, and pulled the trigger. More rocks and bottles crashed around us.

"Peeking around the corner, I could see a number of people milling about inside the office where light was streaming out through louvered window vents. 'Are those our staff in there?' I asked.

"'No! That is the enemy!' one of the night watchmen told me.

"The only reason I could think of for intruders to be in the office was that they must be trying to break into the hospital safe. That being true, they were without doubt intoxicated and armed with *pangas.* Hospital staff or patients could have been seriously hurt, 'You better leave or I'm going to shoot again!' I warned. "Reaching into my pocket, I pulled out another shell. But as I tried to shove it into the chamber, I fumbled and dropped the shell somewhere at my feet in the dark. So I snatched another shell from my pocket, chambered it, and placed my finger on the trigger. Instead of shooting into the air this time, I lowered the muzzle toward the open office window and fired. Someone yelled, and people scattered after that second shot.

"We waited, my heart pounding. We crouched there in the darkness for several minutes before someone called out to tell us, 'They are all gone.' So we went up and found where they'd broken into the office by smashing the door. Once inside they had actually pried open the safe. Fortunately our treasurer had already counted out the day's receipts and put them in another safe in the administrator's office so Ezekiel could take and deposit the money in the bank early the next morning. All they'd found in the business office safe that night was a small bag of Kenyan coins. When I'd shot they must have dropped that, because the coins scattered all over the floor.

"We tried to call the local police on the old crank telephone there in the hospital office. But the robbers had cut the line. So we sent a message to the police station in Bomet, reporting our break-in. However, the driver for the police car had gone home for the night, so it took several hours before the officers finally arrived. In the meantime, we'd found some blood mixed with saliva on the floor of the office, which led me to speculate that one of the bird shot pellets had penetrated someone's lip or cheek. The police followed a spotty trail of blood with the tracks of about twenty men along the dirt road above the hospital. The trail ended at the main road out at the top of the hill.

"The police had no idea where to go from there. When I explained to the chief what had happened, how I'd shot in the air initially, he scolded me. 'You must shoot to kill, Dr. Steury, shoot to kill.'

"I explained that I had no intention of killing anyone. I merely wanted to scare the band of robbers away. But the policeman just shook his head and walked away muttering, 'Shoot to kill.'"

Ernie finally got to bed that night, but when he awakened the next morning he immediately remembered the shotgun shell he had dropped in the grass by the chapel. In Kenya, the law required gun owners to account for every shot fired by keeping the empty shells. So he headed up to the hospital grounds right away to look for it. In the daylight he had no trouble spotting the shell, but when he bent over and picked it up, Ernie suddenly froze. "What I thought was a shell filled with birdshot was really a slug intended for bigger game. I didn't even know I had one of those in my box. I realized as soon as I saw it that it must have been the Lord who caused me to drop that shell, because if I'd had that in my gun when I shot through the window, someone might have died."

Ernie knew the events of that night would make one more story to share in his testimony when the Steurys went home for their next furlough. How he thanked the Lord for his double protection that night: first, that the money had been moved out of the safe before the thieves broke in and that the missionary doctor at Tenwek had not killed anyone over a few dollars worth of coins.

When people back home expressed alarm or concern about the danger Ernie faced confronting that gang of thieves in the dark that night, he would share with them the same assurance he gave when people expressed concern about hazards such as poison snakes, wild animals, and waterfalls, about the uncertain ramifications of difficult decisions on his patients or his family, or about the threat of illness the family itself had faced during that third term with his malaria, Sue's hepatitis, and a brief bout Cindy had with tuberculosis.

"The safest place in the world," Ernie would always tell people, "is in the center of God's will."

What he didn't realize was that confident faith, which had served him so well for the fifteen years since he had come to Africa, that certainty about being in the center of God's will, was about to be tested as never before. Not at Tenwek. The challenge came once the Steurys returned to America for their upcoming furlough.

Chapter 12

THE LORD PROVIDES

Two Years in the States

The Steurys had much good news to report to their supporters as they looked back over their most recent five-year term (1969–74). Ernie reported, "Two new wards were built for our isolation and maternity patients. We now have better facilities in these areas than ever before. The new lab extension has not only enlarged our laboratory facilities but has also supplied a physiotherapy room and much-needed office space. This past year 5,500 inpatients were admitted, and," as Ernie was always most excited to report, "more than 1,500 people found the Lord. There seems to be a real hunger for the things of God among the Kipsigis people."

Wherever the Steurys spoke about their work at Tenwek Hospital, they explained how much was being accomplished with so little. And as they always tried to do on their furlough travels, they emphasized the opportunity for additional ministry in Kenya if they could further expand the hospital work—in terms of facilities and staff. But in the fall of 1974, the responsibility for recruiting new donors for Tenwek and rallying their own supporters to continue their financial backing of the Steurys themselves weighed a little heavier than usual on Ernie's shoulders.

Naturally the Steurys had been thinking for some time about the added cost of higher education for Cindy, who was starting Asbury College, and eventually the other children. Sue recalled, "Ernie would pray, 'Lord, we don't know how we'll pay for college. We're depending on you.' And then he tried not to fret about it. But I probably did enough worrying for us both."

Many of Ernie's doctor friends back in the States were more aware than most people of the financial sacrifice he had made to go into medical missions. Some of them would say to him, "Doesn't it ever worry you how you will pay for your kids' education?" But Ernie believed God would provide. And indeed He did, in a variety of ways. One way included some of those doctor friends who were so impressed by Ernie's commitment that they told him that when his children were ready to come back to the States for college, they wanted to help.

So more than ever before, the Steurys were mindful of how dependent they were on the generosity of others. A cousin of Ernie's, who had just retired and planned to try apartment life and do some traveling, offered them his own beautiful home to live in there in Berne while they were back in the States. Everyone enjoyed a house with more room than they had ever had before. The three younger children especially loved being able to come home from school every day.

But even their positive public school experience contributed to the constant consciousness of the family's financial status. "Based on the salary we received from WGM, our children actually qualified for the government's free lunch program," Sue said. "We were glad they didn't have to feel embarrassed. But we were surprised to learn they considered it such a privilege that everywhere we went it seemed Jon and Nate were proudly informing people that their school gave them their lunches 'for free.'"

That was just one circumstance among many events during that furlough that seemed to conspire to keep financial issues at the forefront of Ernie's mind, as well as the minds of other family members.

"As children growing up, I don't think any of us ever considered ourselves poor," Jon Steury said. "We always had what we needed, and usually what we wanted, except for those not-in-your-wildest-dreams kind of things—like horses, motorcycles, and trampolines—which we never expected anyway. Our parents had certainly never given us a sense that we were sacrificing anything to be missionaries.

"But now, as the new kid in my junior high school back in Berne, I wanted to fit in. And I was convinced that what I needed in order to fit in was a hot new ten-speed bike like so many of my classmates had. I saw one at K-Mart for 104 dollars. But when that bike was the only thing I put on my Christmas list that year, my parents told me that was probably going to be out of their price range and pressed me for additional ideas. Only reluctantly did I give some other suggestions, and not until I made it clear that the only thing I really wanted was that bike.

"Fortunately for me, I guess some friends gave Mom and Dad extra money for their personal use that December. My folks were able to get me that ten-speed I'd wanted. I was thrilled."

But that experience seemed to have sensitized Jon in a new way to the sacrifices the Steurys had made. And it may have set the stage for another family experience Sue recounted. A successful local physician in Berne, who had a big house on a hill outside of town, had invited the Steurys to come out to his place and bring the children to fish in his private lake, and one day the family took the man up on his offer. However, just getting onto the property required stopping to buzz for admission at a big gate that blocked the driveway. There Ernie and the family were instructed to come to the house to introduce themselves before going down to the lake to fish.

The gate and the intercom made a powerful first impression. But it wasn't until the Steurys headed up the drive and the huge house came into sight that Jon announced to his awestruck siblings, "See what all we could have if Daddy had a practice here in the States!"

Without even a moment's hesitation, ten-year-old Nate spoke up to observe in a rather matter-of-fact way, "But we wouldn't be happy, because that isn't where God wants us, and we wouldn't be doing His will."

According to Sue, "Nate's response meant so much to Ernie and me. He and I talked about it later—how it was one thing for us to understand our calling and the reasons for our commitment. To believe we were doing what we did because God had called us. But how much more it meant to know that our children not only understood, but accepted that as well."

In May of 1975 the entire family took a trip to Asbury College in time for the graduation ceremony. There the Steury children, and a lot of other people, gained some understanding about the significance of their parents' work. During the graduation exercises, Ernie's alma mater conferred upon him its first honorary doctor of science degree. A portion of the citation's text said: "Rarely has any individual gone from the halls of Asbury College who more completely epitomizes the missionary spirit and passion of this institution than does Ernie Steury. He not only is a doctor of competence and commitment who ministers with great humanitarian compassion to the people of Kenya, but also has a fervent passion for souls. It is with pride that Asbury College this day honors one of her sons whose life and labors reflect continually upon his alma mater great credit and honor."

Not long after that accolade, World Gospel Mission recognized both Ernie and Sue in the September 1975 *Call to Prayer* with a special "Spotlight on Dr. & Mrs. Ernest Steury: Right Place, Right Time." The large magazine spread included photos showing both Ernie and Sue ministering in Kenya, a picture of the entire family, and a shot of Ernie accepting his honorary degree at Asbury College. The story recounted Ernie and Sue's callings to the mission field and presented an anecdotal picture of their work at Tenwek ministering not just to the Kipsigis people but also to fellow missionaries. The article also referenced the history of Tenwek by commenting: "When one recalls the many years in which faithful prayer band members continually interceded for a doctor to go to Kenya, it is not surprising God found the man He was looking for. Few could have foreseen during that waiting period that God was choosing carefully—He was choosing an evangelist/doctor, not just a doctor."

Unlike during the two previous furloughs, things seemed to be operating smoothly at Tenwek—despite Ernie's absence—so Ernie asked and received the mission agency's permission to stay in the States an extra year so he could brush up in the field of medicine and surgery.

Ernie felt there had been so much progress since he had graduated from medical school that he needed to catch up on all the latest developments in order to offer the best possible care to his patients at Tenwek. He looked into the possibility of doing a year in some surgical residency program because so much of his work at Tenwek was in surgery. But all of his doctor friends in the States as well as missionary doctors he talked to advised against a residency program. "That would be crazy, Ernie," they told him. "You'd spend most of your time holding a retractor for instructors who haven't had nearly as much experience as you've had."

Most of them agreed: The best and fastest way to catch up on changing medical techniques and treatment was just to practice for a while in an American hospital setting. Ernie's friends at Caylor-Nickel Clinic in nearby Bluffton, Indiana, gave him that opportunity. For eight months of his second furlough year, they hired Ernie to do general surgery and family practice in a state-of-the-art medical facility that had such a reputation that it was often referred to as "Little Mayo" in that part of the country.

Not only did that experience bolster Ernie's confidence and medical skills, it provided multiple benefits for the entire Steury family. A second year in the States enabled them to see Cindy through her first two transitional years of college: first at Asbury and then at Marion College (now Indiana Wesleyan University), which offered a nursing program.

For Sue the greatest blessing of that two-year furlough was not only the proximity to their college daughter but the chance to be a family again. For two straight years the boys would come home from school every day. Debbie's second- and third-grade years in the Indiana public schools put off for two more years the day Sue dreaded when she would have to send her youngest off to boarding school. And the family got to celebrate Thanksgiving together both years, which never happened in Kenya, where the third Thursday of November wasn't considered a national holiday and the children were always away at Kijabe finishing up their first school term of the year.

Ernie's opportunity to work those months in American medicine offered the Steurys yet another significant benefit—this one financial. With WGM's blessing, Ernie opted to give up his mission wages for eight months to accept the salary offered him as a temporary employee of the Caylor-Nickel Clinic. Ernie and Sue were able to help pay some of Cindy's college costs and purchase a used car for their own use now, with the intention of leaving it for Cindy when they headed back to Africa.

"One day when a doctor friend paid Ernie to cover his practice for him," Sue said, "Ernie brought home more pay than we received for an entire month in Kenya!" While the Steurys considered the added income a well-timed blessing, Ernie couldn't help feeling conflicted by it. "He told me he thought it would be difficult to ever work in the States, where he would have to determine how much to charge patients," Sue continued. "At Tenwek he didn't receive a penny from patient fees, which paid only a portion of treatment costs. All missionary salaries were paid by WGM from the funds we raised for our own support.

"'It would be so difficult to charge patients for my service,' Ernie would say. 'The prices are so high here in the States. People can't afford to get sick, and they can't afford to die!'"

His work at Caylor-Nickel Clinic accomplished all that Ernie had intended or hoped for. And more.

The family practice work, and especially the experience in general surgery, did bring him up to speed on the most recent advances in office procedures, surgical techniques, and prescription medicine. Everything he learned from working alongside his American colleagues gave Ernie added confidence that he could provide better care than ever at Tenwek when he headed back to Africa. But it was the professional affirmation and personal feedback he received from those same colleagues that first made him wonder if he should go back.

Ernie seemed to elicit two basic reactions from the doctors he worked with: First, they let him know they were very impressed with the breadth of his medical knowledge and experience. They recognized and marveled at his skill as a surgeon, which they considered all the more remarkable when they learned his surgical techniques were for the most part self-taught. Second, they felt compelled to try a variety of approaches to convince him he really ought to stay in the States. "You've spent fifteen years as a missionary to Africa. You've done your time, Ernie. Now you can do something for yourself and your own family."

"Why don't you stay with us, Ernie? We could really use you here."

"You could serve God here. Indiana needs Christian doctors too, you know."

A half dozen different colleagues made comments like these in separate conversations, all on the same day, near the end of Ernie's scheduled time at the clinic. He went home that evening wondering if that was a coincidence, and if it wasn't, what did it mean? The administrators at the clinic had made it clear he had an open invitation to come back any time—for as long as he wanted. The husband of one of Ernie's cousins, a successful physician with an established practice in Michigan, offered Ernie a partnership if he would stay and work with him—at a starting salary that sounded mind-boggling.

Of course Ernie told Sue about the comments from his colleagues as well as the opportunities offered. He admitted the idea of staying had its appeal. "But I don't feel I've been released from my calling," he told his wife.

What he didn't say to Sue, because he didn't know what to make of it himself, was just how serious a struggle was going on inside of him. He had never doubted God's call to become a medical missionary to Africa, and he still didn't. He had seen how God had used him at Tenwek. He knew there was a lot more work to be done there. But for the first time in his life, he had begun to wonder if God really was expecting him to carry on the work.

Even as he finished his tenure at the clinic and accepted a few more speaking engagements to create additional interest and raise a little more prayer and financial support for the ministry, Ernie wrestled with these unprecedented feelings of doubt and tried to analyze the reason for them. *Why didn't he feel the same excitement he'd felt before leaving on his three previous terms?*

Knowing they would be leaving their oldest daughter behind may have been one reason it was harder to pack up this time. And two straight years of being back in the States, together as a family with the younger children coming home from school every day, made it harder to think about sending Jon, Nate, and even Debbie off to boarding school just weeks after they got back to Kenya. Two years of practice in America with all kinds of medical resources and modern technology, twenty-four-hour-a-day electrical power, not having to work at such a demanding pace, and being able to expect a full night's sleep on a regular basis made the prospect of returning to Tenwek with all its challenges and responsibilities seem more daunting than ever. Ernie hoped the problem wasn't a spiritual one—that he wasn't merely being tempted by the allure of an

American lifestyle and all the material things that could mean for him and his family.

But the truth was, Ernie didn't know why he was struggling so. After years of serving the Lord in Africa and seeing time and again how God always provided the physical, emotional, professional, financial, and spiritual resources he needed, Ernie felt guilty about any feelings of doubt. And that guilt was magnified as he continued to speak about the ministry at Tenwek and as he and Sue sent off the last pre-departure prayer letter in July of 1976 to tell their supporters: "We are excited about returning to Kenya! We feel that this is where the Lord wants us, and we are looking to the Holy Spirit to guide and use our lives as we serve Him there. Please pray for us as we travel to Kenya and return to our work."

Ernie did a lot of praying of his own during that time. And he needed to because, despite his uncertainties, the Steurys continued packing. They left for Africa on Friday, July 20, 1976, as planned. When they arrived back in Kenya three days later, the joyous welcome they received from missionaries and Kipsigis alike warmed their hearts. But it wasn't enough to dispel Ernie's doubts.

Still, Ernie didn't want to burden Sue with his feelings because he knew she was facing an emotional struggle of her own. The occasion she had been dreading for years was fast approaching: The school year was about to begin, and their youngest child would be going off to boarding school for the first time. The fact that they'd been able to delay this day of reckoning until Debbie was ready to start fourth grade didn't make it any easier at all.

The drive to Rift Valley Academy to get the children settled into a new school year prompted a wide range of emotions inside the Steury vehicle. Jon and Nate, while not exactly glad to be starting school, were excited about seeing old friends again after two years in America. Debbie naturally felt apprehensive and even fearful at the thought of being so far away from her parents. Sue was just trying not to fall apart emotionally at the prospect of giving up her last child, her youngest daughter, for the sake of God's calling on her life. And then there was Ernie, still wondering if he were supposed to be doing this again and realizing that if he had stayed in the States, none of them would have to make this sacrifice.

Somehow they all got through the moving into dorms and the eventual and inevitably emotional goodbyes. Sue admitted to being a "basket case" all the way home, perhaps more than a little angry with God over the expectation that once again ministry seemed to take precedence over family.

When they got back to Tenwek that night, Sue couldn't bring herself to walk into their house. Instead, she sat on a stonewall at the edge of the yard and announced, "I'm not going back into that morgue."

Ernie didn't know what to say or do. Then Sue finally relented, stood up, and walked through the front door into their empty house.

Eventually Ernie got Sue to talk about her feelings, and that evidently helped him to open up his heart as he finally admitted, "Honey, I'm really having the hardest time feeling good about being back here at Tenwek. I'm struggling because I'm wondering if I was supposed to stay in the States. Maybe God really was trying to tell me something with all those offers I was getting."

"I'd never seen Ernie so discouraged by anything," Sue said. "It was like we were living under this dark emotional cloud. So he and I started praying together every day about each other's struggles. Even then it took maybe three more months before that cloud finally began to lift."

The Great Physician

Time, the demanding hospital routine, and daily exposure to the deep and ongoing needs of the people around him helped remind Ernie why God had called him to Tenwek in the first place as well as why he stayed.

One day Ramona Thomas's Land Rover ambulance from WGM's Maasai dispensary at Naikarra rolled into Tenwek. She helped a crippled young Maasai warrior climb out of the back seat and hobble painfully into the hospital. As Ernie began to examine him, Ramona explained that her patient had injured his ankle two years earlier. He developed chronic osteomyelitis (bone infection) and had received treatment at several government dispensaries and clinics without significant improvement. He had eventually been admitted to another hospital where surgery had been performed, again without improvement.

Ernie noted the extensive infection evidenced by marked swelling and redness. "It was obvious that treatment would be difficult and a cure almost impossible," Ernie remembered later. "I was about to ask Ramona to tell the Maasai man there was little or nothing we could do for him, when the patient started speaking. Ramona translated his words, 'I have come to Tenwek because I know that God will help me get well here!'

"What could I say? With the patient coming to us with such faith, certainly we missionaries could believe God for the healing of this ankle!"

Ernie gathered a number of the hospital staff to pray for this man before he was taken to surgery for an extensive operation to remove all the infected tissue. Every post-surgical dressing change revealed encouraging improvement in the man's condition. Within a few months the wound had completely healed with no evidence of infection at all. Ernie discharged the Maasai man with a set of crutches and strict instructions not to put weight on his newly healed ankle for several more weeks.

Some months later, Ernie journeyed out to Naikarra for a regular dispensary visit. While there he helped lead an evangelistic worship service in a nearby Maasai village. During that service a middle-aged man approached Ernie and insisted the missionaries not leave the village until he returned.

Ernie recalled: "I watched as he disappeared over the hill. Wondering at this strange request, we continued with the service.

"Several minutes later I saw the man returning with another Maasai warrior who was carrying a goat on his shoulders, its front and back feet tied tightly and grasped in his hands. That man with the goat was our former patient, now walking without even a sign of a limp, bringing us a gift of love and gratitude. Christ had again proven to be the Great Physician."

God's Mighty Power

A few years before, Marilyn Van Kuiken had admitted a young Kipsigis man she knew at a glance was desperately ill. Zakayo was 5'10" and weighed only 115 pounds. He couldn't keep any food in his stomach, and his hemoglobin had fallen to 7 (from a normal 12–18). X-rays showed a large mass filling his abdomen, and when Ernie examined him, the diagnosis became obvious. The young man was full of cancer. Inoperable. Ernie sadly informed the family there was nothing they could do but take Zakayo home and care for him as he died.

But Marilyn had become burdened for this young man's soul. "Before Zakayo was discharged," she said, "I talked to him about the Lord. How God had sent Jesus to earth to die for his sins, so that he could live in heaven with Him forever. He was very open to what I said. With tears in his eyes, he prayed and asked Jesus into his life. Then he went home with his family to die."

Two or three months later, Marilyn received a surprise letter from Zakayo saying, "I am still following the Lord, and I am now well." He was looking for work and wondered if there were any positions open at Tenwek. When Marilyn mentioned the letter to Ernie, he suggested she ask Zakayo to return to the hospital for a follow-up examination.

Several days later he arrived on a bicycle he had ridden from his village twenty-five kilometers away, balancing a box of fresh eggs on the back as a gift for Marilyn. The staff could hardly believe this was the same man. Zakayo now weighed 145 pounds, his hemoglobin was 15, and he could eat anything and everything. When Ernie re-examined him, the abdominal mass was completely gone. "We were all thrilled and praised the Lord," said Marilyn, "because we knew He was the one who had done this, not us. Zakayo realized it as well. Through tears of joy he told us he knew he was alive only because of God's mercy.

"We found a job for Zakayo. He trained as a lab assistant and ended up working at Tenwek for more than fifteen years. His testimony resulted in many people from his village becoming Christians. His cheerful smile and his readiness to work were a constant blessing to us all," Marilyn said. "Whenever we looked at him, we saw the evidence of God's mighty power." Indeed, Zakayo served as a daily reminder to the medical staff that at Tenwek Hospital, sometimes even when they couldn't treat, "Jesus healed."

The Door Is Always Open

One evening long after dark, Ernie finally finished his rounds and decided it was time to head home for the night. He walked through the familiar terraced hospital compound in the darkness, down the sidewalk to the lower gate. He let himself out and was just locking the door behind him when two men on bicycles came rolling into the small circle of light cast by the single light bulb hanging outside the hospital gate. As the men coasted to a stop, Ernie noticed one of them had a child in a sling on his back.

"*Chamagei*!" Ernie greeted them and then asked in Kipsigis, "May I help you?"

"Yes," replied one of the men. "We are lost. We have a very sick child here. Can you please tell us how to find Tenwek Hospital?"

As Ernie explained that they were at Tenwek, he turned right around in his tracks, reopened the gate, and took them into the hospital. He treated the child successfully, and a few days later the men took a healthy little boy home.

But Ernie never forgot the encounter he had had with those men in the dead of night. For years he used it as an analogy when he spoke, making the point for his listeners that there were many people (and not just African people) still lost in spiritual darkness that didn't know where to find the help they needed. Some of them were just outside the gates and didn't even know it. They just needed someone to open the door and invite them in.

Tenwek's Spiritual Ministry

From his earliest days in Africa, Ernie had always told his hospital staff that medical treatment was only part of Tenwek's goal. To be the kind of mission hospital God wanted, they needed to be just as concerned about the spiritual condition as they were the physical health of everyone who walked in the door. "We don't just treat the physically sick; we need to help the sin-sick as well."

Now beginning his fourth term in Africa, Ernie became more concerned than ever about Tenwek's spiritual ministry. Perhaps one of the biggest reasons for this was an exciting and very significant staff person. In 1975 while the Steurys were on furlough, the Africa Gospel Church had appointed Reverend David Kilel to serve as full-time chaplain for Tenwek Hospital.

Soon after Ernie had arrived at Tenwek, he arranged for the hospital to hire a layperson from a local Africa Gospel Church congregation to serve as hospital chaplain. This in no way released him (or the other medical staff) from the responsibility and privilege of addressing patients' spiritual issues. Ernie just believed, even after he became fluent in Kipsigis himself, that patients could better communicate and identify with someone who shared their culture and background and that there would be real advantages if they understood this wasn't just some "white man's religion."

The national chaplaincy program had been a distinctive and effective part of Tenwek's ministry for years. Busy as the hospital was, doctors and nurses had a limited amount of time to spend with each patient. While they routinely witnessed to and prayed with patients, it was the chaplain whose job it was to follow up and spend time in the wards answering questions and offering additional spiritual guidance and counsel to interested individuals.

The chaplain also took charge of daily services held each morning in the hospital's chapel located in the courtyard at the center of the hospital grounds. In the beginning, chapel attendance had been mandatory for all patients who were well enough to be there. Then after Kenya's independence, it was suggested chapel become voluntary. However, that change caused no significant drop-off in attendance. Patients and their families were drawn to the sound of singing every morning, and the crowded chapel services continued to be an important and effective means of spiritual and evangelistic outreach.

Ernie was especially pleased to have David Kilel, not just another layperson but a fully ordained minister, as the new hospital chaplain. David came with excellent qualifications. Not only had he recently completed his formal training at Kenya Highlands Bible College in Kericho, he had already earned a reputation among the Kipsigis and the missionaries as one of the sharpest and most promising young spiritual leaders in the Africa Gospel Church. And David was excited about being at Tenwek.

The two men shared a genuine burden for the patients. "Dr. Steury challenged me to be faithful to the Lord and to my calling," David explained. "He always said, 'David, there is no reason to have Tenwek Hospital without the gospel. I don't want any patient leaving here without hearing about Jesus.'"

Ernie took to David Kilel like a son. "He loved me," David recalled. "We became friends. We regularly prayed together about patients, the hospital, even about personnel problems. He became my closest brother in the Lord." The result of that partnership between the American missionary doctor and the young Kipsigis chaplain paid great dividends for the kingdom of God, as over three thousand patients and visitors went forward for prayer in the chapel services or accepted Christ as David witnessed to them at their bedsides during 1977.

Yet David and Ernie's concern for their many new converts didn't end when the people left Tenwek. They worried that many of these baby Christians were returning to home villages that might not have a church or anyone to nurture them in the faith. So the two men prayed constantly about how to follow up with the many people who made spiritual commitments while they were hospitalized at Tenwek.

David's chaplaincy work expanded so quickly that he soon took on a full-time assistant. Although he was more than willing to visit with former patients in their homes, that was difficult to accomplish since people came to Tenwek from all over Kipsigis territory. It would take many hours and sometimes more than a day to walk to the most distant villages. He needed a vehicle. But he and Ernie agreed a car would be very expensive, and not all villages were even accessible by road. So the hospital provided the chaplain with a *piki-pik* (Swahili for motorbike) that became a vital part of Tenwek's unique follow-up ministry.

The Visitor

Early one morning as Marilyn Van Kuiken walked to work, she suddenly came face to face with a full-grown male baboon in the hospital courtyard. The animal had escaped the previous day from a cage at the nearby secondary school where it had lived in captivity for eight years. The baboon eventually found its way onto the hospital grounds, roaming around, creating chaos, terrifying patients and staff, avoiding repeated attempts by Ernie and the staff to ensnare or drug it, and then evading the security guards all night long.

Now here he was, in the middle of the sidewalk, aggressively baring his four-inch fangs and walking right toward the wary nurse. Marilyn knew that adult baboons are capable of killing a person, that their jaws are powerful enough to crush a human skull.

"I stood very still, praying and trying to decide what to do," Marilyn said. "But he walked right up to me and grabbed my left leg with his hand. When I tried to pull free, he opened his mouth to bare his teeth at me again and tightened his grip on the calf of my leg."

"Oh Lord, help me!" she prayed. Then she reached down and took firm hold of the baboon's face. It looked up at Marilyn and opened its mouth as if it were really going to bite her. Then, just as suddenly, it let go, ambled a few feet away, and sat down.

Realizing it wouldn't be safe to leave the animal sitting in the middle of the hospital courtyard, Marilyn stood where she was and directed a staff member to run down to her house and bring back a banana. When she got the fruit, she tossed a small piece of it toward the baboon. When he picked it up and popped it in his mouth, Marilyn whistled softly and showed him what she had left. Walking cautiously, she led the creature toward the doorway of the empty minor surgical room, threw the rest of the banana inside, and when the baboon went for the fruit, she quickly slammed and latched the door.

Immediately she sent for Ernie. When he arrived, the two of them discussed their next step. The longer the animal was confined, the greater the risk he would do serious damage to the room and the equipment inside. And if he hurt himself in the process, he would almost certainly become more agitated and violent. They agreed that they needed to sedate him. But this was a frightened, unpredictable wild animal; it wasn't safe for anyone to approach him.

Ernie had an idea. He went to the surgical supply shelf and returned with a bottle of ether and some rags. He carefully opened the ether, soaked one of the rags with it, tossed the wet cloth into the room through a vent window, and waited. Nothing happened. He soaked another rag and threw it in. They could still hear the animal moving around. After several rags went in, things got quiet.

At that point Ernie went into the room to inject the baboon with a more powerful anesthetic. However, the animal aroused and jumped at him, knocking him backwards out of the room. Ernie quickly slammed the door and went back to his previous ether-soaked-rag strategy. "I don't remember how many rags it finally took," Marilyn said. "But Ernie used up two bottles of that ether before deciding to check on the animal again."

This time the plan called for Ernie to enter the room holding a blanket in front of him to throw over the baboon's head if he attacked. Two of the national staff followed him in, carrying pieces of rope to bind the animal's hands and feet. The baboon seemed to be out cold. But Ernie wasn't taking any more chances. He injected the creature with a whole syringe of powerful anesthetic as the other men tied up the animal.

By now a crowd of people were pressed up to the doorway to see the baboon. They were merely curious, but they also blocked Ernie's retreat from the room. "I need to get out!" Ernie called, in a bit of a panic as he could feel himself going under from the lingering effects of the ether.

When the crowd failed to give way, Ernie almost had to fight his way out, pushing and shoving to get to fresh air. Realizing what was happening, Marilyn began pulling people away from the door to help clear a path. Ernie stumbled out of the room and almost fell into a sitting position on the sidewalk.

A couple of the hospital guards grabbed the unconscious animal and rushed him back to his cage at the school before he woke up. What Ernie hadn't told anyone was that he had purposefully overdosed the baboon in hopes that it wouldn't survive because it had been and could again be a serious threat to the people at the hospital as well as the high school students who regularly made a sport of teasing and harassing the poor caged animal. When the school headmaster called to ask why the baboon hadn't awakened yet, Ernie acknowledged that he "might" have given it too much anesthesia.

The animal never did wake up. So the school's science teacher, not wanting to lose an opportunity, hung the carcass up in a tree just below the mission compound and left it for the crows to pick clean so that he could use the skeleton for display in the science department of the high school. It seems the school staff had the last laugh in that incident as the smell of decaying baboon wafted across the compound for days.

Professional Helpers

In May, two Ugandan doctors, refugees fleeing the brutal regime of the Ugandan tyrant, General Idi Amin, joined the Tenwek staff. A visiting medical student also came from the States from April to June. So for a while before Dick Morse left on furlough, there were five doctors at Tenwek. "Which was really great while it lasted," Ernie said. "It just didn't last long enough."

Later in the summer, a doctor from Texas filled in for Ernie for a few weeks around the time of his daughter Cindy's marriage to Daniel Tolan at Tenwek. Not long after the Texan doctor went home, one of the Ugandans went elsewhere. A few months later the other left for further training, and the full load of hospital work fell on Ernie again.

"One day as we met to pray together, I could see how tired he was," David Kilel remembered. "So I asked, 'Dr. Steury, why don't you request other physicians to come from home to help you? You are finishing yourself!'

"He said to me, 'David, I have been talking to them, but they don't want to come. Perhaps they are too comfortable where they are. I don't know.'

"'Let us pray about that,' I said. So we got down on our knees and asked God to please provide the doctors Tenwek needed."

Pacemakers and Peacemakers

Even for a man of Ernie Steury's commitment and faith, after almost two decades of physically grueling, soul-draining work, it was hard to understand why God had not sent the professional medical help so obviously needed at Tenwek, especially when He provided in so many other obvious ways for patients and missionaries alike. Ernie always enjoyed citing this example of God's provision.

The large pool of blood on the floor startled Ernie as he walked into the men's ward early one morning in 1978. *What in the world happened here?*

Who had bled so badly? When he asked the patients, they pointed toward an elderly gentleman in a nearby bed. His face was badly swollen, and blood oozed from several places where his teeth had punctured his lips.

The patient had arrived the previous evening, and when he had awakened and got out of bed in the night to go to the bathroom, he fainted, fell face-first onto the concrete floor, and severely injured himself. Ernie examined his wounds and then felt his wrist to take his pulse. It was only 30! When he listened to his heart it sounded regular, but confirming the rate of 30 beats a minute made the diagnosis an easy one. The man had a complete heart block.

Ernie learned the man had been misdiagnosed and treated at several dispensaries for epilepsy because he would often stand up and faint and at times convulse.

In the States they would have given this patient a pacemaker. But Tenwek didn't have one. And the only Kenyan Ernie knew who had one went overseas to have it implanted. So for the next few days, he treated the man with a variety of drugs without improvement.

Later that same week, Ernie was summoned to the women's ward to see a sick lady. When he examined her he was surprised to find she had a pulse of only 35. Another complete heart block. This was the second in one week, and he hadn't seen another one during twenty years at Tenwek. How his heart ached for these two patients; there was no hope for them without pacemakers.

As Ernie pondered their predicament, the Lord reminded him of MAP, International, an organization originally started by the Christian Medical Society that supplied medicine and equipment to many hospitals throughout the world. Maybe they could help!

He sent a cablegram to the States, asking MAP for two cardiac pacemakers with electrodes that could be inserted into the heart through a vein. He explained he could not afford to pay more than one hundred dollars for each.

Ten days later Ernie took a visiting doctor and his family to the airport in Nairobi. There was a cablegram waiting for him there that read:

PEACEMAKERS ARRIVING 10/11 NAIROBI ON KLM, FLT 591 AT 9:10 AM.

This seemed almost too good to be true. As he reread the cablegram he noticed the misspelled word, with the "E" crossed out. And he thought, *Wouldn't it be wonderful if we could order peacemakers and implant them into the hearts of people?* Then he realized the wonderful truth is that they did have a Peacemaker, Jesus Christ, who was changing the hearts of patients at Tenwek Hospital every day.

Ernie took the devices back to Tenwek, and three days later everything was set up for the man's surgery. The surgery took place in the X-ray room so that Ernie and his assistants could watch the fluoroscope to guide them as they threaded the electrode into a vein in the shoulder and then down into the man's heart. The surgery went slowly because the old X-ray machine kept malfunctioning, and Ernie had never done the procedure before. But when he finally got the electrode in place and the connections were made, he slipped the pacemaker into its pocket under the skin and then turned to watch the screen of the heart monitor. First he saw a little spike of the pacemaker, and then a steady 72 heart beats a minute. Everyone present exclaimed, "Praise the Lord!"

Two days later Ernie operated on the woman. Just as in the first surgery, the electrode passed into the heart, they connected the pacemaker, and the pulse rate immediately jumped to 72 beats per minute. But after thirty seconds her pulse rate plummeted again to 35. Ernie worked for the next two hours trying to get pacing again without success. When they finally had to quit, everyone was disheartened. Ernie wondered, *Is there something wrong with this particular pacemaker? Or is there too much scarring inside the heart for the electrical impulse to stimulate the heart muscle?* As he explained the potential problems to the patient after the unsuccessful operation, her response was, "God knows; if He wants me to get well, He will help you find a way to do it, but if not, then I am ready to go and be with Him."

Ernie wrote a letter to the Medtronics Company, which manufactured the pacemakers, explaining the problem. They sent the type of electrode that could be surgically implanted directly into the heart muscle. The lady was taken to the OR, where Ernie attached the electrode to the heart itself and then connected it to the pacemaker. Immediately the woman's heart rate jumped to 72 beats a minute. This time it stayed there.

Since both patients were Christians, when Ernie told the story he liked to say: "The Peacemaker is keeping their hearts at peace while the pacemakers are pacing their hearts. God is so good." He certainly provided two patients at a remote mission hospital out in the African bush with the modern technology they needed to live a normal life again.

Maasailand Miracle

God also provided for the needs of His missionaries in amazing and unusual ways, like the time Ernie, Cindy, and Jon took some college students from the Summer Career Corps (WGM's volunteer summer missions program) out in the Land Rover. They were traveling to Maasai on a camera safari to observe and photograph African animals in the wild.

According to Jon, "We had left Naikarra after a long morning's work at the dispensary and stopped at a rocky outcropping for a picnic lunch. When we got out of the vehicle, we heard the hiss of a flat tire. Dad changed the tire, using the spare, and we proceeded on toward home after we'd eaten. Crossing the Loita plains, Dad decided the young people with us might like to see a natural hot spring that was a few miles off the road. As we got out of the vehicle at the springs, we again heard the hiss of a tire. A second flat. That's when Dad discovered that no one had checked the hospital vehicle to make sure it had all the necessary emergency supplies. There was no patch glue (or patching gum, as the British called it) to repair the punctures.

"We hiked over to a nearby hunting camp and asked if they had any gum. They didn't, but suggested Dad moisten the patch with gasoline in order to melt the rubber enough to bond with the tube. We did that, then Dad pumped up the tire and, because it seemed to be holding, put it back on the vehicle. Then we drove off. But a short while later, still out on the vast plains of Maasailand, the patch gave out and the tire went flat again."

There they were in the middle of the Maasai Reserve with a bunch of American college students in a Land Rover with two flat tires and no way to fix them. Ernie prayed for guidance, and then he studied the horizon, trying to decide whether he should start walking. He wondered just how many miles of rolling grasslands and how many prides of prowling lions were between him and the nearest road and how long it would be till he could flag down a vehicle for a ride to a town big enough to have a gas station or a store that would have the necessary supplies to fix the tire.

As he surveyed his surroundings, Ernie noted a dark speck and a tiny cloud of dust in the distance. The dust drew nearer and the speck grew steadily larger until it gradually took on the recognizable and unlikely shape of a motorcycle and rider. It was roaring right toward them over the wild Kenyan countryside, sending herds of animals scattering in every direction as it came.

Moments later the African gentleman riding that motorbike pulled to a stop near the Land Rover and inquired if anything were wrong. Ernie explained the situation and asked if he had any tire-patching gum. The man smiled and handed Ernie a brand new tube. "I have another container that is almost full," he explained. "So when I stopped and bought this at a store in the last town I passed through, I really didn't know why. Now I do. You can keep it."

Ernie thanked him and turned toward the Land Rover. When he turned back to say something else, the man was gone. No roaring motorcycle engine. No cloud of dust. "It was like he just disappeared," Ernie said.

"Afterwards," Jon said, "Dad said he often wondered if that was a time we had entertained angels unaware." Angel or not, the experience served a grateful missionary, not to mention a van load of nervous college students, as a memorable reminder of God's ability to provide.

A New Source of Doctors

Early in 1978 Ernie received correspondence from a fledgling group called World Medical Mission; it was inquiring about Tenwek's size, the qualifications of the hospital's missionary doctors, and other details concerning medical staff. But Ernie knew nothing about the organization nor had he ever heard of its director—someone by the name of William Franklin Graham III—who had signed the letter. Since Ernie was too busy to take time to research these people or respond to their query right away, he set the letter aside to deal with it another time.

Some weeks later Ernie received a communication saying the director of World Medical Mission and one of its founders were in Africa visiting mission hospitals, and they would like to stop in and see Tenwek. Ernie was always glad to show any visitors the ministry and facilities at Tenwek. This seemed like an easy way to discover who and what World Medical Mission was, so he agreed to an appointment.

When the day came, the visitors' private plane buzzed the mission station to announce their arrival and alert someone to come pick them up. Then the two mission officials landed just up the road at the local Bomet airstrip. Ernie gave the men a full tour of the hospital before taking them down to his house, where the Steurys and the Morses planned to serve them a nice lunch.

Dr. Lowell Furman shared why he and his brother, Dr. Dick Furman, had founded World Medical Mission: They wanted to expose American doctors to third-world medical missions by sending them overseas (at the doctors' own expense) for varying lengths of time. Their plan was to offer mission hospitals access to the services of specialists they didn't have on staff, to provide overwhelmed missionary doctors some temporary relief in handling heavy caseloads, and to serve as temporary fill-ins for medical missionaries going on furlough or needing time off for personal or professional reasons.

While that certainly sounded appealing, Ernie and Dick still didn't know much about these visitors or their organization. Was this anything more than just the pipe dream of a couple of well-to-do, well-intentioned doctors? Lowell Furman certainly seemed like a nice, sincere man. But did he and his brother Dick have the necessary resources for World Medical Mission to actually deliver what he said they wanted to do?

Ernie turned to Mr. Graham, the surprisingly young director of World Medical Mission, who was accompanying Dr. Furman on the tour. He asked, "How do you expect to acquire the names of enough interested Christian doctors willing to invest their time and money to do this?"

"From my father's mailing list," Franklin replied. "We've already sent out some correspondence explaining our idea, and we got a very encouraging response."

"And who is your father?" Ernie asked.

"Billy Graham."

Franklin Graham and Lowell Furman were probably a little amused at the missionaries' surprise. "It came as quite a shock," Sue admitted. Ernie had read the signature on the letter, *William Franklin Graham III*, but he had never made the connection. Maybe it shouldn't have, but this revelation gave a whole new air of legitimacy to World Medical Mission in Ernie's mind.

Dick Morse shared how he had come to Christ during one of Billy Graham's crusades in Boston back in college. Out of curiosity Ernie asked if Franklin thought he might someday take over his father's ministry.

"No way, Ernie," Franklin laughed. "There's not a ghost of a chance for that. I couldn't do what my dad does. I'm not a preacher."

The conversation moved back to Tenwek's medical needs. With the Morses just recently returned from furlough and plans for a series of short-term doctors from the States to visit Tenwek over the next few months, Ernie told Franklin and Lowell he thought his staffing situation looked unusually good right then. But he was certainly glad for the contact and would definitely be open to working with World Medical Mission in the future.

He had no idea just how important that contact would prove to be. Nor did he imagine how soon that future would come.

Before the year was up, however, the short-term help Ernie was expecting fell through, and he decided to contact World Medical Mission and tell Franklin Graham he was now ready and willing to take him up on the offer of help—if he had any doctors he could send to Tenwek. That request was fueled by a number of factors that had recently ratcheted up the pressure Ernie felt.

The first factor was an all-too-familiar challenge—the never-ending growth of the medical ministry at Tenwek, which had another record year in 1978. The staff had admitted 7,817 inpatients; seen 23,060 outpatients; and performed 502 major surgeries. The chaplain's office saw almost 3,500 patients and relatives seek spiritual help, a large percentage of these being first-time conversions.

At the same time the workload increased, plans for some of the visiting doctors Ernie had been counting on fell through. Ernie had also been elected to serve as acting field director, overseeing all of WGM's work and missionaries throughout the country of Kenya—one more reason for Ernie's call to Franklin Graham for help. World Medical Mission soon began sending visiting doctors to work at Tenwek for a month at a time, sometimes even longer. Those visiting physicians helped Ernie and Dick handle a patient load that promised to make 1979 even busier than the year before.

News from Back Home

One day during some WGM field meetings in late June of 1979, Ernie was summoned to the hospital office. A few minutes later, someone slipped into the meeting and whispered to Sue, "There's a telephone call from your daughter."

She hurried right up to the office. "As soon as I heard the call was from Cindy, I knew something was wrong," Sue said. "Even in 1979 phone service to Tenwek was so iffy and expensive that international calls were few and far between. And Cindy had managed to get through just a few weeks before on my birthday, so another, unscheduled, call wasn't a good sign.

"When I walked into the office and saw Ernie sitting with the phone to his ear and tears streaming down this face, my heart just sank. As he continued listening on the phone, he jotted one word down on a piece of paper in front of him: 'MOTHER!'"

Ernie's mom had died unexpectedly days before. His sister Clara had wired to Kenya to inform Ernie. And as soon as Cindy had received word, she sent her own telegram.

When they finally got a call through, only a half hour before the funeral service was set to begin, Clara gave Ernie the devastating news and told him about the telegrams. Ernie assured her no such telegrams had arrived. He didn't blame his sister or his daughter. "But as hard a blow as it was to get that sad news," Sue said, "the toughest part of all for Ernie was not finding out until minutes before the funeral." Not that he would have been able to get home in time for the service. That probably would have been logistically and financially impossible. But it would have been emotionally helpful to work through that decision himself. Having no time and no choice made the shocking news that much harder to take.

Another Doctor for Tenwek

Dr. David Stevens, the college student who had stayed with the Steurys in the summer of 1972, was under appointment with WGM to become Tenwek's third full-time doctor even as he finished his final year of residency in family practice. David, his wife, Jody, and their two children, Jason and Jessica, would not arrive in the country until sometime in 1981, but Ernie wished it could happen before his next furlough beginning July 1980.

As excited as he was about the prospect of a young new doctor joining the Tenwek team, Ernie knew realistically that just one more doctor wasn't going to be enough. The ongoing help of World Medical Mission volunteer doctors was always welcome, but there was always more work than the staff could handle.

The greatest challenge for the present and the future of Tenwek Hospital remained the size of its task. It was still the only hospital for three hundred thousand to four hundred thousand people in that part of Kenya. It served 8,955 inpatients and 24,300 outpatients during 1979, delivering 1,251 babies and performing 597 major and 1,589 minor surgeries over the course of that year. The fact that 3,500 people sought spiritual help at the hospital certainly heartened Ernie, but it did nothing to reduce his workload.

In fact, he reported in a letter to supporters in the spring of 1980 that the preceding two months had been "the busiest months of our lives. We keep thinking if things don't slow down we will have to drop out of this rat race. But then we manage with God's daily supply of strength to carry on. The influx of patients at the hospital has been unreal. One of the nurses decided to count the other day and just see how many patients . . . There were 400+ in our 130 beds—so many she wished she hadn't counted. The sad part about it is that so many of them wait so long to come in and then expect miracles which is difficult for the doctors and nurses who do everything they can to save them but many do not make it."

On top of his medical work, the acting field director position was becoming a real burden. While honored by the confidence his fellow missionaries had in him for the job, Ernie and Sue were anxious for him to get out from under that responsibility. Being field director meant Ernie was the mission's representative in dealing with the Kenyan government and the U.S. embassy in Nairobi. He was responsible for everything from informing missionaries of news and policy from headquarters to resolving any interpersonal conflicts or personnel issues. He was also the official liaison between the mission and the Africa Gospel Church and supervised the finances of WGM's work around the country, which required at least one trip a month to Nakuru to review the books with the treasurer.

All of these responsibilities contributed to Ernie's serious exhaustion during the final months of his fourth term. According to Sue, "Ernie was burning the candle at both ends. And it was starting to take a real toll. I even saw it in the mornings when we had our devotions at the breakfast table together. Some days I'd read and then he would pray. Other mornings he would read and I would pray. But sometimes he would just begin to cry and not be able to finish his prayer."

Ernie didn't tell Sue at the time just how concerned he was about his own emotional state. But he remembered his father's struggle with depression, which started at about the same age, and he knew that a couple of his siblings had struggled with depression in recent years. So he worried that this emotional turmoil was a symptom of an even more debilitating problem.

"I sensed he was at his wit's end," Sue said. "So I didn't tell him about the disturbing mood swings I was struggling with at the same time because I didn't want to burden him. I just had to pray that I'd survive the physical and emotional ordeal of packing up for one more intercontinental move, pretty much by myself. And that we would both hold up through Jonathan's graduation and the trip back to the States where maybe we could get a little rest."

But as furlough time approached, disaster struck when Dick Morse came down with a serious case of hepatitis. Since the most crucial part of Dick's treatment was several weeks of bed rest and then an additional period of limited activity, Ernie decided there was no way he could leave his colleague. "I know him too well," he told Sue. "If some emergency comes in, Dick will get out of bed to take care of it. And he just can't afford to do that."

Ernie suggested to Sue, "Honey, why don't you go on back to the States with the kids and get them started in school." (Jonathan was beginning his freshman year at Asbury College that fall.) "I'll come on as soon as Dick is on his feet again or once we get some other doctor out here to help him."

Sue didn't think much of that idea. "*I will not leave you out here!*" she informed her husband. "You need to go home every bit as much as I do. We will just have to pray and trust the Lord to take care of this situation." Sue couldn't remember how long it was after she said that when there was an answer from heaven—literally.

The midday routine of Tenwek was disrupted by the sound of a small airplane buzzing the mission station. "Of course we all went outside to see it turn to make another low pass," Sue recalled. "As it swooped over again, someone with sharp eyes shouted, 'They just threw something out.' Then I spotted a small falling object which actually landed on top of our house.

"We had to go to the hospital's industrial department to borrow a ladder so Ernie could climb onto our roof and retrieve whatever it was. He found a piece of paper wrapped around a Kenyan one-shilling coin, to give it a little weight. Unfolding the paper, he found a scribbled note: 'I'll be at the airstrip. Come and get me. Franklin.' "

Franklin Graham had been in Nairobi and providentially had decided to drop by Tenwek to see how things were going. He found Dick sick in bed with hepatitis, a hospital absolutely overflowing with sick patients, and the stressed-out Steurys wondering how to leave or whether to reschedule their desperately needed furlough.

Franklin instantly assessed the situation and immediately phoned his secretary in the States to ask if World Medical Mission had any visiting doctors scheduled for Tenwek anytime soon. She checked and told him, "No, but there is one heading over to the Africa Inland Mission (AIM) Hospital at Kijabe in a couple of weeks." So Franklin called AIM to ask how badly they needed help and explained why he wanted to know. They informed him they were pretty well covered, so if Tenwek needed a visiting physician, they would be fine. Franklin's secretary called the doctor, a veteran of several previous short-term experiences with third-world medical missions. He was not only agreeable to the change of plans, he said he could move up his departure date a week in order to get to Kenya before Ernie had to leave.

Franklin Graham was shocked by the overcrowded conditions he found at Tenwek. In fact, he was as concerned about that as he was about calling in a replacement to fill in for Dick Morse.

"You're bursting at the seams, Ernie!" he commented as he followed him on a tour through the wards. "What are you going to do about it?"

"I don't know," Ernie honestly replied. "We've been discussing the possibility of a new building with new men's and women's wards, a larger pediatric ward, two new operating rooms, an intensive care facility, and more room for growth. It would be our biggest construction project yet. But we can't do anything until we get more money."

"And how do you plan to do that?" Franklin wanted to know.

"I guess we're just going to have to pray it in," Ernie told him.

Franklin was so moved by the need he saw: Bed after bed containing two or three patients, patients lying under the beds and in the aisles. It was nothing unusual by Tenwek standards, but Franklin just kept shaking his head and taking pictures.

The Steurys headed home for furlough as scheduled. They were encouraged by the way the Lord had provided again for Tenwek's need for doctors through this new and promising association with World Medical Mission and Franklin Graham, never imagining what else that relationship was about to provide.

Chapter 13

Dreams Coming True

One day not long after the Steurys got back to the States for their furlough beginning in 1980, Ernie got a phone call from Franklin's secretary, who excitedly related a remarkable story.

Upon his return from his African trip, Franklin had received an invitation to appear on Jim and Tammy Faye Bakker's television show *Praise the Lord* (*PTL*). Franklin almost turned down the invitation. The Bakkers had recently gotten some negative publicity, and he had always made it a policy to avoid the appearance of aligning his organization with other Christian organizations embroiled in controversies. But at the last minute Franklin changed his mind, thinking this might be an opportunity to let a broader audience hear about the ministries of World Medical Mission and Samaritan's Purse. He would go on the show just this one time. In order to illustrate those ministries for *PTL* viewers, he carried with him a number of his Tenwek photos, blown up to poster size.

When Franklin walked into the *PTL* studio, a producer handed him a waiver to sign before he went on the air. Basically what it said was that all monies that might come in as a result of his appearance on the program would go to *PTL*.

Franklin hadn't come with the idea of receiving any money for his appearance. But the whole waiver thing just didn't sit well with him. His secretary told Ernie, "Franklin almost turned around and walked right out the door."

The Bakkers had already announced their guest list, however. People were expecting him, and Franklin didn't want to create any negative press of his own. So he went on the air.

The interview wandered in several different directions before Jim Bakker finally asked a question that opened the door for Franklin to talk about

World Medical Mission and its goal of supporting medical missions around the world. He mentioned his most recent trip and pulled out the enlarged Tenwek photos. The studio cameras zoomed in for full-frame shots of two and three and four children in each bed of the hospital's pediatric ward. The viewing audience saw smiling maternity patients proudly showing off their newborns from pallets on concrete floors. As he flipped through the photos, one after another, Franklin talked about how great the need was and all that Tenwek Hospital could do if they had five hundred thousand dollars to construct a modern new medical building.

Jim Bakker was obviously moved as he looked at those pictures. "You know, Franklin," he said. "I believe our *PTL* viewers could help with this project." Then he turned to the camera. "If every one of you watching this program today would just send in one dollar, we could build this hospital building. Franklin, where should they send their dollar?"

Franklin gave World Medical Mission's post office box address in Boone, North Carolina.

"And Ernie!" Franklin's secretary exclaimed. "The responses are still pouring in. We've had to rent a bank vault to store all the bags of mail until we can hire some Appalachian State University students to help us get them all opened!"

Most of those envelopes did indeed contain a single dollar bill. But as the amount grew from fifty- to one hundred- then two hundred thousand dollars and kept right on climbing, Ernie said to Franklin, "That's going to cost you a fortune just to process."

Franklin assured him that World Medical Mission wouldn't take a cent of what was donated. "But if you let us put it in the bank until you're ready to begin building, we'll use the interest to help pay for the thank-you receipts we're going to send out to every contributor." Ernie readily agreed to that and called an architect.

Soon after Ernie and Sue's furlough began and the children were settled in school, Ernie was admitted to the Caylor-Nickel Clinic for an apparent heart problem. But a thorough work-up, complete with angiograms, showed his heart was in good condition. The diagnosis: a peptic ulcer and evidence of severe fatigue. A year's furlough looked to be just what the doctor needed.

Sue diagnosed herself early that fall. "The battle with my own emotions which had troubled me at Tenwek continued after we got back to Indiana," she said. "I finally went and had a check-up of my own with one of our physician friends there. I told him about suffering from horrible mood swings." The doctor confirmed Sue's recent suspicions that she was going through menopause and assured her all the feelings she had been worried about were indeed common symptoms.

Despite the usual heavy furlough schedule of speaking engagements and another three-month stint brushing up on Ernie's medical skills while working with Caylor-Nickel Clinic, the couple's furlough time in the States helped restore the emotional and physical health of both Steurys. They were thrilled to become first-time grandparents that fall when Rachel Marie was born to Cindy and Daniel Tolan. Christmas and Easter were special times of memory making with the entire family together again.

Expectations for the future held new excitement for the entire Steury clan. Cindy's family was moving to Winston-Salem, North Carolina, where Daniel had been accepted into medical school at Bowman Gray. Jon planned to head back to Asbury for his sophomore year. After his senior year at Rift Valley Academy, Nate would be returning to the States for college. Debbie couldn't wait to begin high school with her old friends at RVA. Ernie and Sue were hopeful that an expanded Tenwek staff would lighten the load over previous terms and that the big new building in the works would finally ease the crowding.

Work on the new building began shortly after the Steurys returned to Tenwek. While progress seemed so slow that it was sometimes hard to see any significant headway, just watching the amount of excavation being done offered Ernie a sense of hope. Bigger and better things lay ahead for the medical ministry of Tenwek Hospital.

What a difference Ernie felt already with the arrival of Dr. David Stevens. Finally the hospital had three full-time doctors. Not that three was actually enough to meet all the needs, but it would now be possible for one of the doctors to leave the hospital (for a day, a week, or even a year furlough) without dumping an impossible load on one doctor. In fact Ernie and Dick Morse would kid Dave Stevens about how much better things were than they used to be when Ernie was the only doctor for three hundred thousand people. It was much more manageable now: Ernie needed to take only a hundred thousand people, Dick could handle the second hundred thousand, and Dave could care for the remaining hundred thousand. Piece of cake!

Of course what happened was what always happened whenever Tenwek expanded staff or facilities. There were more people with more needs to be ministered to and unusual challenges for the medical staff, who continued to trust God to provide the wisdom and the tools to meet them.

Dave Stevens remembers one such medical challenge.

A Medical Challenge

One day a woman brought in her newborn daughter who "had been born at home a few days previously with part of her brain hanging out in a small membrane covered sac on the back of her head. I can still picture the mother removing the cloth in which she'd wrapped the little one and asking if there was anything we could do. None of us had ever seen this rare congenital defect, much less attempted to treat it.

"So Ernie looked it up and found that without surgical correction the child would certainly die of infection. He learned also that even with the best neurosurgery, one-third of these children die, one-third live with brain damage, and only one-third could expect a normal life. After carefully reviewing the surgical procedure, Ernie explained the risks to the baby's mother. Her response, as she handed over her child was: 'God has given me this child. If He should decide to take her back, that is His will. Do for her what you can.'

"The staff prayed as Ernie attempted a surgery he had never seen performed before, asking our heavenly Father to guide the knife with his hands.

"A few days later, when we sent that baby home, she was completely normal. The Great Physician had answered our prayers."

A Leg for Stanley

While some patients stood out because of their unusual diagnosis, others left a lasting impression because of their memorable character.

Stanley was a Kipsigis boy who broke his leg playing soccer at school. X-rays clearly confirmed the fracture, but they also revealed a tumor in his leg that had weakened the bone at the point of the break. The tumor was malignant and required that the leg be amputated as soon as possible to reduce the chances of the cancer spreading throughout the boy's body.

Ernie explained to the family that Stanley's leg would never heal and that his only chance for a healthy life was to amputate the diseased leg. Everyone seemed to understand except Stanley's father. "Just give him an injection and a plaster on his leg," he said. "He will be all right."

Ernie wished it were that easy. He tried again to explain to the father why amputation was the only choice. After considering the idea for a few seconds, the man picked Stanley up and walked out the door to take him home.

Two days later Stanley's family brought him back and asked Ernie to do the amputation because Stanley was crying day and night from the pain. The father wasn't with them this time, but everyone assured Ernie he would agree to the operation rather than see his son suffer.

During Stanley's recovery from the surgery, several of the medical staff shared the gospel message with him. "One day," Ernie recalled, "he very beautifully opened his heart and life to Jesus. And when we discharged him from the hospital some time later he told me, 'Doctor, the Lord must have something very special for me to do; He helped you remove the bad disease, and now He has given me a new life.'"

Occasionally Ernie saw Stanley for follow-up appointments. He became a strong Christian leader among the students at his boarding school, even teaching Sunday school there. He eventually transferred to the high school at Tenwek and became a frequent visitor and a blessing to many at the hospital. Every Sunday Stanley would rise at 5:00 a.m. and walk on his crutches the five miles back to his former school to teach his Sunday school class. He also made a powerful spiritual impact at home; eventually, his entire family, with the exception of his father, became Christians.

One day Tenwek received a large crate of hospital supplies and equipment from World Gospel Mission headquarters. In the shipment was an artificial leg.

Ernie's first thought was, *Wouldn't it be great if this leg would fit Stanley?* But he knew that was impossible because an artificial leg needed to be custom-made for an individual; careful measurements had to be made to fit a particular person. So he set the leg in a corner of his office until he could decide what to do with it.

Several days later he saw Stanley. Without making it obvious, Ernie stood beside the boy and made a mental note of the level of Stanley's knee and hip compared to his own. When he returned to the hospital, Ernie went to his office and held up the artificial leg next to himself, and it appeared the leg might be about right.

He sent word to the school for Stanley to come see him as soon as possible. When he arrived, Ernie took him to the office. Stanley's eyes grew wide as he looked at the leg Ernie brought from the corner. He had never seen an artificial leg made like this one, and this one was white. To Ernie's great delight, the leg fit perfectly.

Stanley too was thrilled. He said, "Doctor, isn't it wonderful? The Lord helped you remove the cancer so I could live, then he gave me a new heart so I could serve Him, and now he has given me a new leg. God must have something very wonderful for me to do."

The shorts he was wearing, part of the required school uniform, in no way covered the artificial leg Ernie had just put on. As Ernie looked at the exposed hinge at the knee and the straps he said, "Stanley, there is a problem. You cannot wear shorts with this leg; we will have to get you long trousers."

Stanley's face clouded as he said, "I don't think that is possible. You see, I have just been elected leader of the Christian Union. And if I wore long trousers I would be breaking the rules of the school."

The boy's spiritual commitment moved Ernie. "What a tremendous Christian witness. He would rather give up the leg than be a bad testimony for Christ. I assured him I would speak to the principal about the matter."

Permission for the long trousers was willingly granted, and several days later Stanley came to see Ernie with a pair of long pants rolled up under his arm. They went to the office, and in a few minutes Stanley was dressed in his new trousers and wearing his new leg. What a thrill it was for Ernie to see him looking so great and standing there without any crutches.

"Stanley," Ernie said, "there is one more problem; do you have another shoe?"

"No, Doctor," he replied. "I never buy two shoes. I have just one made for my good foot."

Two months earlier a work team of volunteers from the States had been at Tenwek to help with the building. When they left, one of the men gave Ernie a pair of size eleven shoes, saying that he did not want to carry them home with him. At the time, no one on staff wore that size, so the shoes had just been sitting in the office. Ernie picked them up and asked Stanley to put one on his good foot. He did, and it fit perfectly. Ernie put the other shoe on the artificial foot, and it too was a perfect, size-eleven fit.

Stanley again started praising God for what he had done. God had done it all!

Several months later, Stanley wrote to tell Ernie he was now riding a bicycle. Later he wrote again to tell Ernie that his father had accepted the Lord. What wonderful news![1]

Success and Growth

The mission's medical facilities at Tenwek and its clinics at Kaboson and Naikarra treated 10,924 inpatients and 72,473 outpatients in 1981. And more patients and families sought spiritual help at Tenwek in 1982 than ever before—more than 4,100 according to the records kept in the chaplain's office. This made the hospital ministry a major key to the successful work of World Gospel Mission, which was celebrating fifty years

1 Stanley's remarkable story is told by Dr. Mel Cheatham, *Come Walk with Me* (Nashville: Thomas Nelson, 1993).

of ministry in Kenya that same year. The Africa Gospel Church, which traced its denominational roots back to the long labors of Willis Hotchkiss, now boasted over three hundred congregations with more than twenty thousand members for WGM's golden anniversary celebration.

Even as the mission and the church celebrated the past, the slow but steady progress on the new medical building directed Ernie's primary focus toward Tenwek's future. Plans for the three-story building (which would be the largest structure for miles) included a number of classrooms to be used for a new school of nursing, an idea that had been discussed for years and could help meet an incredible need for better trained hospital staff. But, of course, every new plan to meet some need eventually created new needs of its own.

The huge new building was no exception. For all the blessings it promised, it also meant increased demands on Tenwek's current assets. The addition of nearly a hundred new beds would require more nurses, ten to fifteen registered nurses for the Kenyan field. WGM had only seven at the time, and three of those were scheduled for furlough the following year.

Of course more career nurses at Tenwek would require more staff housing because all residences were full at the time. The nursing school would also require housing. A new water tank and water filtration system were already under construction to meet the demands of all that additional housing, plus the requirements of the new building, which would almost double the floor space of the current hospital. Electrical demands of all the new buildings were going to strain the hospital's power supply like never before, which led to a renewed discussion of plans for a possible hydroelectric plant at the base of the falls, a seemingly impossible dream.

The new building continued to go up at Tenwek under the capable supervision of the Steurys' long-time colleague, Gene Lewton. Ernie personally checked on the progress every day and chronicled the entire process. He sent photographs to Franklin Graham, who relayed them on to the *PTL* show so those viewers could see how the dollar bills they sent were being used. Many of Ernie and Sue's friends in the States wrote to tell them about regularly seeing the photos and hearing updates on the building going on in Kenya.

But the growth of the hospital's physical facilities wasn't all that encouraged Ernie early in that fifth term. Never in his twenty-plus years of service had he enjoyed so much professional help. Even when Dick Morse went on furlough, there were still at least three doctors at the hospital because Dr. Marty Graber fell in love with Tenwek and decided to stay on past his two-year appointment. With the added assistance of several visiting doctors provided by World Medical Mission, Ernie found time to begin making plans for a dream he had been incubating in his mind for years.

Community Health Care

For more than two decades, Ernie had battled just to keep his head above water at Tenwek, trying to treat the patients who came through the hospital doors. There just never seemed to be time to address the greater healthcare needs of the Kipsigis people. He had learned early on that most of what he did at the hospital was treating the symptoms without addressing the physical cause of his patients' problems.

Most of the conditions Ernie treated were preventable. Measles, whooping cough, tuberculosis, malnutrition, malaria, and dehydration due to gastroenteritis caused 50 percent of the deaths among children at Tenwek. The staff attempted to educate people about these diseases when they came to the hospital with their families. Ramona Thomas had instituted an immunization program that provided hundreds of immunizations a day in the outpatient clinics, but the underlying problem remained.

Ernie and his medical staff had realized for years that the only way to effectively change the health habits of the Kipsigis people would be to go out in the community and educate them. But the chronic shortage of staff had made that impossible. There was never enough time to treat all those sick people who came to the hospital, let alone go out into the villages and countryside to provide preventative resources. But that was what Ernie proposed to do now. And he thought he had found the perfect people to do it.

Susan Carter had come to Tenwek in 1980 on a two-year short-term assignment, filling in for nurses on furlough. By the time her term was up, she felt burned out by the overwhelming demands of the hospital schedule. Before she left, Ernie told her how much he appreciated her good work and that he hoped she would consider a career appointment. Susan told him she didn't think she was cut out for the kind of hospital nursing required at Tenwek. But when he told her a little about his dream for a community health program, Susan informed Ernie that if he would promise she could work in community health, she would return to Tenwek at the end of her furlough in 1983.

Ernie hadn't worked with Dave Stevens very long before he recognized the young doctor's initiative, his sense of vision, and his motivational and leadership ability. He and Susan Carter seemed the perfect team needed to conceive and launch the community health program. When an unexpected resource became available to Tenwek, Ernie was convinced it was time for this new venture.

Dave Stevens remembered being the only doctor on duty at the hospital one busy afternoon when he was told a *mzungu* (an expatriate, non-Kenyan, white person) wanted to see him in the outpatient clinic. No visitors were scheduled, so Dave's curiosity was piqued. "As soon as I finish this procedure, I'll be up." A few minutes later he was shaking hands with Dr. Mark Jacobsen, a young Christian physician from the International Health Department of Johns Hopkins Medical School. Mark explained that he was on a two-year assignment to Kenya to start three pilot programs for the community-based distribution of family planning supplies. (At that time Kenya had the highest population growth rate of any country in the world.) The plans for one of Mark's three pilot projects had fallen through at the last minute, and he had heard through the grapevine about Tenwek's new community health initiative.

Dave explained the dream of starting a community-health program to help educate the Kipsigis people in basic nutrition, clean drinking water, sanitation, and similar subjects in order to improve the region's quality of life and reduce the cases of preventable diseases such as gastroenteritis, malaria, and malnutrition (treatment of which absorbed an overwhelming proportion of the resources at Tenwek). Dave told the visiting physician that Tenwek's plans were preliminary; the hospital didn't have much money or expertise. They had expected to learn as they went along.

"Suddenly," David Stevens recalled, "here on our doorstep in rural Kenya was an expert from Johns Hopkins, arguably the best school for public health in the entire world. Mark was not only willing to offer advice on setting up a program, he already had funding available through USAID [United States Aid for International Development], which ended up providing us with more than $150,000 for the first three years of our program. That money turbo-charged Tenwek's community-based healthcare program, which went on to become a model for similar programs around the world and helped revolutionize the people's health status in that region of Kenya."

The whole concept was brilliantly simple. After surveying a number of Kipsigis villages to confirm what the Tenwek staff already felt were the most common health issues, Susan Carter and three national assistants began visiting villages throughout the region. They explained the basic idea and enlisted church and community leaders to set up community health committees. Those health committees, after a two-day training session in their communities, selected seven respected and capable people to become volunteer community health helpers.

Those workers were then given a month's worth of intensive instruction on how to use creative psychosocial teaching methods such as stories, skits, dramas, and practical demonstrations to communicate important community health concepts. Then those newly trained helpers went back to their home communities to spend two or three half-days each week communicating what they had learned to one hundred of their neighbors.

Half of that time was spent teaching preventative health measures: the importance of boiling all drinking water, the need to dig latrines and refuse pits away from family huts, the value of building cooking fires on a raised area in the middle of a hut to prevent so many babies and toddlers from rolling or falling into the flames, the purpose of constructing a simple rack made of sticks to keep eating utensils and cooking bowls up off the contaminated ground while they dried. They also spent a fourth of their time teaching or providing curative measures: dispensing a few basic medicines and instructing people how to treat scabies and malaria, showing parents how to mix a simple rehydration drink from boiled water and sugar to prevent so many children from dying of dehydration, demonstrating basic first-aid techniques that could keep minor cuts and burns from becoming dangerous infections. The final quarter of their time was devoted to evangelism, spiritual training, and counseling.

In the first year of Tenwek's community health program, the staff trained fifty community health helpers, established eleven community health committees, and made over six thousand home visits. The plan was to keep growing the program up to five thousand home visits a month within the next couple of years.

Ernie was thrilled with the early results, even if it was way too early to see the program's impact in reducing the patient load at the hospital. In fact, a 1983 malaria epidemic brought hundreds of people a day in for treatment at the out-station dispensaries and up to fifty admissions a day at Tenwek Hospital. At times up to five hundred patients overflowed the 130 beds until people were sleeping under the eaves of all the buildings and on the floor of the chapel as the staff began to wonder if those new wards would ever be done.

The good news was that Chaplain David Kilel reported 4,008 seeking spiritual help during 1983 and another 4,064 during just the first six months of 1984. With money provided by Franklin Graham's Samaritan's Purse, the hospital was able to send Kipsigis Bibles home with new believers.

Newfound Funding

By early 1984 the roof was going on the big new ward building, and work was moving along on the five-unit apartment building for staff housing. World Medical Mission, Samaritan's Purse, the Billy Graham Evangelistic Association, and a number of other donors helped provide a steady flow of funds to move these projects toward completion.

"We actually experienced a quantum shift in our fund-raising strategy through the process of building that new big ward building," David Stevens recalled. "When we realized how much money it was going to take to finish and furnish such a facility, I sat down one Sunday afternoon and wrote a three-page proposal to the Young Foundation. That may have been Tenwek's first foundation request. A few months later when we received a letter awarding us $50,000 a year for three years to build and equip our nursing school classrooms, I told Ernie, 'This was a lot easier than deputation!' From then on, due to the high cost of expanding our medical facilities, we began to approach government aid programs and foundations for funding of larger projects and used mission support money for evangelism and for smaller projects such as staff housing."

In the meantime, the old facilities remained filled to 211 percent capacity for 1984 as more than eleven thousand patients were admitted to the hospital. More than sixty babies were born at Tenwek one very busy week. And Edna Boroff reported nearly two thousand maternity patients for the year, including the fifteenth set of triplets she had personally delivered during her time at Tenwek.

New Doctors to Share the Work

When David Stevens and his family went on furlough in 1984, Ernie naturally had to shoulder a bigger share of the load again. But the challenge was easier than ever before because of short-term doctors Bob Wesche and Marty Graber, now serving at Tenwek with WGM. A steady stream of visiting doctors from World Medical Mission also continued to come to the hospital to help.

The memorable exploits of one of the doctors who came for a month in 1984 were talked about at Tenwek for a number of years afterwards. Dr. Don Mullen, a cardiovascular surgeon from Wisconsin and a member of the WGM Board, *just happened* to be at Tenwek when a patient came in with stenosis of the mitral valve. His heart valve was scarred shut (probably the result of rheumatic fever) and wasn't allowing enough blood through the left atrium into the heart.

In order to perform the necessary surgery successfully, the surgeons needed a heart-lung machine to allow the blood flow to bypass the heart while they performed cardiac surgery. But such sophisticated equipment was not available out in the remote reaches of Africa. Neither were there any logistical or financial means to get the patient to another facility that could perform the surgery.

The patient was about to die, so Don Mullen attempted what seemed like an impossible operation for a mission hospital. It was probably the first procedure of its kind ever performed in any mission hospital in Kenya, perhaps even in all of Africa. With Ernie's assistance, Don opened the patient's chest and sewed a purse-string suture, similar to the part of a small draw bag, in the left atrium of the heart itself. Then he made a small incision through the wall of the heart inside the ring of the suture, quickly stuck his finger through the incision, and pulled the drawstring tight around his finger to keep the patient from bleeding to death. Then, using just the tip of his finger, which was now inside the man's beating heart, and operating totally by feel, Don opened the mitral valve by gently breaking the scars between the leaflets. When he finished, he loosened the suture just long enough to withdraw his finger, pulled it tight again, tied it off, and closed the patient up. The man fully recovered.

Before Dr. Mullen returned to the States, he and Ernie successfully performed two more of those operations. Ernie would tell those stories for years, marveling at what he had seen and how God had brought the right man with the right skills at the right time to save the lives of three people who would have certainly died.

Don Mullen's experience was part of the inspiration for a long-standing joke the career doctors at Tenwek used on visiting physicians. During orientation of new staff, the straight-faced veterans would say, "Make yourself at home while you are here. And please be sure to let us know if there is anything you need in the way of medical supplies and equipment . . . and we'll be glad to tell you how we learned to get along without them."

Computer Technology

Another exciting development at Tenwek was the introduction of computers. Dave Stevens started the process by discussing with a visiting computer expert his own frustration in keeping up with medicine and supply prices, knowing the hospital's financial status and maintaining an accurate inventory by hand. He also wanted to produce a monthly newsletter, publish teaching materials, and keep a database record of activity for the community health work. Tenwek would be the first mission hospital in Africa to begin using computers.

After researching which computers would be best suited in terms of cost, versatility, reliability, and portability, the consultant purchased a couple of KayPro II computers, which utilized a CP-M operating system. Then he and Dave began developing some specialized programs that would be needed at Tenwek. Dave started implementing the system in mid-1984. Although he knew the computers wouldn't do anything that the staff couldn't do themselves, the machines would save thousands of hours, increase the accuracy of financial records, and enable the staff to make better business decisions for the hospital. Instead of addressing hundreds of prayer letters by hand, the staff could simply press a button and print labels. Year-end reports that previously took days to prepare could be done with a few computer commands. Word processing saved missionaries valuable time with tasks such as preparing health helper training lessons and printing graduation certificates, allowing them to do additional ministry work.

The hospital conducted business with 150 different companies, had 160 nationals on payroll, and kept separate accounts on each of the building projects. By applying appropriate technology to third-world problems, Tenwek was taking a step in the right direction. As the many hours spent in record keeping were shortened, the staff had more time to be about the most important work of all—winning souls for Christ.

Along with all the other improvements being made at Tenwek in the mid-1980s, a team of telephone workmen came from the States to install a new intercom phone system that connected the various hospital departments to each other and to all the residences located on the station. Gone were the days when the night duty nurse had to send a night watchman with a lantern to awaken a doctor to perform an emergency C-section. No longer would Sue have to send one of the children up the hill to the hospital after dark to find out how much longer it would be before Ernie came home for supper. Messengers no longer had to search from one end of the hospital to the other to find a doctor when one of his colleagues wanted to consult with him.

Dedication and Celebration

Much progress had occurred at Tenwek since Sue and Ernie arrived in May 1959. Back then the "hospital" consisted of 35 beds in four wards and one small examining room. In 1984, there were 130 beds, a good laboratory, X-ray facilities, ultrasound, operating room, physiotherapy, delivery room, and an outpatient department. In 1959 Ernie was the only doctor; now there were five doctors and five nurses, as well as 146 national staff members to help.

In 1983 builders had started construction on the new building Franklin Graham had raised money for on *PTL*. A year later the roof was on and the interior was being finished. The added facilities would include 110 more beds, two operating rooms, a recovery room, and a small intensive care unit. The lower floor would provide space for four classrooms of a new nursing school that the hospital hoped to open in late 1985.

The nursing school was going to be government-approved for training enrolled community nurses. Graduates of the program would complete a three-and-a-half-year curriculum and would then be qualified as midwives, community health workers, and ward nurses. They would also be discipled in the Christian life so they could share Christ with their patients.[2]

By March of 1985, the last-minute details of finally finishing the new hospital building and planning a big dedication ceremony were pushing Ernie and Marilyn Van Kuiken to their limit. They were hoping Kenya's President Daniel Moi would attend the ceremony. The long-awaited day finally arrived. March 9, 1985, dawned clear and beautiful without a cloud in the sky. President Moi arrived at Tenwek about 11:00 a.m. After signing the guestbook, he planted a tree in front of the new building, then cut

2 *Call to Prayer*, June 1984, World Gospel Mission.

a ribbon and declared the Reverend Johana A. Ng'etich Medical Centre officially open. (The building was fittingly named after the old Kipsigis pastor who used to stay up and pray for Ernie when he saw the operating room lights on in the middle of the night.)

Ernie then gave President Moi a personal tour of the new building and part of the old hospital. President Moi told Ernie that Tenwek had always been a special place for him since he had proposed to his wife on the porch of one of the missionary's homes when she had been a student at the Tenwek girls' boarding school.

An estimated twenty thousand people, including many government officials, attended the ceremonies. National television and the republic's major newspapers covered the event, reporting that in his speech to the crowd, President Moi praised the missionaries for their good work, especially in the field of medical health.

During his speech the president announced that the Kenyan government would supply a national doctor of Tenwek's choice and pay his salary to work at the hospital. That was wonderful news to Ernie, who experienced yet another joy later that day when his son-in-law, Dr. Daniel Tolan, assisted him in performing the very first surgery in the new building.

As Ernie walked into the big bright modern OR in the new medical center, he couldn't help thinking how much had changed since he had performed his first surgery in Tenwek's original operating room—the one that was so small his scrub nurse had to duck under the table to get to the other side of his patient. Things really were better now, and the credit for the improvements belonged to God.

The progress at Tenwek wasn't over. An even more remarkable development was about to change Tenwek Hospital and the lives of its staff forever.

Chapter 14

POWER FOR TENWEK

In July 1984, many months before the new ward was finished, Ernie, almost jokingly, had said to Dave Stevens, "Dave, while you're home on furlough, why don't you raise the funds to build a hydroelectric power plant?"

They both knew Dave would have almost no spare time in his busy speaking schedule, so Dave chuckled as he told Ernie, "Sure, no problem!"

Yet neither one of them really considered the issue of getting Tenwek more power a laughing matter. In fact, Dave Stevens said, "One of the greatest frustrations for me, and a serious hardship for our patients, was the fact that Tenwek only had electricity seven to eleven hours a day.

"There were no public utilities or private power companies in our part of Kenya. The hospital generated its own power—50 kilowatts of it. You could hear that generator hum all over the hospital and living compound. It kicked on around six each morning, but was off a good part of every afternoon. In the evening it was on till five minutes before nine when the lights blinked. That was the sign to turn on a battery light or find matches to light a candle or lantern.

"The fuel to run the generator cost so much to truck in that it consumed 25 percent of our limited hospital budget each year. We simply couldn't afford to run it any more. And whenever oil prices went up, we would have to cut the hours back even farther.

"You can probably imagine some of the limitations this placed on the medical care we could offer. We couldn't operate a true intensive care unit without power. We couldn't run respirators or electrically monitor critically ill patients through the night.

"What's harder to imagine is what it was like [before we got our phone system that could be run off of batteries] to be roused from sleep in the middle of the night by the sound of tapping on your window and the glow of a lantern held high outside by a night watchman who has been sent to summon you for some sort of medical emergency. And then walking by flashlight back up the hill and into a darkened building where each ward was only dimly illuminated by the flickering flames of one or two kerosene lanterns hanging from the ceiling.

"Our hospital staff found it difficult to even wade through the dark sea of humanity on the wards at night, let alone provide adequate around-the-clock medical care for our patients by lantern light. I can't count the number of times—long after the light of morning stirred the crowd—someone would realize the lump under that blanket hadn't moved. And we'd find a patient who had died unnoticed during the night.

"What we wouldn't have given to have the electricity needed for constant monitoring, for alarms that buzzed, for suction machines. Or even a single incandescent light bulb in each room to ward off the darkness.

"We did have a little 5,000 watt, gasoline-powered generator we could afford to run at night, but it only put out enough power to run one or two incubators. Some nights we would have three premature babies in each at the same time. But that obviously created a problem in spreading disease. And then we had to worry about what to do when another preemie was delivered. How do you decide which baby should live and which one is going to die?

"Patients were literally dying for the lack of electricity. I remember the sad case of a young child on whom we'd had to perform a tracheotomy. Because we didn't have electricity at night to run suction, and we didn't have enough nursing staff to man the wards twenty-four hours a day, I taught this girl's mother how to use a foot pump to suction the tube periodically throughout the night—until we turned the generator on the next morning. The manual suction didn't work nearly as well as an electrical one would. But when morning brought enough daylight that we could blow out the single kerosene lantern hanging from the ceiling in the middle of the ward, we found the mother asleep. The little four-year-old girl's trach had gotten clogged, she'd been unable to breathe,

Ernie M. Steury was the seventh child born to David and Mary Steury of Berne, Indiana, January 3, 1930.

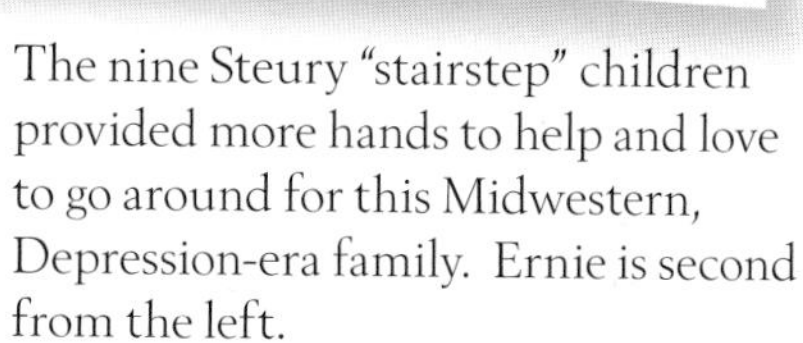

The nine Steury "stairstep" children provided more hands to help and love to go around for this Midwestern, Depression-era family. Ernie is second from the left.

:rnie married Jennie Sue Groce in August 1954, at the beginning of his second year in ned school.

Ernie and Sue became proud parents of Cynthia Ruth in January 1957, during Ernie's last year of med school.

In 1959, Tenwek "Hospital" consisted of two 20 x 20 foot buildings (right, foreground). The hospital's first major expansion, the Gertrude Shryock Building (above) was completed in 1962.

Ernie and Sue Steury raised their family of four children in this small cement block home, just down the hill from the hospital.

At its completion in 1985, the Johana Ng'etich Medical Centre was the largest structure for miles, with 110 beds. The new building also contained two ORs, a minor surgery room, a critical burn unit, an ICU, six semi-private rooms, offices, and classrooms for a proposed nursing school.

This aerial view shows the hospital compound when Ernie and Sue retired in 1994, nearly forty years after their arrival at Tenwek.

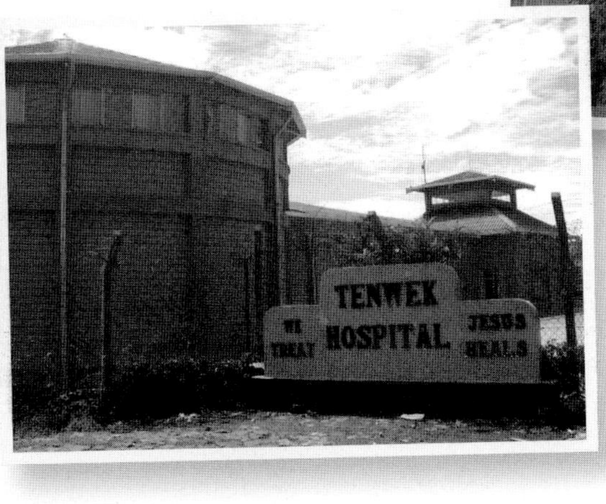

The old familiar sign (with the newest surgical theatre building behind it) still stands as a testimony of hope to patients as they come down the road to the hospital.

Before a second doctor arrived, Ernie, with only the able help of his nursing staff (left to right)—Ramona Thomas, Eldamae Kemper, Edna Boroff, and Eddie Goff—provided primary medical care for more than 100,000 Kipsigis people for ten years.

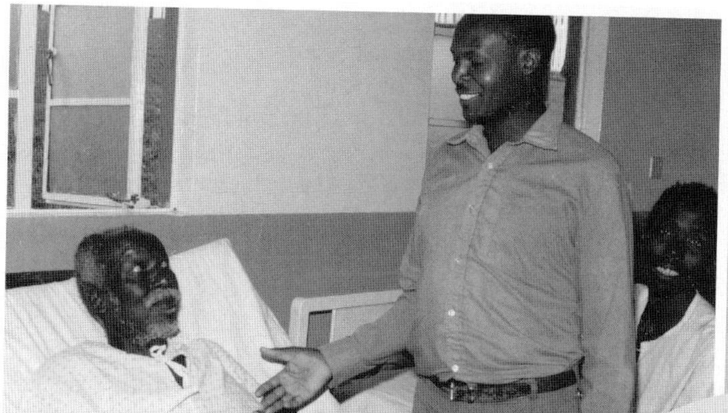

Longtime Chaplain David Kilel caught and shared Ernie's passion for the hospital's spiritual mission.

Occasional safaris provided both rare family time and a source of meat for the missionary staff. Pictured here with Debbie and Nate, Ernie bagged this Cape buffalo, a dangerous animal that often caused injuries, bringing more patients to Tenwek.

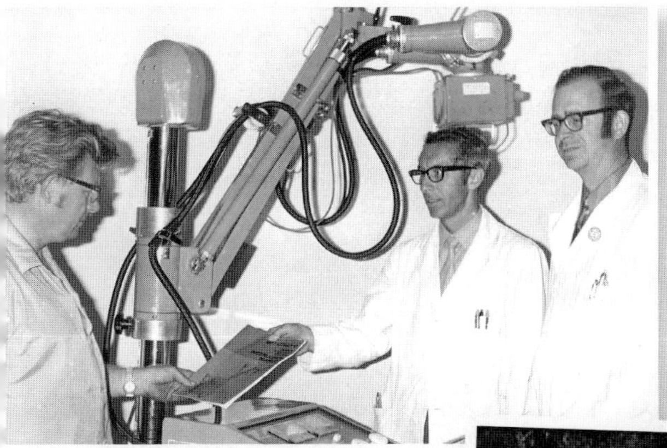

Ernie and Dr. Richard Morse (right) receive instructions on the operation of a new portable X-ray machine, donated by a British tourist club whose members had been treated at Tenwek after a tragic accident.

n addition to his medical duties, :rnie conducted regular evangelistic vork, preaching and even baptizing :onverts in the nearby river.

Cindy quickly discovered some distinct advantages to growing up in Africa, including the opportunity to have some unique pets.

;ue and Cindy spend time together vhile they wait for Ernie to come ıome from the hospital.

The young doctor known as Mosonik soon earned the respect of the Kenyan people, who presented him with a traditional headdress, making him an honorary Kipsigis warrior.

Ernie (pictured with his daughter Debbie) and other WGM missionaries before him dreamed of harnessing the power of Tenwek's falls.

The Steurys and their Tenwek missionary family sent home this 1972 holiday greeting. Back row, left to right: Nurse Marilyn Van Kuiken, Cindy, Nurse Jeannine Spratt, Sue, Ernie. Front row, left to right: Dick, Betty, and Ricky Morse, Debbie, Jon, Nurse Edna Boroff, Nate, Carol Trachsel and Sara Hill, medical technologists.

Ernie's friend and prayer partner, Rev. Johana Ng'etich, gives a call to worship on his igondit (traditional Kipsigis "trumpet").

Before Nurse Edna Boroff came to Tenwek, the Kipsigis people believed triplets were cursed, so the second-born would be killed or abandoned to die.

Edna with the first-known surviving set of Kipsigis triplets. She raised the middle child at Tenwek for over a year to disprove old superstitions and end the tribal practice of infanticide.

The Steury family posing outside their home.

Ernie's reputation as a doctor quickly spread throughout Kipsigis land. He was recognized and welcomed everywhere he went.

A local Africa Gospel Church pastor greets new arrival Ernie and asks him to preach on the Steurys' first Sunday at Tenwek, May 1959.

Before Tenwek Community Health educated the Kipsigis people to build their fires on raised platforms, out of the reach of toddlers, Ernie often treated burn victims like this little girl. The health program decreased the number of these types of injuries significantly. Before treatment, this patient could only scoot across the floor. After treatment, she could walk.

After years of nursing experience in the Ethiopian bush, Marilyn Van Kuiken arrived at Tenwek in 1968. She became Aunt Marilyn to the Steury children and a dear friend to Ernie and Sue.

Ernie enjoyed more room (and more help) in the OR as each new, improved building was added.

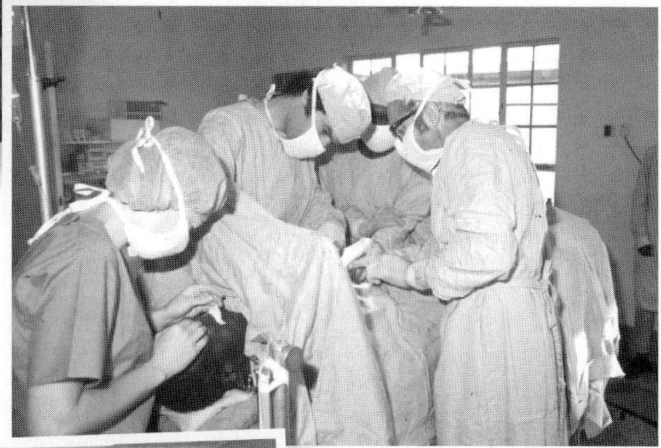

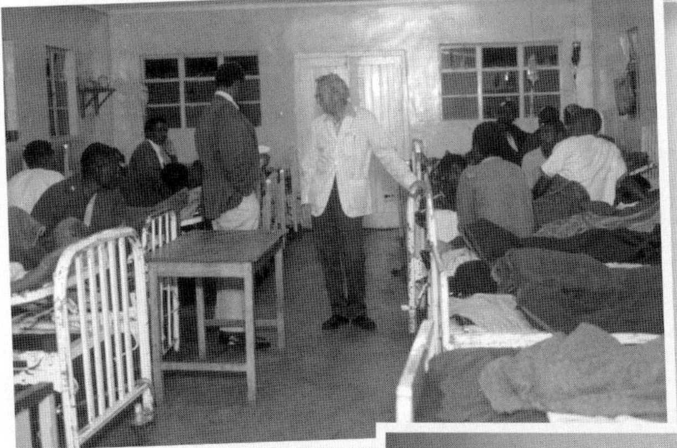

No sooner would Tenwek add capacity than the new facilities would fill to overflowing. In 1966, the hospital averaged 186 percent occupancy. During 1980, patient occupancy ran at 233 percent.

Before Ernie assembled this donated autoclave, he often had to sterilize surgical instruments in Sue's pressure cooker.

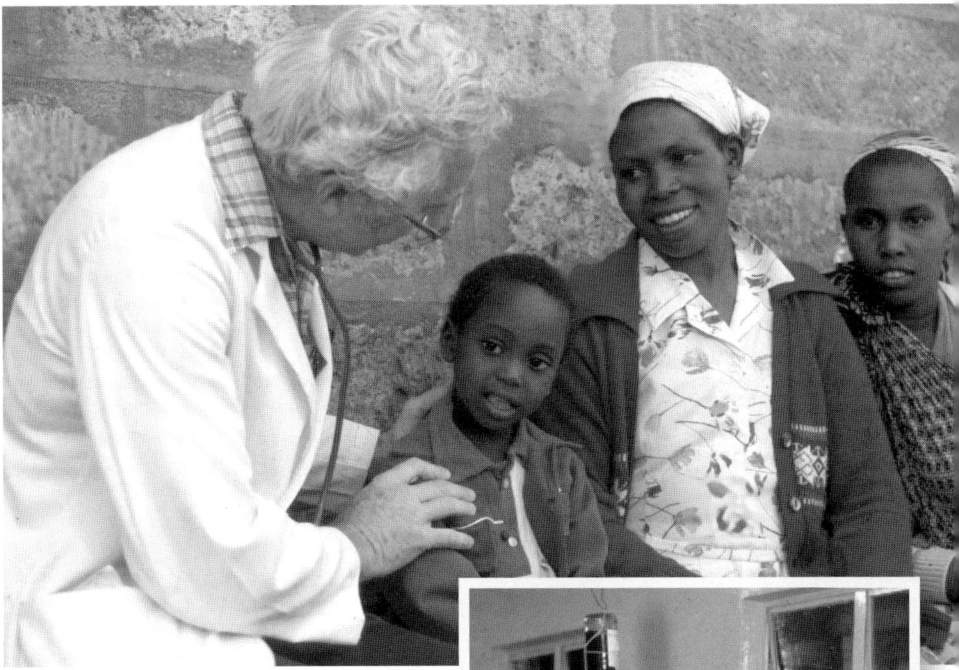

At the end of a long day of scheduled and emergency surgeries, there might be a hundred outpatient cases waiting to see a doctor. Then, of course, there were always rounds.

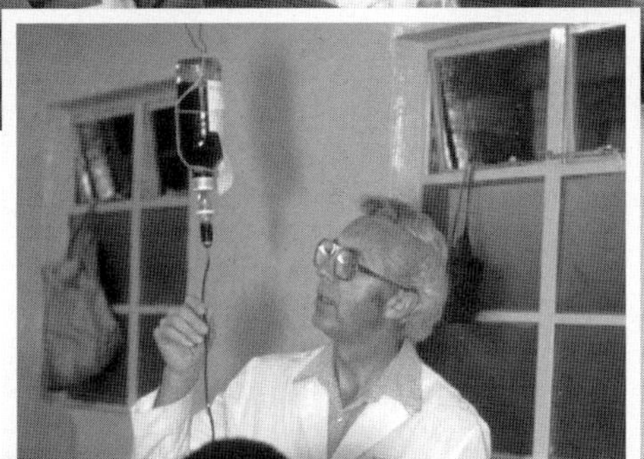

Patients often walked for many miles, sometimes past government clinics, to be treated at Tenwek. Their explanation: "Here the hands are kind."

When Tenwek completed its own hydroelectric dam in 1987, the electricity flowed, changing hospital medical care and everyday life forever.

Ernie gave President Daniel Arap Moi a personal tour of the hospital when he came for the dedication of the Johana Ng'etich Medical Centre.

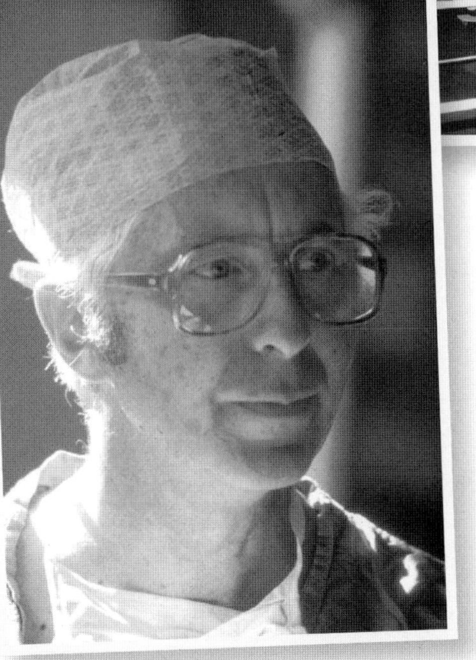

Over the years, Ernie Steury's compassion, commitment, and humble example inspired and taught thousands of physicians around the world what it meant to practice medicine in partnership with the Great Physician.

Steven Mabatu says the simple kindness of a cup of tea convinced him "Dr. Steury was a man I could trust and pattern my life after." After working with Ernie at Tenwek, Steven was appointed a Kipsigis chief in his home region.

Ernie's medical treatment saved the lives of thousands of patients over the years, and Tenwek's community health program drastically improved the health and lifestyle of hundreds of thousands of people throughout southwest Kenya.

Ezekiel Kerich risked ancient tribal taboos to work at Tenwek as the first hospital administrator. According to Sue, "Ernie and Ezekiel bonded like brothers."

People would come from all over Kipsigis land believing, "If we can just touch Mosonik, we will get well."

After laboring alone for many years, Ernie greatly valued the physician colleagues who eventually joined him (left to right): Marty Graber, Bob Wesche, Dick Morse, and David Stevens.

The emergency caesarian delivery of this woman's baby was the first surgery performed at Tenwek in 1959. Ernie noted, "The Lord was with us! If mother and baby hadn't survived, it might have been a long time before the Kipsigis people would have trusted me to operate on another patient."

When Ernie appointed Dr. David Stevens his second-in-command, he planned that Dave would take over leadership of the hospital.

After Sue began teaching evangelism skills to community health workers like these, she felt she had finally found her niche.

Ernie not only directed the medical ministries at Tenwek, he oversaw the constant expansion of the facilities. Here he answers questions for missionary builde Billy Wayne Fuller.

From the beginning, Ernie's goal was to nationalize Tenwek Hospital. He was thrilled to hire Steven Mutai to replace retiring hospital administrator Ezekiel Kerich. Stephen eventually became CEO.

After a surprise visit from Franklin Graham in 1978, World Medical Mission, Samaritan's Purse, and the Billy Graham Evangelistic Association partnered with Tenwek on many new endeavors.

Ernie and Sue with their four adult children (left to right): Cindy, Nate, Jon, and Debbie

Susan Carter's years of experience coordinating Tenwek's community health program made her a logical choice to become executive director of Tenwek Hospital when Ernie retired.

With great skill and diplomacy, Ernie regularly represented Tenwek by speaking and consulting with the national leaders of the Kenyan government. In 1997, President Moi granted Ernie his adopted country's highest honor (right): the Order of the Grand Warrior of Kenya.

During his last days in Kijabe, Ernie rallied to enjoy a visit from a contingent of old friends and medical colleagues representing MAP International and the Christian Health Association of Kenya.

and she was dead. Simply because her mother had fallen asleep in a dark ward and the manual pump was inadequate. But ultimately because we didn't have the electricity to run the equipment that would have kept the child alive."[1]

By 1984 Tenwek's need for a reasonably priced and constant source of electricity was desperate. The annual cost of diesel fuel for the generators was more than sixty thousand dollars. And the new ward, which would nearly double the size of the hospital, was going to require more power than the generators could produce, which meant diesel fuel costs in the coming years were projected to go far higher.

The meager patient fees the hospital charged couldn't cover the increase in cost. Something had to be done. But Ernie had no idea where to start, except to pray that the Lord would again find a way to provide for Tenwek's ministry and to charge Dave Stevens with doing whatever he could on his furlough.

Neither Ernie nor David saw any real reason for hope on the horizon. But no sooner did Jody and Dave Stevens get back to America than God answered Ernie's prayers and got the ball rolling in a most unusual way.

"Jody and I were living in our hometown of Wilmore, Kentucky, that furlough year when I was interrupted by a knock on our front door early one August morning. Opening the door, I saw Marilyn Kinlaw standing on our front step, in her housecoat, her hair in curlers, and a baby on her hip. Marilyn's husband, Denny, was a physician friend; they'd been to Tenwek during his residency. So she knew our needs.

"'David,' she said, 'I was having my devotions this morning and God told me to come over here and say something to you.'

"Now, I'm not exactly used to having people drop by with messages from God before eight o'clock in the morning. Actually, this was a first. Yet Marilyn had obviously disrupted her morning routine with her children because God had prompted her. So I said 'Come on in.'

"Marilyn stepped inside the door but declined to take a seat. 'I'm in a hurry,' she explained. 'I've got to get back home and take care of the kids.

1 David Stevens, *Jesus, M.D.* (Grand Rapids: Zondervan, 2001).

But God told me to let you know that there's an engineer here in town today from World Radio Missionary Fellowship; they operate radio HCJB in Ecuador. I heard they built some sort of hydroelectric plant there. I thought maybe he could somehow help you in building the hydro plant Tenwek needs.'

"I said, 'Let me get you a cup of coffee. Come in, Marilyn, and sit down for a minute.'

"'No, I really can't, David. I've got to go.' She told me the engineer's name and where in town he was staying. Then off she went back to her home."[2]

Soon after his visitor left, David Stevens headed across town to meet the engineer Marilyn thought had something to do with building a dam in South America. When Dave introduced himself to Bruce Rydbeck and briefly explained Tenwek's need for a hydroelectric dam, this engineer smiled oddly and told him, "David, I was having my devotions this morning and praying to God saying, 'Lord, it would be great if you would give me a chance to work on another hydroelectric project like we did down in Ecuador.' I just can't believe there would be another opportunity like this!"

Dave could see the excitement on Bruce's face as he went on to say, "I'll tell you who we need to get hold of right away. Can we get a couple of phones where we can both get on the line?"

Dave put Bruce in his car and drove to his own parents' house. Bruce got on one phone to place the call, and Dave picked up an extension. They were telephoning a civil engineer with Duke Power Company in North Carolina, which Bruce told Dave was one of only three power companies in the United States that built their own hydroelectric projects. This man had helped Bruce and provided expert advice when HCJB had built their hydro project high in the mountains of Ecuador.

Hugh McKay answered the phone. Bruce greeted him warmly, then introduced Dave and briefly explained his need to build a hydro plant for Tenwek Hospital in rural Kenya. There was a long pause before Hugh said, "Dave, I was just sitting here at my desk, leaning back in my chair, enjoying a good cup of coffee." (It was about 10:00 a.m. by this time.)

2 Ibid.

And I was praying, 'Oh God, give me another chance to do what we did down in Ecuador.' Then the phone rings, and it's you and Bruce!"

Hugh too was now excited. In just a matter of minutes, both he and Bruce had already grabbed onto this vision of a hydroelectric plant for Tenwek. Dave could hardly believe it! "But," he said, "I could feel it; something incredible was going on here. I definitely got this spine-tingling sense that God was already at work."

"Dave, have you got a piece of paper?" Hugh asked over the phone.

"Sure," David told him.

"Then take this down. Here's what we need to know," and he began rattling off a bunch of information he wanted Dave to gather for him. Exactly how high was the waterfall? How much water flowed over it per minute? How much did the flow change from season to season through the year? And a whole lot more.

Dave was practically reeling from the speed of all that was happening. Part of him wanted to stop and say, "Whoa! This idea is still impossible. We don't have the funding. No one at our mission has any expertise in this at all." But Bruce and Hugh were excitedly talking about this possibility and that option—how this would be just like, or how it might be different from, what they had done in South America.

Dave took the checklist of requested information Hugh McKay gave him over the phone that morning and sent it over to Tenwek. Ernie was working desperately to finish the new ward, so it took a few weeks for the folks in Kenya to collect all the data and send it back.

The next step was a feasibility study. Could the idea work or not? How could it be done? What was it going to take?

A plan like that would cost a lot of money Tenwek didn't have. But Hugh McKay told Dave, "Don't you worry—just leave that to me." Three weeks later he sent Dave a sixty-page feasibility study, complete with diagrams, pictures, and graphs, based on the Tenwek data. Hugh had spelled it out plain and simple. Step by step.

Reading that feasibility study, Dave slowly began to believe the impossible might happen, that the vision could come true—until he got to the bottom line where Hugh had given his rough estimate of the cost: six hundred thousand dollars.

Dave's immediate reaction was, *Oh, man! How many churches am I going to have to visit to raise that kind of money?* Then he remembered his experience with the foundation that provided the last of the money needed for the ward building.

So he sat down and tried to think of any and every possible alternate source of money. He knew or had heard of people in eight different foundations, so he decided to write each of them a formal proposal letter. He worked hard writing that appeal, got input from a number of people, and sent it off by the end of September 1984.

October went by and nothing happened. November came and there were still no replies. Hugh McKay and a couple of other engineers wanted to go over and check out the actual site. But they needed money for airfare; they had already ordered their tickets for the third week in November and had requested time off from work. They needed to see the falls, to look at the location, and determine for certain if everything in the formal proposal was actually going to work.

Two days before the engineering team was scheduled to take off, they still didn't have money for their tickets. That same day Dave Stevens got a phone call from Joe Luce. Joe's family owned the Blue Bird Corporation, the big bus manufacturer in Georgia, and had been faithful supporters of WGM over the years. Thinking Joe would be interested in the power project, Dave had sent his family's foundation a copy of the feasibility study and the formal proposal.

Joe told Dave later, "David, when I called you that day I told myself, 'There is absolutely no way they can do this at Tenwek. It's impossible. It's too expensive. No one in WGM knows how to build a hydroelectric plant. They don't have the resources or the manpower.' But you seemed so sure you could do it. So I thought, 'I'll give him twenty thousand dollars. If that's gone, it's gone. But at least he can try.'"

Part of Joe Luce's twenty thousand dollars paid the way for the engineering team to fly to Kenya, and Ernie showed them the hospital and the falls. When they came back they were absolutely convinced the plan would work.

December went by, and nobody sent any more money. January was almost over, and still no funds. Dave spoke at a mission conference with someone from World Vision, the large Christian relief and development agency that works all over the world. Dave asked the World Vision representative if his organization ever got involved in projects like Tenwek's. He suggested writing their U.S. headquarters, so Dave sent them a proposal and got an immediate reply, "You need to apply through our Kenyan World Vision office in Nairobi when you get back to Kenya."

David Stevens described his feelings five months later when he and his family went back to Kenya to begin their second term: "Our year of furlough, which had begun with Ernie's challenge and gotten off to such a memorable start—with Marilyn Kinlaw's early morning visit and the subsequent connection with Bruce Rydbeck and Hugh McKay, the plans, the proposal, the seed money from Joe Luce, and the confirmation that our plan would in fact work—ended on a rather discouraging note. Because nothing else had happened. We still didn't have any money for the project. I had sent out forty more foundation proposals and not one had stepped up to help us."

Some people had faith, however. Bruce Rydbeck had asked his mission organization, World Radio Missionary Fellowship, if he could help Tenwek build a hydroelectric plant. When WRMF generously gave Bruce permission, Ernie and Dave took most of the remaining seed money to buy tickets for him and his family to move to Kenya.

Though Dave had little hope World Vision would be able to help, he stopped at their office in Nairobi when he arrived back in Kenya. They told him, "We have never funded anything like this. We do child welfare projects. But if you want to send in a proposal, we'll take a look at it. But don't get your hopes up."

There was another roadblock just as big as funding: Tenwek didn't have official government permission to begin building a hydroelectric dam on the river. When Ernie had started inquiring about the process, he had been told it would take two years to get the paperwork approved before construction could begin on any hydroelectric plant. There would be forms to sign, reports to be filed, studies to be conducted, inspections to be made, committees to meet. It sounded like bureaucracy at its best.

So Ernie went to another government office. And another office. Then he went back to each of them again. But the discouraging word never changed. "It'll take years to get an answer. And the likely answer will be 'no.' No private organization has ever built a hydro plant the size you propose. We think it is impossible for you to do."

Finally, somebody had a brainstorm. Tenwek already had an official government license to generate power for the hospital from a diesel generator. So what if they stopped asking approval for constructing a hydroelectric dam and just asked permission to change their source of power? Ernie went in to the appropriate government office, showed them the license Tenwek already had, granting them the right to generate their own electrical power, and asked if they could get an official okay to switch from an old and inefficient diesel generator to a hydroelectric power source.

The officials told them, "No problem. If you want to change your power source, that's fine!" Ernie didn't bother to mention that the hydroelectric power source didn't exist yet. An official signed a simple form, and Ernie took that form back to the government office that had first denied permission and told them, "Look! The power board has given us permission. Why can't you?"

In less than a week, they did. But approving the concept was one thing; getting final approval to start the actual construction of a hydroelectric dam was yet another. More red tape. In September of 1985 that permission finally came through.

By this time there was very little of Joe Luce's seed money left. But since the next step was to build an access road down to the falls, Ernie and Dave decided to start hiring local Kipsigis men to do that arduous job. Without dynamite or even a bulldozer, the workmen began to widen the footpath that ran along a narrow ledge high above the river. On one side was the drop-off and on the other, solid rock.

Tenwek bought picks and shovels. The men built fires to heat the rock and then poured cold river water on the hot stone to crack it. Slowly a road wide enough to get construction equipment and materials down to the falls began to take shape. Work on the project proceeded, even though Tenwek still didn't have any resources to begin the next step.

Two days before the money ran out and they were going to have to shut down the work, Dave Stevens received a phone call from the director of World Vision in Nairobi. He said, "Dr. Stevens, with little hope I decided to send your proposal to our main office in the States anyway. Low and behold, they have approved it. I've got a check for fifty thousand dollars. I want to fly out tomorrow and give it to you." And that was enough money to keep the construction going.

The entire project ended up costing over eight hundred thousand dollars. Early estimates were low because the government changed some specs and because no comparable project had ever been attempted in Kenya. Not one of the forty foundations that had been approached when Dave's faith was wavering ever gave Tenwek any funding for the hydro project. All the necessary money eventually came in from the first eight foundations he had contacted. And according to Dave, "Every bit of that eight hundred thousand dollars came in just when we needed it to keep the construction on track," which taught him, he said, "that even if all we think we can manage is a mustard-seed worth of faith, effort, or talent, once God pitches in, mountains will move. Dams will rise. Electricity will flow."

Even though no one at Tenwek knew how to build a dam, God supplied people who did. Another engineer came from Australia to build the powerhouse. A specialist in heavy equipment volunteered from Canada. God brought people from all over the world to do this project. But the first step in building the dam itself was to hire a hundred Kipsigis men to start chipping at the riverbed with chisels and hammers. For weeks during dry season when the river was low, the water was diverted by sand bags while they dug an eighteen-inch deep trench into the bedrock all the way across the river. The engineers explained: "This is the most important step in the entire project. If you don't get down into the bedrock, it won't matter how much concrete you pour. The dam will move when the waters come. We need a firm foundation."

Instead of hiring an outside construction company, Tenwek bolstered the community's economy by employing local labor for building the dam. And there was a lot of labor. Transportation prices were so high and the roads so bad that it was more cost effective to pay hundreds of local

Kipsigis workers to make the necessary gravel by breaking up river rocks with hammers than it was to truck it in.

There were always a lot of people and a variety of activities going on down at the construction site. Many of the missionaries, as well as a lot of local people, would walk down every day or so to see what progress was being made.

WGM missionary builder Billy Wayne Fuller managed all the on-site construction: the volunteers, national staff, capable engineers, and construction people. Bill Wright, an electrical engineer from HCJB, lived and worked at Tenwek for six months. Eric Moore, a project manager from HCJB, came and went during the project. Ross Chatfield and his wife came from Australia to Tenwek to help build the powerhouse. And then there was seventy-year-old "Uncle Charlie" Snyder, a mechanical wizard from Canada who rebuilt a bulldozer and made a crane to lift the penstock, installed the turbine generator, and personally repaired the hospital's diesel generators time after time.

Dave Stevens kept all the project's books on his home computer in the evening and tried to pursue and raise the funds as they were needed, while still practicing medicine and serving as the hospital's medical superintendent during the Steurys' furlough, which began in 1985. At times Dr. Stevens felt overwhelmed by the enormity of the task. "Believe it or not," he said, "we made every bit of the concrete for our hydroelectric project in a half-cubic-yard cement mixer. If you know anything at all about construction, you realize that's the size mixer you would use to pour a patio. But that's all we had to build a 150-foot-long dam that was forty feet high and more than twenty feet thick at the base. Impossible? No. But it helped me imagine what it must have been like to build the pyramids.

"We had three lines of men at once converging on that mixer. One line brought sand, another rock, the third cement. They'd each dump their load in the mixer, another man would add water, and someone else would allow the minimum turns before dumping the contents of the mixer into one of the wheelbarrows waiting in yet another line. Then the finished cement would be wheeled on the run out onto the dam and poured into wooden forms. At crucial points of the dam's construction, crews poured cement like that for twenty-four to forty-eight hours straight. It took everybody working together to make it happen."

One of the challenges Tenwek faced in developing the hydro plant and trying to decide on the most efficient turbine was the seasonal fluctuations of the river. During the rainy season there was often enough water flow to generate a couple of megawatts of electricity. But there would be times during the dry season when there would be only enough water to generate 50 kilowatts. Most turbine generator sets require a full water flow all the time to work efficiently. So it took a lot of research before those managing the project found a German system that could operate efficiently with widely varying flows and could be synchronized to work in tandem with the hospital's diesel generators during the dry season. The fact that the perfect set to meet Tenwek's needs *just happened* to come from Germany influenced a German foundation to pay the $225,000 the generator cost.

Workers had started building the road down to the construction site in September of 1985, and by the following August, construction on the dam was finished. So was the powerhouse. All that remained was the turbine generator set, the shipment of which was delayed until the end of 1986.

While all this construction had been going on down in the valley, on the hillside high above the Nyangores River, the medical work of Tenwek Hospital not only continued, it grew like never before. With the opening of the new ward, the hospital's occupancy rate dropped from 180 percent in 1984 to just 110 percent in 1985. A large guesthouse and a five-unit apartment building for staff were also completed and occupied. But the expansion didn't stop there. A dormitory/dining complex for nursing students, a large meeting room, another six-unit staff apartment complex, and an addition to the maintenance building were all under construction.

In 1985 the hospital served 10,165 inpatients and 54,130 outpatients. The doctors performed a thousand major surgeries, and more than two thousand babies were delivered at Tenwek. A third chaplain had to be employed to deal with 8,258 seekers.

Statistics for 1986 were even higher. Inpatients totaled 12,720; outpatients, 62,134; major surgeries, 1,070; and deliveries rose to 2,499. Four full-time chaplains dealt with 9,662 seekers. (This made the average over a three-year period to be about nine thousand a year.)[3]

By the beginning of 1986, the community health program had also grown to include over one hundred volunteer community health helpers. These workers gave more than thirty thousand immunizations and made more than fifty thousand home visits where they taught better health practices, treated common diseases, and shared the gospel through their own witness and by using simple picture books on salvation, growing in the Lord, and the work of the Holy Spirit. With an estimated average household of seven individuals, this meant 350,000 people were impacted in their homes by this one program in 1986. And the numbers of trained volunteers continued to grow.

Furlough

While all these exciting things were happening at Tenwek, the Steurys began their furlough in the summer of 1985. In and around their usual long list of speaking engagements, Ernie and Sue managed to celebrate exciting times with family and friends, including both of their sons' weddings. Nate married Elinda Enright a few weeks after Ernie and Sue returned to the States, and Jon's marriage to Vera Seaman took place in November. By December they all looked forward to gathering in Berne to celebrate the family's first Christmas together in several years. But a routine physical exam at Caylor-Nickel Clinic in mid-December impacted those plans when doctors discovered a small malignant tumor in Ernie's colon.

During a December 20, 1985, surgery, doctors removed about a foot of Ernie's colon, but they felt confident they had removed all the cancer.

---

3 Burnette C. Fish and Gerald Fish, *A Place of Songs* (Marion, Ind.: World Gospel Mission, 1990).

Ernie was well enough to come home from the hospital a couple days after Christmas. But four days later he developed complications and was readmitted to the hospital on January 1, 1986. On January 3, Ernie's fifty-sixth birthday, he underwent surgery again for a bowel obstruction. What was scheduled to be a forty-five-minute procedure turned into a four-and-a-half-hour ordeal.

Untold numbers of people were praying for Ernie: WGM prayer bands; friends around the world, including all of his missionary colleagues back in Africa; and tens of thousands of Kipsigis Christians in hundreds of Africa Gospel Church congregations throughout Kenya. On January 17, Ernie had his third major surgery in less than a month, this time for a suspected pelvic abscess. On February 9, after forty straight days in the hospital, Ernie came home again.

Since the Steurys spent much of the first half of 1986 recovering from Ernie's physical ordeal, the mission extended their furlough to the end of the year. Ernie worked again at the Caylor-Nickel Clinic for the months of September and October for his usual brush-up on recent medical developments. As always, the experience gave him an added sense of confidence and encouragement to take back to Kenya with him. And there was more encouragement than usual this time because the surgeon friend who had performed all three surgeries on Ernie did a biopsy of his colon as a precaution, and all the tests came back normal. So Ernie and Sue were cleared to go.

While on furlough they had seen their children mature and grow in their desire to serve God. This knowledge helped Ernie and Sue face the prospect of going back to Kenya without any of their children for their sixth term. But the thought that Jon and Vera and Cindy and Daniel would soon be joining them as missionaries in Kenya also gave them a real sense of pride, not to mention something exciting to look forward to.

Mosonik and Tapkigen (the name the Kipsigis women gave Sue during their third term in Kenya means "The One Who Always Returns") received an especially warm and joyful welcome-back from missionaries and Kipsigis who saw this latest return of the Steurys as a definite answer to their prayers. Then Ernie and Sue hit the ground running in Tenwek as 1987 began.

All Systems Go

They could hardly believe all the changes that had taken place on the station while they were gone—new staff and new buildings everywhere they looked. And the dam! Ernie had seen photos of the progress, but pictures didn't begin to do the structure justice. The dream had become a reality in his absence. What a difference the hydro was going to make for Tenwek and its ministry!

The generator set had finally arrived on Christmas day. It would have gotten there Christmas Eve, but one of the trucks hauling it out from Nairobi got stuck in the mud on a dirt road twenty-one kilometers from Tenwek. On Christmas morning several missionaries in a four-wheel-drive Land Rover used picks and shovels and chains to get the driver back on the road and led him to Tenwek by a better route.

All that remained was the careful alignment of the turbine and generator with the penstock and the rest of the project, some additional wiring, programming the computer controls, and the final testing. Electrical engineer Bill Wright from HCJB radio in Ecuador had come to Tenwek for six months to help synchronize the electrical system and the computer controls. Everything needed to be working in time for the dedication ceremony with Kenyan President Daniel Moi, scheduled for February 21, 1987.

Eight days ahead of schedule, everything was in place. At 4:10 p.m. on February 13, 1987, everyone involved in the project gathered in and around the control room at the maintenance building near the hospital. The switch was thrown, and electricity from the new hydro plant flowed to all parts of the hospital and to every building and house on the base. "What a thrill it was to see the lights come on," Ernie said. "Everything worked perfectly. A dream first conceived by Willis Hotchkiss and WGM's first missionary, Robert K. Smith, plus many prayers over fifty years were finally realized."

Then the diesel generator was shut off, and the familiar noise that had sounded from the hillside at Tenwek for decades finally faded away. Ernie led the group in a prayer of rejoicing and thanksgiving.

Plans for the formal dedication the following week had to be changed when President Moi canceled his appearance due to the sudden death of a close personal friend. But so many mission officials, former missionaries, and other dignitaries from around the world had already arrived that Ernie decided to go ahead with an "unofficial" dedication service of praise and worship down by the dam. Several hundred people from the hospital, the local community, and other parts of Kenya joined in the service.

Numerous people spoke about different aspects of the project, frequently using words like "miracle," "dream," and "answer to prayer." Dave Stevens talked about the amazing way God had brought all the people and pieces of the puzzle together to complete what so many people considered an "impossible feat" in just eighteen months. Ezekiel Kerich represented the hospital and the community when he pointed out that the whole project, like the hospital ministry itself, had been done for the ongoing benefit of the Kipsigis people. Joe Luce, representing the WGM board and the Blue Bird Corporation's foundation, which made the first donation for the project, said a few words. He commented on how easy it is for Christians to limit God by their lack of faith and how this power plant would be a lasting monument to God's power and faithfulness to His people. Other missionaries and local officials spoke. The head of World Radio Missionary Fellowship, the parent organization of radio HCJB in Quito, Ecuador, who had loaned three engineers to Tenwek for the project, brought greetings from missionaries around the world. Ernie read additional greetings from several individuals who wished they could be there, including pioneer missionary Robert K. Smith himself.

Ernie closed the service with a special dedicatory prayer. Then he led the many visitors and the crowd of local people on a grand tour of the powerhouse to see the generator and turbine in operation.

What a difference this was going to make for Tenwek Hospital. As Robert Wesche said in a support letter later that spring, "Intravenous drip monitors, mechanical volume respirators, gastrointestinal suction units, and other items are coming out of storage now that we have 24-hour electricity."

Not only would the modern, first-class 320-kilowatt hydroelectric plant improve the medical care offered at Tenwek Hospital, it promised to transform life for all those who worked there. "Suddenly we could do things we'd never done before," David Stevens said. That first night when the lights didn't blink and go off at nine o'clock seemed such a novelty that Jody and I were up until one in the morning. Nothing reminded us to go to bed. Our newfound source of power definitely took some getting used to. It seemed almost too good to be true."

Generous Friends

In the days that followed the celebration of the new hydroelectric plant, Ernie and Sue had the special privilege of playing host to the visitors who stayed at Tenwek a little while longer. And as they always liked to do with first-time visitors from the States, they took a daylong safari out to the game park in Maasai to see the animals. Two of the guests who went with Ernie and Sue that day were Joe Luce and his wife, Marilyn.

Because of the Luce family's long involvement with WGM, Ernie and Sue had known of Marilyn and Joe for many years. But they had developed a special bond with them during their furlough back in 1980–81. During the Steurys' deputation travels, they made a stop in Georgia to speak at WGM's Southeast Celebration at St. Simons. The Luces were regulars there. So one evening in the dining room, Joe told Ernie and Sue he had wanted to talk with them and invited them to join him and Marilyn at a table for four.

As they began to eat, Joe said, "Ernie, I've heard you talk many times about your work at Tenwek. But I've never heard your testimony as to how you became a missionary doctor and how you and Sue ended up with WGM in Kenya. Would you mind sharing that story with us?"

Ernie was always glad to tell how God had worked in his life over the years. So he started by talking about his upbringing on a small Indiana farm. He recounted how God had kept him from joining the U.S. Navy at the last minute, how he had felt called into missions, and how his pastor had recommended Asbury College. He told about how he had seriously dated the daughter of missionaries to Sierra Leone and how everyone assumed they were meant for each other—until he had felt led to break off their relationship before he left for college.

Sue told her own story about how she and Ernie found each other at college and shared a calling to Africa. Ernie told how he had assumed he would be a missionary preacher, but his roommate, who had always dreamed of being a doctor, talked him into considering premed. Ernie described for the Luces how he had searched for some way to pay for medical school and had finally appealed to Dr. George Warner, president of World Gospel Mission. He recalled how Dr. Warner had told him WGM had no scholarship money for medical students, but he would mention the idea at the next board meeting, and how before that meeting ever took place, someone had unexpectedly given ten thousand dollars to be used for that purpose. That was the gift that had made it possible for him to go to medical school and graduate debt free so he could go to Africa as a medical missionary and be Tenwek Hospital's first doctor.

Ernie stopped his story at that point and said, "Joe, I never did know where that money came from. But I've heard so many stories over the years about your father's generosity and how he liked to designate large amounts of money to special projects . . ."

Marilyn Luce, who had been tugging on her husband's arm, spoke up and asked, "Did Dad do that, Joe?"

Joe made sort of a negative motion with his head and gestured for his wife to wait as Ernie had continued, "So Sue and I always kind of wondered if maybe your dad gave that money . . ." Ernie paused.

By this time he and Sue and Marilyn were all watching the tears roll down Joe Luce's face. Joe turned and smiled at Marilyn. "Don't you remember, honey? Back in 1953. We didn't have a lot of extra money. But we felt God telling us to send a gift to WGM?"

Joe and Marilyn Luce had sent the ten thousand dollars. They had never known how it had been used or by whom. Ernie and Sue had benefited from that money, but they had never known who or where it came from. Almost thirty years later, both couples had found out what had happened at the same time. As they sat together around that dinner table, Joe Luce wasn't the only one with tears in his eyes.

"Ernie and I always felt a special bond with Joe and Marilyn after that," Sue recalled. "And they felt the same way about us. The Luces became some of our dearest friends."

This added to the significance of Joe's gift for the hydro project and made it a special joy for the Steurys to take their friends on that safari adventure out to Maasai. At the end of that memorable day together, enjoying the awesome beauty of Africa and its wild animals, Ernie and Joe stood together with their heads and shoulders sticking out the top hatch in the back of Gene Lewton's four-wheel-drive pickup during a long and bouncy ride back to Tenwek.

"Ernie," Joe Luce asked his friend, "what are your plans for retirement?"

"I haven't really thought about it," Ernie told him.

"Where do you plan to live?"

"I don't know," Ernie replied. "We don't have a place."

The conversation went in a different direction from there. But that little exchange on a dusty ride over the Maasai plains would eventually take on significance for both men that would only be revealed years later.

It started Joe Luce thinking, *I bet there are a lot of missionaries like the Steurys who have invested their entire lives in missionary service and have made little or no provision or plans for their retirement years. Somebody ought to do something about that!*

It also started Ernie thinking about how, as he was beginning his sixth term of service in Africa, he was a lot closer to the end of his career than he was to the beginning. That, along with all the wonderful changes taking place at the mission, added a new sense of urgency regarding the need to be thinking about Tenwek's future. He was more convinced than ever that the hospital's greatest days of ministry still lay ahead.

Special Care for Special Patients

The Kipsigis people and missionaries alike benefited from the new and improved medical facilities as the result of the most recent developments at Tenwek. Almost thirty years after Ernie Steury had to boil his surgical instruments in Sue's pressure cooker before his first emergency surgery, the hospital's new Johana A. N'getich Medical Centre not only contained two operating room suites complete with sterilization equipment, it also housed Tenwek Hospital's very own intensive care unit (ICU). That unit didn't offer the degree of specialized care available in an ICU in a hospital in the United States, but it did permit the staff to closely supervise and give special care to very ill patients.

The first patient to be placed in the ICU was a little girl recovering from brain surgery. Dr. Mel Cheatham, a visiting neurosurgeon from Ventura, California, diagnosed a malignant tumor causing obstructive hydrocephalus. He removed much of the tumor from the fourth ventricle of her brain, and she was placed in the ICU for careful monitoring. A few weeks later she had recovered enough to go to Nairobi for radiation therapy to shrink the remaining tumor. The Tenwek staff prayed that the treatment would give her several more years of life free from the intense pain she had been suffering when she came to them for help.

On the first day the ICU was opened, Edna Goff rushed to Tenwek from the Kaboson Health Center (the hospital's outstation clinic) with a boy who had fallen in a river while having an epileptic seizure. Some boys who were with him managed to pull him from the river and ran for help. He woke up following his seizure, but over the next two hours he began having difficulty breathing. His family hurried with him to Kaboson several miles away, and by the time they arrived, he was having bubbling respirations. It was evident that he had nearly drowned, and now he was having lung complications. Edna and the boy's older brother placed him in Edna's vehicle, and they began the twenty-five-mile journey to Tenwek. During the one-and-a-half-hour journey over bad roads, the boy suffered increased difficulty breathing. Just as the vehicle pulled up to the hospital doors, his respiration stopped completely.

The staff rushed him to the ICU, which had been open only a few hours. An anesthesiologist who had accompanied Dr. Cheatham to Tenwek quickly inserted an endotracheal tube and suctioned some of the fluids out of his lungs. He was suffering pulmonary edema as a result of his near drowning and required positive pressure breathing and frequent suctioning over the next several hours. A chest X-ray showed infiltrates from the pulmonary edema and pneumonia. But the boy's condition improved, and he woke up enough during the night to manage to pull out his endotracheal tube and say that he was hungry. The Lord had allowed him to live long enough to reach Tenwek Hospital and had provided the staff and equipment in the ICU to give him the care he needed during the first critical hours. After a couple days he was able to walk from the ICU to the pediatric ward, and after another few days, he went home.

Chapter 15

ENVISIONING THE FUTURE

Everyone was excited about the new facilities, the luxury of round-the-clock electricity, and the improved medical care those developments promised for Tenwek's patients. Even before the hydro project was finished, Ernie and his staff had drawn up plans for a new outpatient clinic that would focus on maternal-child health care. The needs in outpatient care were obvious to anyone who ever visited Tenwek. Sick people, young and old, lined up outside the hospital every morning—in part because there just wasn't room inside to put them all. Every year the Tenwek medical staff was seeing well over fifty thousand outpatients in two small rooms allotted for that purpose.

For some time now Ernie and the staff had been discussing these needs and planning the answer—a new complex that included a dental clinic, an eye clinic, a TB clinic, a whole suite of examination and treatment rooms, and a number of administrative offices in addition to an outpatient/maternal-child health care unit. The hospital also desperately needed a new maternity ward. Tenwek's current thirty-bed maternity ward regularly housed sixty to seventy patients and delivered more than 2,500 babies a year.

The estimated cost of one million dollars for the two-building complex would make this expansion Tenwek's largest project yet. WGM was hard pressed, however, just to raise enough money to house the growing number of workers required to staff the new Ng'etich medical building. There was no way could they expect their regular supporters back in the States to come up with so much money for yet another expansion. So this time Ernie made an appeal to the government for its assistance. When the U.S. ambassador to Kenya and the director of USAID in Nairobi visited Tenwek to see the hospital and the progress on the hydro plant in January of 1987, Ernie spelled out the dream for a new building and asked if USAID might help sponsor the project. He prayed their recommendations to Washington might result in a significant grant. Shortly after the U.S. ambassador sent a cablegram to Washington urging American officials to give Tenwek the grant, USAID promised to come up with half the funding.

The hospital then applied to EZE, the German foundation that had funded the generator set for the hydro plant, for the remainder of the construction costs of the two new buildings. Final approval from both sources came through before 1987 ended, and construction was begun. About the same time, just down the hill from the hospital, the Africa Gospel Church began building a new and bigger sanctuary to replace the Hotchkiss Memorial Church, which was in need of major structural repairs.

New construction was hardly the only thing happening at Tenwek. The even more "permanent" aspects of ministry too continued to mushroom, particularly with the community health program, which had a big impact on the eight thousand new believers in 1986. The growing volunteer force, already 125 community health helpers, was having an immediate impact throughout the area, both physically and spiritually. Due to the immunizations and the instruction provided by the workers, the number of measles cases at Tenwek had been cut in half, and whooping cough cases were only a fifth of what they had been in preceding years.

With all of the building and development going on at Tenwek, Ernie began thinking about his legacy and the significance of his life's work in Africa. Some of his reflections were included in a June 1987 *Call to Prayer* article entitled "Temporary."

"I tried to fashion a temporary instrument to remove the small bean that had been in a little girl's ear for three months. Someone had already tried to remove it, but it had absorbed moisture and was wedged tightly in the ear canal right on the eardrum. I took a paper clip, straightened one end of it, and then bent it at a sharp right angle—just long enough to slip past the bean and gently lift it out. It worked perfectly, and the bean came out without difficulty. I walked past the waste can and threw the paper clip away—I was through with it. It was just a *temporary* instrument.

"I walked down the ramp to the *temporary* building which served as our female medical ward. It had been put up when we demolished a ward that stood where we were going to build our new ward and operating suite. Even though it was serving a purpose, I was glad that we didn't have any other *temporary* wards.

"I looked around and saw many *temporary* things. Several children were using crutches *temporarily* because they had surgery for osteomyelitis, a severe bone infection. The little children who had been burned at home were wearing bandages *temporarily* until their burns were healed or the skin grafts had taken. The intravenous fluids which were running into several patients' arms were there only *temporarily* until they could again take fluids and food by mouth. The little baby in the incubator was there *temporarily* until the little body could grow strong enough to cope with the cold, cruel world.

"Our large new ward had *temporary* scaffolds built all around it so that the building could be put up. Without the *temporary*, much of the permanent would not be in existence. As the *temporary* was taken away, it was thrilling to see what is permanent.

"However, many things which seem permanent around us are really just *temporary*—even health. The one thing that is permanent at Tenwek Hospital is the spiritual fruit. The spiritual ministry has changed the hearts and lives of many patients and families who have come to the hospital. Homes and communities have been changed, and new churches have been started as new Christians returned to their homes. Last year over eight thousand people found the Lord here at Tenwek. During the first six months of this year, many more have put their faith in Christ. The sign outside our hospital still reads: We Treat—Jesus Heals. The healing patients receive here is not just of the body, but also of the soul—the one thing in life which is permanent."

Midway through 1987, Sue took over the evangelism training and began supervising the evangelism efforts of the community health program. That opened up a whole new ministry for Sue. She went out into the Kipsigis communities throughout the region, training local community health committees and helpers how to more effectively share their faith with others. Many of the new volunteers accepted Christ in Sue's training classes; then they in turn won others as they went out into their communities.

After thirty years of raising four children and being limited to ministry tasks that could be integrated with her family and homemaking responsibilities (hospital bookkeeper, postmistress, station hostess, VBS director, Sunday school teacher, women's group leader, and speaker), this new assignment proved an exciting opportunity for Sue. "It was like I had finally found my niche," Sue said. "I just loved the interaction with the nationals. And the positive response was so rewarding."

Ernie's role and title at Tenwek also changed. He was appointed executive officer of the hospital by the board of governors. In this role he was responsible for all the staff of the hospital. Others on the staff who shared the load were medical superintendent, Dr. David Stevens; administrator, Mr. Ezekiel Kerich; and nurse-in-charge, Mrs. Connie Ojiambo. Ernie praised the Lord for his gifted and dedicated staff, who worked together well. As chairman of the station, Ernie was also responsible for keeping the rest of the missionaries informed about mission matters and taking care of plans, problems, and projects.

More than ever before, Ernie realized how his own role at Tenwek had evolved—and was still evolving. For so many years when he had been the only doctor *to do* the medical work, everything and everyone had depended on him. Now it was his role to see that the medical work *was done.* And there were now, thankfully, others to help shoulder the load.

There were, of course, tradeoffs. Spending a much bigger percentage of time on administrative tasks meant less time doing what Ernie loved most—directly interacting with his patients. Yet Ernie realized his age (almost sixty) and his recent health issues made it reasonable that he commit less time and energy examining, treating, operating on, and caring for patients and more time supervising and directing a growing team of well-qualified doctors and nurses to do those things.

Not that Ernie was ready to hang up his stethoscope or pack away his surgical instruments. He always preferred people-work to paperwork. So he got out of the office to make his rounds in the wards and take his turn in the OR as often as he could. But during those years in the mid- to late-1980s, the administrative load seemed to grow even faster than the hospital and its ministry. More and more of Ernie's people-work focused on personnel rather than patients.

Changing Roles, Changing Relationships

Ernie's relationship to his staff was also shifting. When Ernie had arrived at Tenwek back in the 1950s, the nursing staff had been older than, or at least as old as, he was. For twenty years Dick Morse had been a trusted colleague and partner in ministry. He was a few years younger than Ernie, but he too had been a professional contemporary whose children, like the children of other WGM missionaries working at the Bible college in Kericho and elsewhere in Kenya, had always referred to the Steurys as Uncle Ernie and Aunt Sue, just as the Steury children had referred to Ernie and Sue's missionary colleagues as Uncle Dick and Aunt Betty (Morse), Uncle Gene and Aunt Marion (Lewton), Aunt Marilyn (Van Kuiken), and Aunt Edna (Boroff).

But a significant change began to take place now as the expansion of Tenwek's hospital ministry brought an increase in staff. Since many of these new medical staff members were a full generation younger than Ernie and Sue, their children began affectionately calling the Steurys Grandpa Ernie and Grandma Sue. "We served as substitute grandparents to a lot of the missionary kids at Tenwek," Sue said. "Even as we became surrogate parents to a growing number of the people we worked and rubbed shoulders with every day—expatriate missionaries and nationals alike. I remember one Kipsigis staff woman in particular who spent countless hours visiting in our home and in personal counseling and sharing time with me. Ernie and I loved her and her husband and talked to them and advised them like they were our own children. They actually called us mother and father. And their children addressed us as grandma and grandpa. Our hearts were broken when we learned this husband was being unfaithful to his wife. Ernie went and confronted him. The young man sought forgiveness, and his wife took him back. But when the marriage didn't last, we grieved with her for the whole family."

Relationships with other missionaries presented other challenges and opportunities for the Steurys. Sue took on the primary responsibility for Kipsigis language training for some newcomers, and that process helped foster the mother-figure role she played especially in the lives of young women missionaries. "My heart went out to the single women," Sue said, "because I knew some of them had to give up relationships to answer their call to come to Tenwek as missionaries. As a teenager, I had thought I would have to do that as well. So I felt especially grateful to God for Ernie and was more than willing to be a sounding board for any of the young female missionaries who needed someone to listen to their concerns.

"Ernie always supported me in this interpersonal ministry. Whenever it was appropriate, he'd join me in these interactions. We regularly invited one or more of the single missionaries over for meals. And many were the times when Ernie would be the only man among several women sitting around the table in our home. He never seemed to mind. We loved these young women and so appreciated the professional, personal, and spiritual commitments that brought them to Africa to work with us."

The "parental" role Ernie and Sue assumed with their generation-younger colleagues seemed especially appropriate and understandably exciting for them when their son and daughter-in-law, Jon and Vera Steury, became the newest WGM missionaries in Kenya during the summer of 1987. Their assignment, as trained educators, was to spend the first few months learning the Maasai language before moving to the Naikarra station to teach in the African Gospel Church's first secondary school for the Maasai people.

To have a second generation of Steurys serving as missionaries in Kenya was a real source of pride for Ernie and Sue, especially when Jon cited his experiences in missionary boarding school and in his own family as the primary tools God had used to shape him into a person willing to be used by the Lord on the mission field. "I think of those early days when we went out to Maasai as a family, on hunting and camping trips, and for Dad to treat people at our outpatient clinic there," Jon recalled. As a kid I never dreamed I'd be coming back there to live and serve as a missionary teacher. But that was when I first began to love the Maasai land and the Maasai people."

For Ernie and Sue, the passing of time was underscored not only by the arrival of a new generation of missionaries but also by the departure of those who came before them. Indeed, when longtime missionary nurse Edna Boroff retired, WGM recognized her contribution to medical missions in Kenya by staging an actual "passing of the torch" ceremony as part of her retirement celebration. Edna had come to Tenwek in 1947, back in the days when many patients and visitors arrived by oxcart over dirt and mud roads. For forty years she had charge of the maternity ward—a dozen of those years before she ever had a doctor to back her up. During her tenure at Tenwek she had personally delivered eighteen to twenty thousand babies—two to three times as many as a busy American obstetrician delivers in an entire career.

Edna helped deliver nineteen babies in one day. Over the years she delivered seventeen sets of triplets and, during a single term, 121 sets of twins. During her last term in the mid-1980s, she delivered 4,130 babies. She was practically an institution at Tenwek and throughout that region of the country. The Kipsigis people knew and loved Edna.

By the time she retired, many women who had been delivered by Edna, and probably more than a few whose mothers were delivered by her, were having their own babies delivered by the little nurse from Ohio. These mothers were so honored they named their children after her—boys as well as girls. In fact whenever Edna went anywhere in that part of Kenya, whether to a game park or a hotel, chances were good they would insist she would get in free because the manager or someone else on the staff had been delivered by Edna or had a son or daughter or a niece or nephew delivered by her. She was an honored guest wherever she went.

The Need for Nurses

On July 6, 1987, Ernie's longtime dream of having an ample supply of Kenyan nurses was coming closer to fruition with the opening of a nursing school at Tenwek. The first class contained thirteen students who all did well in the first six months of their training. But while they waited for the first class to graduate, there was a continuing need for missionary nurses. An increasing number were required just to help carry the heavier medical load in Tenwek's bigger and better hospital wards. On top of that were the new endeavors like community health and the nursing school that required R.N.s with specialized qualifications and interests, both to train the national participants and to administer the program.

Ernie learned to rely on a new generation of nurses. And his confidence in new talent was rewarded in the way Susan Carter had coordinated the day-to-day work of community health under David Stevens's direction. The impact of that program was everything Ernie could have hoped for and more. Now he hoped that the long-awaited nursing school could get off to the same quality start. To head that program Ernie recruited a veteran missionary nurse, Mary Hermiz, who had already spent several years working in the Papua, New Guinea, bush. Mary's family had been supporters of World Gospel Mission all of her life. "As an eight-year-old girl I remember praying for a doctor to go to work at Tenwek," she recalled. "When I was ten, Ernie Steury came to speak in our church and actually stayed in our house during his deputation travels. I learned this young doctor heading to Kenya was the answer to our prayers.

"So thirty years later, when he asked me to come and help start the nursing school at Tenwek, it was a chance to work with someone I'd looked up to my entire life. Yet I wasn't at all sure I was the right person for the job until Ernie convinced me."

Mary didn't realize what a formidable job she had until she arrived in Kenya. But she found great encouragement in Ernie's example. "He had the whole administrative load of Tenwek on his shoulders," Mary said. "The ministry was multiplying so fast that it was outgrowing the infrastructure of support. Ernie was overseeing so many different programs and had so much to do. Yet he always had time for the people around him. Not just to listen to them, but to get to know them."

Susan Carter observed, "I'd heard so much about Ernie Steury before I ever got to Tenwek that I thought he could walk on water. Working with him every day, I learned he was human, that he struggled like the rest of us. Yet he lived out his faith in such a way with such humility and patience that I gained even more respect for him as time went by. I think that was true for almost every missionary at Tenwek. He was definitely our leader, but a leader who led by example. Ernie was first of all a servant—to those of us he led and to everyone around him."

Always Time for Others

By the late 1980s Tenwek had a larger staff with more trained medical professionals than Ernie could have asked for, or ever dreamed of, during his first couple of decades in Africa. He no longer felt the burden of sole personal responsibility for every patient who arrived at Tenwek. He no longer had to perform every surgery or be on call every night, or even every third night. Yet some days it seemed that any relief gained from the shared patient load was more than replaced by the increased administrative burden.

In the wake of his bout with colon cancer, Sue and Ernie's colleagues tried to adjust his schedule to reduce some of the physical demands on him. Ernie, however, still had more on his plate than any one person could ever get done. He was constantly on the move—literally as well as figuratively. Everyday he tackled a wide variety of jobs: drafting a new hospital policy; making a tough management decision; consulting with younger doctors on unusual medical cases; discussing a budget challenge; addressing a touchy personnel crisis; compiling an administrative report; taking a regular turn in surgery; counseling colleagues and subordinates struggling with emotional, relational, and spiritual issues; hosting official and unofficial visitors; chairing a field staff meeting of all WGM missionaries in Kenya; keeping tabs on construction projects; making rounds of the hospital wards; serving as liaison between hospital ministries and the Africa Gospel Church; representing Tenwek with government officials and their agencies in Bomet, Kericho, or Nairobi; preaching in local congregations; assuming the role of caring and encouraging father, grandfather, and friend for fellow missionaries and their families; being a devoted husband; and looking after his own physical, emotional, and spiritual health.

There were always too many things to do and too many places to be for Ernie to ever slow down very much—or for very long. "Those of us who worked closest to him realized the pressure he was under," commented

Susan Carter. "He remained ultimately responsible for everything that happened at Tenwek. True, more staff were working in more programs and doing more ministry than ever before. But there were still too few mid-level managers to help oversee and administer it all. So Ernie was involved in everything to varying degrees."

And yet no matter what he was doing, whether he was trying to extricate himself from the never-ending pile of paperwork or rushing across the hospital compound to help in the OR, Ernie had time for others. His colleagues remember his signature response to those who stuck their head in the door with a question or accosted him on the sidewalk with a problem: *What can I do to help?*

"No matter what he was dealing with at the moment, no matter how tired or how rushed he may have felt," Susan Carter said, "Ernie was always ready to give you his full attention. If he was so urgently needed somewhere else that he couldn't stop, he would listen long enough to understand what your concern was and then maybe he'd ask you to walk along with him wherever he was headed. He demonstrated both his humility and his patience in that he was never too busy to set aside what he was doing, shift gears, and listen to others' concerns."

Chaplain David Kilel seconded those observations when he said, "Anyone could come to him at any time. And people did because they could see the spirit of Christ in him. He never acted like a busy, big man in charge of the whole hospital who couldn't be bothered. He always took time to stop and say, 'Yes, what can I do for you?' And then he would listen to the answer.

"I remember praying in the chapel one day with Arap Toli, whose wife had been in the hospital for three months with an unknown illness. We prayed that God would reveal her problem to someone who would know how her condition could be treated. We finished praying, and I looked up just as Dr. Steury walked by. I called, 'Dr. Steury! Wait!' He stopped and I asked, 'Do you know this man?' I introduced him to Arap Toli and explained that we had been praying for his wife, how she couldn't stop vomiting, and how no one knew what to do. Dr. Steury listened and then suddenly turned and walked to the pharmacy, where he found a medicine to give to Arap Toli's wife. Two hours later she had stopped vomiting. In four days she was well and left the hospital. He listened to people because he cared about people. Then he also listened to God."

Ernie's care for others showed itself not just in the humble act of listening but also in his thoughtfulness toward those around him. Mary Hermiz recalled that "Ernie always tried to have licorice candy for me whenever we met in his office to talk about the nursing school because he had found out that I loved licorice. And from time to time, on special occasions or when he wanted to say thank you for something, he would give a missionary colleague a jar of his homemade pickles. He grew the cucumbers in the garden behind his house, and from time to time he'd personally can a new supply. You were the envy of the whole base if you had a jar of Ernie's prized sweet pickles.

"Ernie's barbecued chicken, and the secret recipe he used to prepare it, was perhaps even more famous than his pickles. He would grill the chicken in his yard, and you could smell it all over the Tenwek compound. If you weren't the one invited for supper, you certainly wished you were.

"You know, Ernie raised his own chickens. And occasionally he would slaughter maybe eight or ten at once and invite all the Tenwek missionaries over for a big cookout. As busy as he was, he enjoyed gardening and cooking for other people. I think it was how he relaxed and unwound. And it gave us a chance to see a whole other side to him."

Do You Know Mosonik?

Of all Ernie's missionary colleagues who worked closely enough with him to know him well, Dr. David Stevens had a truly unique perspective on, and relationship with, both Ernie and Sue. Though Dave was a colleague whose children addressed the Steurys as uncle and aunt, he was young enough to be their son. Dave had considered Ernie to be his professional and personal role model ever since he had stayed in the Steury home during the summer following his junior year of college. As an author, Dave dedicated his book, *Jesus, M.D.*, to his parents, his wife, and to Ernie as his mentor because "you personify the Great Physician to me."

Dave wrote of the personal relationships "forged and strengthened in the heat of crises shared" with Ernie and Sue. He recounted the wonderful care Ernie and Sue had personally given to Dave's wife, Jody, during and after the delivery of their third child.

One day Dave and Jody were rushing to Nairobi to catch a flight back to the States for a family emergency when they came to a flooded ravine made suddenly impassable by a thunderstorm upstream. As they waited helplessly, resigned to missing their flight, an old gentleman came out of the bush to strike up a conversation in Kipsigis.

When Jody told him they lived at Tenwek, he suddenly became more animated. "Do you know Mosonik?" he asked, using Ernie's Kipsigis name.

"Yes, we do," Jody assured him. "In fact they call my husband Arap Mosonik! He isn't really Mosonik's son, but he is like a son because he is the young doctor following in Mosonik's footsteps at the hospital."

A huge smile filled the old man's face, then, strangely, he turned, and at a half-trot he headed back into the bush, yelling at the top of his lungs. He was still shouting, his Kipsigis too rapid for Dave to understand, as he disappeared over a nearby ridge.

Within minutes Dave and Jody realized what was happening as people began streaming onto the road. Each one carried rocks. They waded out into the stream to wedge in their load before running back into the bush for more.

They were building a bridge. Dave started down to the river to help, but the old man returned and insisted Dave just relax as he issued more rapid-fire instructions to his crew. Within minutes they began adding logs and rough-hewn boards to the top of the rocks.

Satisfied that everything was progressing as he wanted, the old gentleman turned to continue the conversation. He told them, "When my wife was sick, Mosonik came to her bed many times, even in the middle of the night. I don't think that man ever sleeps. My wife would have died, but Mosonik cut her belly open to make her well. And then my daughter, when she had her first baby, it wouldn't come. So we took her to Tenwek, and somehow Mosonik got my first grandson out. He lived and is growing well.

"We Kipsigis know, if we get sick and go to the hospital . . . and just touch Mosonik, . . . we will get better."

Within minutes the hastily but lovingly constructed temporary bridge was finished. As Dave and Jody crossed the swollen stream and continued their journey to Nairobi, Dave said he couldn't help thinking what an impact Ernie's long years of service had made on people throughout that part of Kenya. His patients noticed, as Dave had noticed countless times, how Ernie would put an arm on their shoulder or hold their hand as he cared for their hurts, their wounds, and their sickness. They noted how gently he probed and palpated. His compassionate touch had made such an impression that people for miles and miles around had come to a conclusion much like the sick woman who grasped the edge of Jesus' robe: "If we just touch him, we will get better."[1]

Leadership Potential

Just as Dave Stevens saw much to respect and emulate in his mentor, Ernie recognized great potential in his younger colleague, who proved his capabilities time and again in his first few years in Kenya, whether it was writing foundation grants for hospital expansion, jump-starting and then spearheading the hydro project to completion, directing the incredibly successful community health program, overseeing the hospital's conversion from American medical standards and practices to British standards and practices in order to meet governmental prerequisites for an accredited nursing school, or taking over administrative responsibility as Tenwek's medical superintendent when Ernie was on furlough. From the outset of his medical missionary career, Dave Stevens had shown the kind of initiative, vision, organizational ability, and communication skills Ernie had been looking for in a younger person he could groom to take his place and assume the leadership of Tenwek Hospital and its multiplying ministries for decades to come.

"It wasn't something Ernie officially announced," Sue said. "But he talked about it with me. The choice was so obvious and David's skills so well suited to the job that I think everyone at Tenwek, missionaries and national staff alike, simply assumed Ernie would eventually hand the reins

---

1 David Stevens, *Jesus, M.D.* (Grand Rapids: Zondervan, 2001).

to David. It was just understood. And it seemed all the more natural and right because Ernie truly did love David like a son."

Health Crisis

Serious consideration of Ernie's successor became a front-burner issue for everyone at Tenwek a lot sooner than expected. A routine barium study conducted in Nairobi during January of 1988 indicated disturbing news. Ernie had cancer of the colon again.

He and Sue discussed the options. A repeat of the earlier surgical procedure seemed like the most promising treatment. One possibility, perhaps the simplest, would be to have the surgery done in Nairobi. That would be cheaper and involve less travel, and Ernie knew of competent surgeons in Kenya. But a different course was decided when Franklin Graham called Ernie and told him two first-class plane tickets from Nairobi to the States had already been purchased. He and Sue just needed to pack their suitcases, come home, and get the best possible medical treatment they could find as soon as possible.

They left within days and arrived in North Carolina on January 23. Six days later Ernie underwent surgery at Charlotte Memorial Hospital to remove another section of his colon. Two weeks later X-rays showed a complete obstruction of the small intestine starting just beyond the stomach. After five-and-a-half hours in surgery, the surgeon gave up and backed out. The bleeding and the adhesions were so severe the surgeon couldn't even identify some of the body parts, and he feared Ernie would not survive if he continued. He said, "It looked like someone poured Elmer's glue into his belly; everything was stuck to everything."

Ernie's surgeon felt he couldn't do anything more for several weeks or months. The news was rather disheartening because it meant Ernie might never eat another meal and could have to take his nutrition through a central line in his jugular vein for the rest of his life. Despite that prospect, which would have precluded his and Sue's ever returning to Africa, Ernie and Sue were wonderfully assured that God was with them. He gave them perfect peace in spite of the problem. Yet they trusted the Lord to work a miracle.

Back in Kenya the Steurys' fellow missionaries and thousands of Kipsigis people were also praying for Mosonik. The reports from the States did not sound good. And the Tenwek staff all knew enough about medicine to understand the serious implications of what details they heard. "We were afraid we were going to lose him," Susan Carter recalled.

Lots of folks back in the States were just as concerned. One Indiana man, the father of a Tenwek missionary but someone the Steurys barely knew, showed up at their apartment door in North Carolina to ask if he could pray for Ernie. He explained that he didn't claim any special healing power, but he had just felt the Lord impress upon him to pray for Ernie. He had done so back home in Indiana. But he had believed the Lord was telling him he needed to go to North Carolina to pray for Ernie in person. The man admitted he didn't understand why he was supposed to do this; he had never had God tell him to do anything like this before. But he had climbed in his car with his daughter, and they had driven all night from Indiana to pray with Ernie.

Sue invited the visitor in, and he prayed for Ernie's healing. The Steurys thanked him for his concern and his prayers. He bid them goodbye, got in his car, and drove back to Indiana.

Ernie and Sue never did learn what God might have been up to in that man's life—to send him hundreds of miles to offer a prayer. But within the next couple of days, it became clear that something was happening inside Ernie's body. One day while Sue was preparing a special chicken dish, Ernie exclaimed that it smelled so good he thought he would like to try a little broth. He figured he could just drain it later from the tube the surgeon had put in his stomach and out through the abdominal wall to drain his stomach and saliva secretions. But he heard his intestines gurgling after he ate; he was amazed when he opened his stomach tube to drain it. There was nothing there! On the doctor's advice, he started taking fluids by mouth; the IV was discontinued two days later, and before long he was back on a regular diet.

During a follow-up exam on July 5, the surgeon commented on Ernie's case to the other medical staff that were with him: "He was completely obstructed and we sent him home on IVs. A short time later, his bowel miraculously opened up; it certainly wasn't anything I did." He was thrilled to see how well Ernie was doing and cleared him to return to Kenya a couple weeks later.

Celebrations

Much was happening at Tenwek before and after the Steurys returned to Kenya in late July of 1988. Ernie was thrilled to see construction progress on both the outpatient/maternal-child health unit and the new maternity ward—what an asset they would be to the hospital once they were finished! The walls were also up on the new Hotchkiss Memorial Church just down the hill from the hospital compound; the builders were waiting for the steel structure to complete the roof.

Even as Ernie slowly regained his strength and stamina, all around him the hospital's infrastructure and ministry continued to grow at a record pace. And that growth carried over into the first few months of 1989.

In April 1989 the Steurys returned to the States for a short visit and for Ernie's one-year check-up with his surgeon in North Carolina. One hour out of Amsterdam, on his flight across the Atlantic, Ernie developed severe abdominal pain. By the time he arrived in Charlotte, he was so ill that he was checked into the hospital within an hour after landing. The initial diagnosis was another bowel obstruction. So of course the first thought was cancer again. But the CAT scans, X-rays, and lab tests showed no evidence of cancer. The obstruction resolved without surgery, and after Ernie was discharged from the hospital on the fourth day, he exclaimed, "Miracles still happen!"

He was out of the hospital in plenty of time to celebrate with Debbie when she graduated magna cum laude from Indiana Wesleyan University (formerly Marion College) with a B.S. in nursing. Ernie himself was honored during May in Minneapolis at the annual convention of the Christian Medical & Dental Societies (eventually renamed the Christian Medical and Dental Associations); this organization, which he had been a member of since medical school, recognized his career of service with their Servant of Christ Award. This award, symbolized by a towel and a basin in reference to Christ's washing of His disciples' feet, is the highest lifetime award granted by the CMDA. (Previous winners included world-renowned surgeon Dr. Paul Brand and former U.S. Surgeon General Dr. C. Everett Koop.)

After their short, but eventful, time in America, the Steurys returned to Tenwek with grateful hearts on May 24, 1989, just in time for Ernie to spend two and a half hours getting briefed by David Stevens, who handed over the administrative reins to the hospital before leaving on furlough.

Once again Ernie's administrative plate looked full to overflowing. As he wrote his supporters, with "visitors, work crusades, budgets, board of governors meeting, schedules at the hospital . . . [and more]—deadlines seem to be the order of the day. Yes, we are busy and happy to be back at Tenwek and able to work with our fellow missionaries and national staff . . ."

Along with all the work, there was plenty to celebrate at Tenwek the remainder of that year. His Excellency Mr. Daniel Moi, the president of the Republic of Kenya, made July 2, 1989, a memorable day when he arrived to officially commission the hydroelectric project and attend the service of dedication for the new Hotchkiss Memorial Church. The 1,200-seat sanctuary was full to overflowing, with another ten thousand people sitting on the ground outside.

Another cause for celebration: Chaplain David Kilel graduated from the Nairobi Evangelical Graduate School of Theology on July 22 with a master of religion degree. After being away in school for almost three years, he was back at the hospital full-time, overseeing a staff of five other chaplains and discussing with Ernie their shared dream for establishing a chaplaincy school at Tenwek to train chaplains for other hospitals throughout Kenya.

In October 1989 Tenwek reached another important milestone when the vice-president of Kenya, the Honorable George Saitoti, came to dedicate the hospital's two newest buildings—the Outpatient/Maternal-Child Health Unit and the big new Edna Boroff Maternity Centre. Edna herself was there to be honored. She stayed in Kenya several weeks after the dedication, working in the new ward that bore her name, adding a few more babies to the thousands she had successfully delivered over the decades. "It looked so natural to see her there," Sue said. "What a wonderful thing for her to be able to come back to see and even use the new facilities."

As exciting as all the physical improvements were, Ernie was even more thrilled by the fact that three new career doctors arrived at Tenwek during the last half of 1989. Ernie was in Kenya for more than twenty years before David Stevens became Tenwek's third career doctor. Now there were three new doctors coming in less than six months: Dr. Hal Burchel with his wife, Ruthann; Dr. Michael Johnson and his wife, Kay; and Dr. Daniel Tolan and his wife, Cindy. This last couple was the arrival the Steurys had been anticipating most—their son-in-law was bringing their daughter home to serve alongside Ernie and Sue at Tenwek where she had grown up.

God Keeps His Promises

As the time for furlough approached, Ernie realized that at age sixty, this was probably going to be his last furlough in preparation for the final full-term of service in his missionary career. With all the changes taking place during his most recent term, he probably spent more time than usual those first months of 1990 remembering the past and seriously considering the future of Tenwek. What a sense of reward he must have felt as he looked around the modern, three-hundred-bed hospital and remembered that first twenty-by-twenty-foot building with an OR barely big enough for an operating table. What a thrill he must have felt working alongside those three new missionary doctors and remembering all the years he had worked alone, wondering if God was ever going to call another physician to help him. What a sense of excitement and anticipation he must have felt as he envisioned Tenwek in the years ahead!

Ernie wrote, "God never breaks His promises! When He called me to be a missionary many years ago, He gave me the promise in Isaiah 41:13, 'For I the Lord thy God will hold thy right hand saying unto thee, fear not, I will help thee.' He has never broken that promise. There have been many times when I faced difficult surgeries or other decisions which I did not know how to handle. His promise was always true—He helped me.

"Some years ago, after we returned from furlough, the devil gave me a very difficult time. It started when friends in the States asked me why

I was going back to Kenya. They reminded me that I had fulfilled my obligation to work in Kenya and it was now time to stay home and make money. I knew that God had not released me from my commitment in Kenya, but day after day, the temptation to return to the States was there. As I trusted the Lord to keep me faithful to His call, He delivered me from the temptation and gave me another wonderful promise. 'The Lord will rescue me from every evil attack and will bring me safely to his heavenly kingdom. To him be the glory forever and ever' (1 Timothy 4:18). When Satan comes with his attacks, I can claim the promise God gave me. What a joy it is to know that He is always there when we call.

"When I was in the hospital with cancer, I wondered if I would ever return to Kenya. I was reminded of the many people who had assured me over the years that they were praying especially for my health. I realized that those people, and thousands of others, were still praying for me. I knew that I could trust the Lord to work out His perfect will for me. What a thrill it was to see His miraculous touch on my body! He has given me the joy of spending a few more years at Tenwek for Him. I know that someday He will take me to Himself, and I will not experience the touch of physical healing. Whether it is to live or die, I know that God keeps His promises and they are all true."[2]

So it was that the promise of one more furlough in preparation for one more term of service in Africa gave Ernie Steury new reason to hope and trust in the God who had first called him to the mission field and then to Tenwek more than three decades before. Ernie knew without a doubt Who had called him to be there—albeit as another temporary instrument. And he felt certain he knew who was to follow in his footsteps to provide the leadership for Tenwek once he was gone. That knowledge gave him great satisfaction and great assurance about whatever the coming years would hold. Little did he know that confidence was about to be shaken like never before.

2 *Call to Prayer,* April/May 1990, World Gospel Mission.

Tenwek Community Development

Things were going well at Tenwek. The hospital's new water filtration system had just been completed, and for the first time in the mission's history, the water coming out of the faucets didn't look like tea. Missionaries reported seeing the bottom of the tub when they took a bath.

Since the Steurys had left Kenya on furlough in June 1990, the new nursing school, which had been started in 1987, graduated its first class of ten. All ten students passed their final exam to be licensed as enrolled community nurses (ECNs), which authorized them to work both in hospital and community settings.

Chaplain David Kilel and Dr. David Stevens helped conduct a seminar in Nairobi for hospital chaplains from around the country. Plans for establishing a chaplaincy training school at Tenwek were already underway.

In addition to the ongoing and burgeoning hospital ministry, the educational/evangelistic work of Tenwek Community Health Outreach and its new and innovative arm, Tenwek Community Development, had taken off and was showing tremendous ministry potential. The community development program had been the brainchild of David Stevens, who envisioned building on the community health model to address the economic crisis. The poor economy impacted all of Kenya, particularly the Kipsigis people in the region around Tenwek, where an acre of land cost two thousand dollars, and the average income was less than four hundred dollars a year.

The high-priced land problem stemmed from the fact that all the good farmland in the country was already taken. Only 15 percent of the country receives enough rainfall to support subsistence farming, and 85 percent of the population lives on that 15 percent of the land. Every available square inch of fertile land was planted, so visitors would often be surprised to see crops planted on the shoulders of a highway. People in Kenya were that desperate to find ways to grow food for their families.

Kenya's birthrate, the highest in the world at the time, was projected to double the country's population within the next decade. So the crisis was only going to get worse. Even near Tenwek, in one of the richest farming regions of the country, it was common to find children who were malnourished simply because their parents had nowhere to grow enough food.

The only way most young men could get any land at all was to inherit it. But the average family plot was ten acres and the average family had five sons, so each son would eventually get only two acres. Those two acres would have to have an incredibly high yield to support just one family. The Tenwek Community Development project intended to help tackle the food production problem using the same basic instruction and multiplication techniques that worked so well for community health.

This new program focused on three specific income-generating activities.

The first was milk production. The Kipsigis cultural belief that cows were the basis of wealth, combined with the shortage of land, had led to overgrazing and poor milk production (only a cup or two of milk a day from the best cows). So Tenwek Community Development promoted the new concept of zero-grazing units. Each family was encouraged to select its three best producing cows and keep them contained in a shed. They would then plant an acre or two of fast-growing napier grass, which quickly reaches a height of two or three feet. Farmers would cut some grass every day; carry it to their cows, which no longer had to wander the countryside burning calories in search of scarce nutrition; and provide water and mineral supplements. These cows now contracted fewer diseases and parasites from other cows since they didn't go to the river with them for water. Soon the cows' milk production (and the farmer's income) would double or triple. Before long a farmer could afford to supplement the feed with commercial dairy meal, and production would go even higher.

The second goal of Tenwek Community Development was to help people improve their cash crops. Double Harvest, a Christian agricultural mission located in North Carolina, donated a large greenhouse and other equipment. Samaritan's Purse helped with shipping and construction. The result was an operation that grew three hundred thousand high-yield hybrid plants at a time in a revolutionary nursery system called *Winstrips*®. The goal was the development of plants with hardier root systems, which meant stronger adult plants and eventually more produce. Tenwek was concentrating on cabbage, tomatoes, onions, and tea, and people were reporting twice as much produce as before. They also grew trees to help reverse the effects of deforestation.

The third community development goal was to help women increase their income by teaching them how to improve their chickens' egg production. Most Kipsigis families had a flock of tough, scrawny birds that ranged far and wide, inside their huts and out, searching for bugs to eat. Even if the chickens managed to lay an egg every week or two, the women were lucky to find it in the bushes before it was too old to eat or sell. Tenwek Community Development raised high-egg-producing hybrid chickens in brooder houses down the hill from the hospital. The staff taught the people to build a simple, cheap, disease-free, raised chicken house out of local materials. Twenty hybrid chickens kept in one of these coops could produce fifteen or more eggs a day. That meant in the fifteen minutes a day it took a woman to feed and water her chickens, she could generate as much income as a man could make in a full-time, minimum-wage job.

Once enough families increased their milk and egg production and had excess garden produce to sell, Tenwek Community Development planned to help the farmers set up local companies, or co-ops, in order to market their produce and get better buys on the supplies and raw materials they needed.

The primary purpose of this new program was identical to the purpose of all of Tenwek's ministries. Development workers would be trained in evangelism and discipleship. They would witness in every home they visited. When would they have a better opportunity to introduce people to Jesus Christ than after they had shown concern by helping the farmers build a chicken coop or a zero-grazing unit? Dave Stevens was excited about this program because this new outreach would especially impact the men in the area, who were often the most resistant to the gospel.

Over the next three years (1990–1993), the Tenwek staff wanted to reach twenty-four-thousand people with this new outreach. They had done their homework and had visited many agricultural and animal husbandry stations in Kenya. They had tried each method to prove that it worked and recruited the first supervisors. They even had funding for the program, having received a grant to cover most of the expenses for the next three years.[3]

Everywhere he spoke during his ten-month furlough in 1990–91, Ernie proudly reported on this new community development program and all the other good things happening at Tenwek. But he also asked his listeners to pray for Tenwek's hospital staff in the wake of meningitis and malaria epidemics that had broken out in the area since he had left Africa. And he informed anyone who was interested of the hospital's ongoing need for doctors, more registered nurses, a dentist, a pharmacist, a maintenance supervisor, and assorted other personnel.

The Steurys' furlough turned out to be just what the doctor ordered. Despite the demands of travel, speaking, and fundraising, Ernie began to feel rejuvenated. And as he slowly built back his physical strength, he and Sue began anticipating their return for one more term of service in their adopted homeland.

Meanwhile, there were other developments taking place back in Kenya, unknown to Ernie, which would have surprising and significant ramifications for him, his future, and the future of Tenwek Hospital. They had to do with Dr. David Stevens and the issue that had been troubling him.

Where Is the Lord Leading?

David thought he had reached the end of his physical, emotional, and spiritual rope back in 1988 when he and his family had originally been scheduled for their second furlough. Then Ernie had his second health crisis, and the Stevens family canceled their plans and stayed at Tenwek to provide the necessary administrative leadership. Mustering up the energy and fortitude to keep going another year after the long-anticipated departure date was one of the hardest things David had ever had to do. He had been carrying his load plus a lot of Ernie's due to Ernie's illnesses throughout much of his term.

---

3 David Stevens, *Call to Prayer,* June 1990, World Gospel Mission.

By the time the extra year ended and the Stevens family finally left on furlough, David was desperate to get out from under the constant pressure and responsibility. When the day came to fly home with his family, David was running on empty—physically, mentally, and emotionally. In his own words, "I wasn't just burned out; I was fried."

His feeling of exhaustion gradually faded over the first few weeks back in America. But, according to David, "a restless, unsettled feeling remained. And there was a sense that God had something else in store, which I found disquieting because I loved what I did at Tenwek. I loved my colleagues and my patients. World Gospel Mission was a fine organization to work with. I found great satisfaction and reward in everything I'd been able to do during my ten years in Kenya. I'd expected to spend the rest of my life and medical career there. And yet there was this feeling that some change was coming. But what could be more rewarding or more important than the work I'd felt called to do at Tenwek? Perhaps if I could take what I'd learned and what we'd done at Tenwek and go broader. But how could that happen? And who with?"

Through his time of questioning, Dave began to think about World Medical Mission. Franklin Graham and his group, who had befriended Tenwek, worked with many different mission hospitals around the world. So not long before the end of Stevens families' deputation, when Dave was going to be in North Carolina anyway, he decided to swing by World Medical Mission headquarters in Boone and at least thank the staff there in person for everything they had done for Tenwek over the years. He told himself, *If it turns out that I can sit down and talk face to face with the director of WMM and Franklin Graham at the same time* (which wasn't likely because Franklin always seemed to be on the road somewhere), *I'll take that as a sign from God to raise the question of future possibilities for working together.*

Ten minutes after David Stevens walked in the front door at World Medical Mission headquarters, he was sitting in an office talking with Franklin and WMM director Guy Davidson. Then he raised the question of someday working with them in some capacity doing something with mission hospitals. Since David was very indefinite about the timing or any specific ideas, he was a little surprised that their immediate response was so positive.

"We merely agreed to keep thinking and staying in touch," David recalled. "So I was taken completely off guard when Franklin phoned me, only a week or so before our return to Tenwek, to offer me the position of executive director of World Medical Mission. I told him I was honored, but that I was expected back at Tenwek within days to take over for Ernie, who was going on furlough. There was no way I could leave Ernie or WGM in the lurch. So I couldn't possibly accept his offer. Maybe sometime down the road if the position was open again."

So the Stevens family had returned to Kenya as planned. And the Steurys had begun their furlough within a week. Then, only a few days after Ernie left, Franklin Graham had stopped by Tenwek during a visit to Kenya. He told David he was more convinced than ever that World Medical Mission needed a doctor as executive director. And because he believed David was the man for the job, Franklin asked him to take some time to reconsider the possibility.

David agreed to do that. "I'll give you an answer by the end of the year," he promised Franklin before bidding him goodbye.

As he got back into the familiar routine of life and work at Tenwek, David found he had little time or inclination to think about the World Medical Mission position. The myriad of daily challenges he faced—running a large hospital, overseeing the community health and development ministries, taking his turn on call, seeing patients, making rounds, and performing surgery—demanded all his attention and energy. And that was even before the meningitis and malaria outbreaks threatened to overwhelm the hospital and its staff for several months. But as difficult as the work could be sometimes, it provided a real and satisfying sense of fulfillment. He truly felt he was making a difference.

So it was that the final months of 1990 seemed to sneak up on him. It wasn't until Thanksgiving that David started seriously thinking and praying about the World Medical Mission position. "I promised Franklin I'd give him an answer by the end of the year," he reminded Jody, his wife.

"I prayed about it all right," David admitted. "Then I sat down and made a list of pros and cons. I came up with a number of reasons for staying at Tenwek—God had called me here. I enjoyed my work. I loved my patients. And my colleagues. They were family. This was home. And then there was Ernie."

David Stevens's "Reasons for Staying at Tenwek" list went on and on. It was so much longer than any reasons for leaving he could think of that there seemed to be no comparison. In stark black and white, the decision seemed obvious. He immediately sat down and wrote Franklin Graham to thank him again for the offer and to say he felt Tenwek was where God wanted him to stay.

"Then I had two of the most miserable weeks of my life," David remembered. "There was this terrible sense of oppression, that I'd made a serious mistake. I didn't understand it at first. I'd prayed about it, hadn't I? Then it hit me. It was as if the Lord were saying, *You prayed. But you didn't wait and listen for My answer!* So I laid out a fleece before God. I told Him, *If Franklin doesn't take no for an answer, if he writes back and tells me he will keep the job open and tells me just to let him know when I would want it, I'll take that as a clear sign of your leading."*

A month went by. No response from World Medical Mission. David was beginning to think his lot had been cast. Finally, in January, a letter came from Franklin. He acknowledged David's decision to stay at Tenwek, but he told him he wanted to leave his offer on the table. If or when David ever changed his mind, he should let Franklin know.

David prayed some more. He and his wife prayed together. This time he waited and listened for over a month, until he felt certain God was leading him in a new direction.

He wrote Franklin saying he now believed God would have him accept the offer. But he was going to have to wait until Ernie got back from his furlough before he could work out the timing. In the meantime, Franklin asked David to accompany him on a trip to Russia that spring to explore the possibility of starting some outreach ministries in and to the newly accessible medical establishment in the former Soviet Union. David came back from that trip more convinced than ever that World Medical Mission was where God wanted him to go next.

Breaking the News

By the time Ernie and Sue returned to Tenwek at the end of April 1991, several of the hospital's medical staff say they had a pretty good idea that Dr. Stevens was going to be leaving Tenwek sooner rather than later. Many more sensed something was in the works.

Yet there had been no official announcement. And it wasn't the kind of subject anyone, even David, wanted to greet Ernie with before he got settled back into the hospital routine. In fact, for months now David had been dreading the talk he knew he needed to have with his mentor. His apprehension was heightened when Ernie informed him of his intention to let David continue to handle more and more of the administration. "You've been doing a great job of that already. I want to spend the rest of my career working more directly with patients again."

The more Ernie talked about his vision for his final term at Tenwek, the worse David Stevens felt. "He was talking about cutting back on his administrative load, getting out from under the burden he had valiantly carried for so long, and looking forward to practicing medicine again. After all Ernie had done for Tenwek over the years, he deserved the chance to finish up his career on his own terms, caring for patients, and at a healthier pace," David recalled. "How could I break the news that I was leaving, knowing once I was out the door, the entire administrative load would all fall on him again? Realizing how much Ernie had counted on me to continue his life's work. Understanding there was no other obvious doctor on staff to take over and carry on all the chief executive responsibilities."

Because he didn't know what to say or how to say it, weeks went by while the younger doctor watched and waited for the right words, the right time, to say something, anything, to Ernie about his personal plans. Eventually David could wait no longer. Most of the other missionaries at Tenwek already knew. While they respected David's need to make the announcement himself, David knew he had to tell Ernie soon, before someone else said something to inadvertently give it away. He couldn't bear the thought of Ernie learning it from anyone else. So the difficult day finally came when David walked into Ernie's office to tell him he was going to accept the directorship of World Medical Mission.

For months David had imagined just how hurt and disappointed Ernie was going to feel. But the pain was even worse than he had expected—for himself as well as for Ernie. "I cried as I told him," David said. "He cried as he listened to what I had to say. Then the two of us just sat in his office and cried together."

Despite the shock and sorrow he expressed, Ernie graciously assured his young protégé, "You need to do what the Lord calls you to do, David." But granting that much of a blessing, which he repeated to David several times over the next few months, didn't settle the matter in Ernie's heart and mind. It continued to remain unsettled as the Stevenses packed the last of their things and left Tenwek for America in November of 1991.

"That was a much bigger blow to Ernie than he ever wanted people to know," Sue admitted. "He never saw it coming. So he was absolutely devastated. I would walk into his office up at the hospital and find him slumped back in his chair, staring into space. In all the years of our marriage, I'd never seen him act so terribly discouraged. Even in the early days at Tenwek when he was the only doctor and the needs he faced seemed absolutely overwhelming. For almost twenty years Ernie had such high hopes for David and the role he believed David would play at Tenwek. Now it was like someone had yanked the rug right out from under him. He didn't know what he was going to do.

"For a while there I don't think Ernie could quite believe that David would go through with his plans. That when the time finally came, he would actually leave."

Sue was probably the only person who realized the depths of Ernie's despair. He told her he thought David was making a serious mistake. One day he asked her, "Do you think David would have done this if his father was still living?" Another time he shook his head and asked Sue, "How many times have I felt burned out?" He didn't think David was giving his own feelings enough time. He believed his young colleague had gotten tired and discouraged and latched on to the first escape hatch he could find.

For a while Ernie attributed part of the blame for David's deciding to leave Tenwek on Franklin Graham for enticing him away or maybe talking him into it. He felt more than a little hurt by that prospect because

Franklin had been such a good friend to Ernie and Sue, and his organizations (Samaritan's Purse and World Medical Mission) had partnered with Tenwek on several projects and had always been supportive of the hospital's various ministries over the years. "Franklin could have found any number of doctors to head World Medical Mission quicker than we can find someone to take David's place at Tenwek," Ernie complained to Sue.

When Franklin assured Ernie that he hadn't set out to take David from Tenwek, that David had approached him first, Ernie felt a lot better toward Franklin. But he found no comfort at all in knowing David had initiated the original discussion about an opportunity with WMM. In fact, learning this truth made Ernie feel even worse. He wondered, *How could Dave have done that?*

As was usually the case whenever a longtime colleague left Tenwek, there were a series of going-away events in which David and Ernie were both expected to participate. They each listened to person after person stand up to praise and commend David, which made him feel even guiltier about leaving so many people he cared about. At the same time, it rubbed salt in what felt like an open wound to Ernie. Then, after everyone else had their say, they all expected Ernie to have the last word, to express his appreciation, love, and blessing on his young colleague. "Those occasions were excruciatingly painful for us both," said David.

Publicly and privately Ernie continued to say how important it was for Dave to do whatever God called him to do. But friends and family say that the day Tenwek bid goodbye and Godspeed to the Stevens family was one of the lowest points in Ernie's life.

Ernie was going to be sixty-two years old the first of the year. He would soon celebrate thirty-three years of ministry at Tenwek Hospital. All that he had been through in recent years had persuaded him it was time to pass the torch. For years he had known he would eventually hand that torch, along with all of his hopes and dreams for Tenwek, over to Dr. David Stevens.

Now suddenly David was gone. And when Ernie looked around, he didn't see anyone he thought could take his place.

Chapter 16

A Time for Farewell

The departure of Dr. Stevens was hardly the only personnel crisis Tenwek Hospital faced at the time. In 1991 Tenwek had several other urgent needs: more national doctors and registered nurses and a national hospital administrator to replace longtime friend and Christian brother, Ezekiel Kerich, who was retiring. Many of the staff were badly overworked, especially those in the nursing school. There was also an international need. Kenya was being flooded with refugees from Ethiopia. The estimate was that 220,000 were already in the country, and many more were coming. This was in addition to the many thousands who were already there from other neighboring countries. These people all needed food, shelter, water, and the gospel. One reason so many thousands of refugees were pouring into the country was because things were better in Kenya. Thirty years of stable government certainly distinguished Kenya from its neighbors. And a big part of the reason things were better in the Kericho district of southwest Kenya was due to the presence and impact of Tenwek Hospital. While Ernie always tried to deflect any of the personal praise and credit he routinely received, he could certainly take a well-earned measure of paternal pride in the legacy of the hospital itself.

Special Honors

After returning from furlough in the States, Sue had quickly resumed her role as evangelism trainer for the community health helpers. Several volunteers found Christ during the training. And when they went into the community to practice what they learned in class, they came back excited to report how they had led several others to faith. On graduation day the students presented Sue with a kerosene storm lantern that was already lit. "We want to give you this lantern," they told her, "because you have brought light into our community and our lives."

Soon after their return from furlough, Ernie and Sue were also invited out to the Kaboson Health Center for a welcome-back party. The national staff prepared a feast and put on a special program during which they gave Ernie and Sue customary tribal gifts. Ernie was honored in a ceremony making him an official Kipsigis elder—signified by the bestowing of a blanket to wear, a fly whisk, a wooden war club called a *rungut* (ROON-GOOT), and a special walking cane. Sue was presented with a dried gourd, pale orange in color and shaped a little like a butternut squash. It had been carefully hollowed out and elaborately decorated and painted. The beautiful container was perfect for mixing and serving the traditional ceremonial beverage the Kipsigis called *mursik*—a gray mixture of raw milk and charcoal aged to a proper sourness and served at room temperature.

The Kipsigis used *mursik* as a curative health drink for a wide variety of ailments. But for obvious reasons, some missionaries privately joked that drinking it made them "moresick." Ernie became quite fond of the drink. "But it's definitely an acquired taste," Sue admitted, "which takes years for most missionaries to develop. If they ever do." So there was more than enough *mursik* to go around at Kaboson that night of the Steurys' special honor.

International Outreach

The ministry at Tenwek provided the Steurys a strong base from which to reach out beyond the borders of Kenya in their later years of missionary service. After almost twenty years of civil strife and the brutal and bloody dictatorship of Idi Amin, the war-ravaged country of Uganda had reopened its borders and reestablished a measure of peace. The Ugandan refugees who had fled into Kenya were now returning to their homeland with such optimism and determination to rebuild their country that World Gospel Mission and the Africa Gospel Church decided they would do what they could to help. Ernie went with a delegation from WGM and the AGC across the border to the west of Tenwek to meet with Ugandan officials and explore the options for service.

Uganda's minister of health was especially interested in medical help and the potential ministry of community health. His country desperately needed someone trained in community health work who could teach part time in the national university. More than a hundred professors, the most educated people in the country, had been killed or fled Uganda during the war.

Another serious problem facing that small, impoverished country was its population of more than two million orphans. The war was only partially responsible for that national crisis. AIDS, which was projected to kill one out of every three Ugandans over the next few years, was already well on its way to wiping out a generation of young adults.

Ernie reported: "In some villages, one or more people die every day. It is not unusual to see some families taking care of five to fifteen extra children who have been orphaned by the death of relatives. These families need help to provide for and educate these children. Their hearts are hungry for the love of people who care and of Jesus who loves them. What an opportunity we have to invest in the lives of these precious children!

"WHERE DO WE BEGIN? We hope to begin by organizing Community Health work in some of the many communities which have no primary health care. God has wonderfully prepared the way for us by giving us a Ugandan registered nurse, Connie Ojiambo, who was our head nurse at Tenwek Hospital for several years. She and her husband came to us as refugees . . . and while at Tenwek they accepted Jesus as their Lord and Savior . . . Now she is back in Uganda working in a government clinic. Early this year we brought her back to Tenwek to train her in Community Health work so she can go back to her own people, and with God's help, duplicate the ministry we have here. Susan Carter will be assisting her in establishing the work by making regular visits and acting as a consultant."[1]

The trip to Uganda wasn't the first, or last, international outreach Ernie took part in. On another occasion he and Reverend Jonah A. Cheseng'eny, the moderator of the Africa Gospel Church, also visited Tanzania to

1 *Call to Prayer,* 1992, World Gospel Mission.

explore the possibility of the AGC and WGM starting churches and opening up ministries there. But because there were serious tensions between the governments of Kenya and Tanzania, the two men couldn't simply cross the border from one country to the other; they had to fly first to Burundi and then go into Tanzania. Unfortunately, the government official with whom they were to meet was called away on the day they arrived. Now they had to find another contact, but that would take time, and what had been planned as a short one- or two-day visit dragged on for several extra days. Hotel and meal costs quickly depleted their resources.

"We ran out of money!" recalled Reverend Jonah. "And Kenya and Tanzania were not exchanging money at that time, so what could we do? Fortunately, Dr. Steury was a man who had learned to live and walk with God by faith for a long time. So we prayed and asked God to perform a miracle.

"Then Dr. Steury decided to go to the bank. I told him I thought it would be better for me to go back to our hotel and stay out of public. I already felt everyone was looking at me with suspicion (and even hatred) because I spoke Swahili with a different accent.

"So he went to the bank alone. And as he was explaining our situation to one of the bank officials, another bank customer standing nearby overheard what he was saying and walked up to Dr. Steury. 'You're an American?' he asked. When Dr. Steury said 'yes,' the man introduced himself and explained that he had been educated in America and now taught at a university in the Tanzanian capitol of Dar es Salaam. When Dr. Steury asked him where he had gone to school in America, the man told him, 'Asbury College.' Dr. Steury told him that was also where he went to school. They began asking each other questions. 'Do you know so and so? Did you have such and such a professor?' After a while the man asked what Dr. Steury was doing in Tanzania. When he heard our predicament, the man took him directly to the bank manager's office. He told the banker to please give Dr. Steury all the money he needed—that he would personally guarantee it. And Dr. Steury could repay him when he returned to Kenya.

"When Dr. Steury came back to the hotel and told me the story he laughed and said, 'I went into that bank like a beggar and came out like a millionaire!' We had prayed and asked God to perform a miracle—and He did!"

Answer to Prayer

Even after David Stevens's departure, there were six doctors working at Tenwek, so Ernie wasn't nearly as concerned about the daily operation of the hospital or the level of medical care for patients as he was the long-range leadership and administration of Tenwek's ever-expanding ministries. He had known for some time that his old friend and colleague Ezekiel Kerich would be retiring as hospital administrator. Ernie felt it important to have an African in that leadership position, but as he considered the current staff at Tenwek, he didn't see anyone he felt could take Ezekiel's place.

"So Ernie believed it was truly an answer to prayer," according to Sue, "when Stephen Mutai contacted him about a position at Tenwek."

A young Kenyan who had gone to India for his education, Stephen had just returned home with an MBA and a desire to start a challenging professional career. Banking had been his first choice because it promised to provide him success and security; but when a friend suggested he inquire at Tenwek Hospital, he contacted Ernie.

Stephen already had a lead on a good position with a major bank, so he said he wouldn't actually apply at Tenwek unless Ernie promised him a personal interview. He thought such a bold attitude might be held against him, but, on the contrary, Ernie seemed impressed that this young man didn't want to waste his time if he wasn't going to get some serious consideration. So Ernie quickly set a time to meet and interview Stephen.

The two impressed each other from the start. Ernie saw a bright, well-qualified, and ambitious young man of Christian character—someone with impeccable credentials and real potential who certainly seemed to be an ideal fit for Tenwek's needs. And Stephen was impressed with Ernie as he shared his vision and his heart for Tenwek's ministry and explained the hospital's philosophy, "We treat, Jesus heals," and as he explained how he had been looking for someone to train as hospital administrator for two years now. Stephen said, "Dr. Steury struck me as someone I wanted very much to work with and learn from—a real man of prayer. I thought to myself, *Now I see what God is doing in my life. This is what He has been preparing me for."*

Ernie too felt God was at work here and decided to hire this impressive young man. Stephen then encouraged a Christian friend who had gone to school with him in India, Geoffrey Lang'at, to also apply at Tenwek. Ernie hired this second young man as well, with the hope that Geoffrey and Stephen could be an effective team, and at the same time doubling the chances that one of them would grow into his role and become the new hospital administrator Tenwek so desperately needed.

Ernie worked closely with both young men, initiating them into the life and ministry of Tenwek hospital. Stephen and Geoffrey very quickly learned of the respect Ernie had earned from the staff and patients. "Dr. Steury was a man who cared for and loved people," Stephen said. "He was a very spiritual man who wanted to pray before any meeting or discussion. And he was always willing to listen."

After six months of on-the-job indoctrination, Ernie sent Stephen to Nairobi for an official hospital administration-training course. And when he came back from that, Ernie began easing Stephen into Ezekiel's position. "He slowly began giving me more and more responsibility. He talked to me and taught me about the various issues I needed to know as hospital administrator," Stephen said. "When he visited government offices, he would take me along so he could introduce me to the officials and I could see how he dealt with them. Dr. Steury enabled me to do my assigned job. He was willing to explain something I needed to understand. He was willing to assist or to show me if there was something I needed to learn how to do. He was a good teacher and supervisor. I made many mistakes, but he was always patient and gentle in the way he corrected me, which was more painful and probably made me feel worse than if he had been hard on me.

"He was truly a man after God's own heart. And sometimes I think he could read my heart and mind. I remember the time, about a year after I came to Tenwek, when I was quite tempted by a high-paying banking position that was open. It was a very good job which I thought I had an excellent chance of getting.

"But after I made an appointment for an interview, I became very disturbed. Very troubled. And Dr. Steury walked into my office, sat down, and said, 'I sense you are struggling with something, Stephen.' I didn't know what to say, but he didn't seem to need me to tell him anything. 'You are in a valley of decision,' Dr. Steury told me, 'I don't know what it is about, but I would like to pray with you if that would be all right.'

"I told him it was, so he began: 'Lord, I want you to help Stephen in any decision that he is going to make, that he would glorify you . . .' By the time he finished, I tell you, I was crying. I cried and cried.

"I confessed to him what I'd been struggling with. And then I sat down and wrote the bank I had made the appointment with to say I was no longer interested in interviewing for their position. They called and wanted to know what had happened.

"What happened was that this man of God challenged me. And from that day on I knew for sure that God had called me to Tenwek and I would stay until He tells me to go."

In the meantime Stephen still had a lot to learn. But he said the most important advice he got from Ernie was the repeated admonition to "be faithful and be honest. If you just try to glorify and honor God in everything you do, people will respect and follow you. And everything will work out."

The hospital administrator position certainly seemed to be working out. "I can't begin to tell you how excited Ernie was to have Stephen and Geoffrey," Sue said. "It just meant so much to him to hear them talk about how they felt God had called them to Tenwek—like Ernie had been called. I think it gave him hope they would have the same kind of commitment to the hospital in the years to come. And that truly encouraged Ernie."

Tribal Conflict

Not all personnel issues at Tenwek proved to be so positive. A crisis in March 1992 not only threatened the staff, it also endangered the lives of the missionaries and the future of the hospital itself.

After thirty years of one-party rule, President Moi had announced the first truly democratic, multi-party election in the nation's history.

Strong feelings quickly rose to the surface as various tribal groups looked at a new and unfamiliar political landscape and began trying to stake out their own claims. In the Kericho district, as in other areas of the country, the predominant tribes began exerting pressure on the out-of-tribers in their midst. In the town of Bomet, threatening posters and signs began appearing in the stores and along the streets. A few troublemakers among the local people evidently wanted to stir up resentment toward outsiders, particularly any members of the Luo tribe that had been bitter enemies of the Kipsigis in generations past.

Realizing animosity was building, Ernie called a meeting of all the missionaries at Tenwek. They gathered one evening at the Steury home for a time of prayer and a discussion of what possible security measures the hospital might need to take to protect the hospital's Luo staff members.

What Ernie didn't know at the time was that earlier that same night, an armed gang had formed and was marching up the road from the river toward Tenwek. The men were carrying *pangas,* spears, bows and arrows, and they were chanting as they came, "Death to the Luos! Death to the Luos!"

Up in the Steury home the missionaries were gathering, and the meeting was about to start when the phone rang. When Daniel Tolan answered it, he heard screaming and shouting on the other end. The desperate voice on the line was difficult to understand, so it took a few moments for him to realize that the home of one of the staff families—the Oguta family, who were Luos—was being attacked.

When Daniel reported to the missionaries what he had heard, Ernie immediately took charge, "You men come with me!"

"Should we take sticks or something?" one of the men asked.

"No," Ernie replied. "We'll take nothing but ourselves." Before he turned and led the men out the door, he directed the women missionaries to stay inside and pray for protection and peace until they returned.

"So that's what we did," recalled Christine Stanfield, a missionary nurse, whose husband, Jeff, oversaw Tenwek's computer operations. "We prayed, we sang some songs, and quoted Scripture promises about the Lord's strength and protection. And Sue Steury even shared some stories she'd heard from older missionaries who had lived through the MauMau rebellion back in the 1950s. How during the height of the violence, some people had claimed to see angels on guard around the grounds at Rift Valley Academy, scaring the mobs away. After hearing that, we began praying, 'Lord, show yourself at Tenwek, however you need to be seen to bring peace in this situation tonight.'"

"We prayed like never before," Cindy Tolan reported. "I know I was terrified by the thought of what they might face. I had a father *and* a husband in the group."

In the meantime, the men were running up the hillside toward the staff housing just above the hospital. As they approached the Oguta home, they saw a mob of twenty to thirty armed men angrily milling around the front of the house. As Ernie approached the troublemakers, they all turned toward the missionaries. One of the men, an obvious ringleader, demanded to know, "Are you Mosonik?"

When Ernie calmly replied that he was, the man asked him, "What are you doing here?"

Replying in Kipsigis, Ernie asked, "What are *you* doing here?"

The man, who had obviously had too much to drink, answered Ernie by shouting, "We are going to kill some Luo tonight!"

As other voices behind him mumbled their agreement, Ernie marched right up to that loudmouthed ringleader. The man's *panga* waved back and forth in the air just inches from Ernie's nose. "You are not going to kill anyone tonight!" Ernie announced in Kipsigis, loud enough so the whole mob could hear him.

The ringleader shouted, "If you don't move, we'll kill you."

"No, you won't," Ernie declared and took another step closer to the men in the front.

Chaplain David Kilel, who had come with the missionary men, said, "I saw one of the troublemakers put his sword right up against Dr. Steury's stomach. But Dr. Steury showed great courage."

Ernie began talking again in a confident, yet lower, voice, causing everyone to grow quiet to hear his words. "You know who I am," he told them in Kipsigis. "I am Mosonik. I am grandfather to some of you. Father to others." He was counting on the Kipsigis culture, which demanded respect for elders. As he talked, he took another step away from the house and up the hill, drawing the mob with him. "You need to listen to what I say," Ernie told them. "You don't want to hurt me. You don't want to hurt these people. They came to work at Tenwek Hospital to help the Kipsigis people. You all need to go home now."

"He just kept quietly talking," Daniel Tolan recalled. "His quiet spirit seemed to gradually calm the men."

Once Ernie had gently and shrewdly maneuvered the mob far enough away from the Oguta home, he turned and instructed Daniel to run back to the house and bring the van to get the family out of Tenwek and down to the police station in Bomet.

Daniel sprinted down the hill to the Steurys' house, grabbed the keys to the Kombi, reported what was happening to the women, and within minutes pulled the van up to the Ogutas' front door, separating the mob and the house. He opened the sliding door on the van, and the besieged family quickly slipped into the vehicle without ever being exposed to the arrows, spears, or even the view of the drunken crowd some distance away in the darkness. As John and Domatila Oguta, their babysitter, their friend, and the three small Oguta children slipped in between the seats, Daniel instructed them to lie low and stay out of sight. He pulled away from the house, went right past where Ernie was still talking to the men, and drove to the Bomet road.

When the ringleader noticed Daniel driving away with what looked like an empty van, he seemed to suddenly remember what they had come for and shouted again at Ernie: "You have tried to deceive us, Mosonik. The Luos are not in that car. They are still in their house, and we are now going to kill them."

With that he angrily headed for the Ogutas' front door, and Ernie followed along saying, "Let's just see." When they got to the empty house, the men finally realized the family was gone.

Ernie announced to the whole crowd again, "You all need to go home!" There didn't seem to be any point in doing anything else. So by ones and twos the angry men slowly slipped away into the dark of night.

Meanwhile, Daniel started toward Bomet as Ernie had instructed him. Suddenly he felt very strongly that he needed to turn back to the Steury house instead. When he and the Ogutas walked through the Steurys' front door, all obviously safe and sound, the women's prayer meeting turned into a praise and celebration service. When Ernie and the other men returned a few minutes later, they found the women still hugging and reassuring the frightened but relieved Ogutas.

The whole group prayed together, thanking God for His protection and the way He had taken care of everyone involved in the situation. It was decided that the safest place for all the Luos and any other out-of-tribers on the compound to spend the night would be up in the hospital's business office. The office was fortified with barred windows and a steel door that could be bolted shut. So all the men left again and walked the Ogutas, sheltered now in the middle of a missionary phalanx, up to the hospital, where they could be locked in and guarded for the night. As they gratefully huddled in the safety of the hospital's administration wing, the Ogutas tried to thank Ernie. Domatila Oguta insisted on recounting the episode for Dr. Steury to know what had happened from their perspective.

She said they had heard the mob approaching and quickly locked their outside doors. But when the angry men began banging on the front door, she and the family's babysitter had taken the three children into the bedroom and hidden them under the bedclothes while her husband and another Luo man, who was sharing supper with them, tried to barricade the door with furniture. She could hear her husband desperately calling for help, so she looked through a keyhole in the bedroom door and saw the outside door beginning to give as the men pounded it with their weapons. She knew the clubs and the *pangas* would soon break the door down.

About that time her husband and his friend had retreated into the other bedroom and tried to barricade the door, which had no lock. Domatila was terrified that if the mob broke through the outer door, nothing would stop them from breaking into the room where her husband was now hiding.

"I remembered that my grandmother and my mother always told me," Domatila said, "'When you don't know what to do, you can always call on the name of Jesus.' So when I was afraid the door was going to break, I just started praying, *Jesus! Jesus! Jesus! Please come help us!* The next time I looked out the keyhole, I saw the hand of God holding back the front door. When I saw that, it brought such peace to my heart, knowing that God would protect my husband and me and our children. That hand was right there before my eyes, Dr. Steury. I saw it, and what I saw will be forever before me until I die."

After he had heard her remarkable story, Ernie instructed some of the missionary men to stay with the Luo folks. They locked the steel doors and collected a number of fire extinguishers to use as weapons in the unlikely event that the mob returned. Then the rest of the missionary men followed Ernie back to the Steury home to let the women know the crisis seemed to be over.

Ernie's reassuring comments concluded with a retelling of Mrs. Oguta's account about seeing God's hand holding the door. And then he offered this observation: "Isn't that a wonderful testimony of how God brought peace to that woman's heart!"

"Ernie hadn't even been there to realize how we'd been praying," Christine Stanfield marveled. "And those were the very words he used, 'how God brought peace.' When we had prayed that God would 'show Himself to bring peace' we had imagined some vision that would frighten away the mob. But that was not how God had answered our prayer. He needed to be seen to bring peace—not to the mob, not to solve the whole situation—but to provide much needed peace to one terrified mother's heart! We were awed."

The missionaries stayed at the Steurys' home a while longer for a time of praise and thanksgiving. Then everyone, except those locked in the business office, went home to bed.

It wasn't until later that the missionaries learned of another reason for praise—more evidence of God's protection on that memorable night. The hand of God had also been on Daniel Tolan when he made the seemingly impulsive decision to take the Ogutas to the Steurys' house rather then the police station. According to witnesses, a second band of armed vigilantes had blocked the road out to Bomet and had been waiting for anyone trying to flee Tenwek that way.

The morning after the disturbance, Ernie met to discuss the problem with the district commissioner. They agreed to send the children in all the local schools home early with instructions to tell their parents there would be a *baraza*—the African community's version of a town meeting—that afternoon. Within hours, thousands of Kipsigis people gathered on a hill-side near Tenwek. The district commissioner and several other community leaders spoke first and reported what had happened the night before. Then Ernie stood to address the crowd. He reminded them Tenwek was their hospital. But he also warned them that if all the out-of-tribers on the hospital staff had to leave, the hospital might have to close (these people made up many of Tenwek's national professionals), and that neither the missionaries nor the other non-Kipsigis workers could stay if their lives and the lives of their families were going to be threatened by violence.

When he finished, a number of local leaders stood and spoke for the community. "This is not what we want," they said. They apologized to Ernie for the behavior of a few young men who had gotten drunk. "We want you to stay, Mosonik!" they said. "We want everyone at Tenwek Hospital to stay. We want to keep our hospital open."

The speeches went on for several hours, and by the time the meeting ended, the inter-tribal tensions around Tenwek had, for the most part, been diffused. The hospital stayed open, and only the Ogutas, their babysitter, and the Luo friend who had been with them during the attack, decided to leave.

According to Christine Stanfield, "It was Ernie's calm wisdom and his influence and leadership that made the difference. His example taught us all so much about how to trust the Lord."

It seemed that even at the end of an illustrious missionary career, there were new experiences to face, new lessons to learn, and no way of anticipating what else might yet lie ahead.

While the open hostility and resulting tensions settled down at Tenwek, there remained an undercurrent of political unrest and scattered tribal clashes throughout the country as the political landscape in Kenya underwent a seismic shift from a one-party government to a multi-party system in the months leading up to the 1992 national elections. Resulting uncertainty led to a significant downturn in the economy, which severely impacted the hospital ministry—along with skyrocketing inflation and a serious drought during the growing season. Many sick people who came to the hospital were unable to pay their bills. And even more people who needed medical assistance didn't seek treatment they knew they couldn't afford. The end result was that Tenwek's patient load and cash flow plummeted to the point that the hospital had difficulty even paying staff and purchasing basic medical supplies.

Despite that economic struggle, the ministry continued to grow. Not only did WGM send another missionary couple to help expand the work in Uganda, but Tenwek continued to train new community health workers: There were now 395 from forty-nine different areas, and the nursing school admitted ten new students who comprised the program's ninth class since the school was founded.

WGM supporters once again came through with enough gifts to Tenwek's "Needy People Fund" to see the hospital through its latest financial crisis. More than two hundred new Christians were baptized in the area during the annual special Christmas meetings held in local African Gospel churches.

The economy continued to present a challenge in 1993. The ongoing drought impacted both the hospital and the people who lived around Tenwek. For months the river was so low that the hydroelectric plant could only operate a few hours a day. Two large diesel generators, recently donated to the hospital, supplemented the hydropower and provided stand-by power for the hospital and the staff houses. But those back-up generators used more than two hundred dollars a day in fuel—adding greatly to the hospital's cash-flow crunch.

The local people suffered more than the hospital. Without the rain needed by their crops to produce a good harvest, many families suffered from malnutrition and disease. Fortunately the new community development programs helped many families make up for their losses. And the community health staff was busier than ever.

In 1993 there were 456 trained community health workers who conducted almost sixty thousand home visits and taught better health practices to over 199,000 people. Almost six thousand new latrines were dug and three thousand home fireplaces raised. More than fifty-two thousand immunizations were given and thirty-five thousand children were examined at clinics. Over four thousand families received special "official" certificates, which they proudly hung on their wall to show their friends and neighbors that they had fulfilled all the requirements necessary to earn one of Tenwek's coveted "healthy home" awards.

Ernie was heartened when he heard such glowing reports of Tenwek's ministry. He was always quick to credit responsible staff. But he was even more careful to remind everyone that the effectiveness of any ministry was reason to praise the Lord and to give Him the glory for everything He had done and was doing at Tenwek.

Tenwek's Chaplaincy Training School

Tenwek's newest program was especially gratifying for Ernie. He and Chaplain David Kilel had been talking and praying and dreaming of starting a hospital chaplaincy school at Tenwek for years. That vision was part of the motivation for the graduate degree David had pursued and earned a few years before. They had been making more detailed plans ever since. But it wasn't until Ernie's last full term of service in Kenya that those dreams became a reality. With some initial funding from Samaritan's Purse, the L. Nelson Bell Hospital Chaplaincy School (named after Ruth Bell Graham's father, who had been a missionary physician to China) had opened its doors at Tenwek. David Kilel, with Ernie's encouragement and full support, was heading up the work. The school would have six to ten trainees at a time. Each student would be a committed Christian young man or woman from throughout Kenya and neighboring countries, all of who felt a call to this particular type of ministry. Eventually the trainees would go back to their own home regions and serve as hospital, prison, or military chaplains there.

Ernie watched with pride as his longtime friend and colleague put the program in place. The chaplaincy training school was David Kilel's dream. His vision and commitment got it launched. His excitement and personal experience as a chaplain fueled the program, as he told his students how God could work in the lives of patients and as he shared the lessons he had learned about being an effective hospital chaplain. Ernie encouraged him and his students.

From time to time, at David's request, Ernie taught in the classroom, sharing a doctor's perspective on patients' needs. He hoped Tenwek's chaplaincy training program would challenge its students toward the same goal he had always tried to have at Tenwek: No patient should ever be treated at Tenwek and sent home without having the opportunity to hear and respond to the basic message of the gospel. Ernie also tried to impress upon the students what a great responsibility they would have as chaplains—how their ministry with patients and their families meant they could minister to many people who would never in their lives come to hear the gospel in a church. The vast majority of the students not only bought into Ernie's vision and accepted his challenge, they could hardly wait to get back home and put what they learned into practice.

Indeed, the message and goals of Tenwek's chaplaincy training school were not only embraced by the students themselves, they were also accepted and greatly appreciated by the hospitals those students represented and by the various denominations and groups administering those medical institutions from throughout Kenya—and eventually Malawi, Zambia, Madagascar, Uganda, Zimbabwe, Rwanda, and elsewhere around Africa.

The new school expanded Tenwek's ministry by opening some surprising new doors. Sue recounted one example when Ernie and David Kilel went to Zimbabwe to talk about the training school and to conduct a seminar for hospital chaplains from throughout that country. Some fifty people had signed up for the session in advance, which thrilled the two men from Tenwek. But they were a little taken aback when over half of those who showed up were from Catholic hospitals—many of them nuns. Ernie and David wondered if there had been some misunderstanding. Did everyone realize the session was going to be led by evangelical Protestants? How would their message be received?

"The fellows decided they wouldn't change a thing," Sue said. "And I remember how thrilled Ernie was by the response. He and David talked about their experience doing spiritual ministry at Tenwek, gave examples of how they shared the gospel in different situations, how they counseled and challenged patients spiritually, what they would ask to open a spiritual discussion, how they would explain the plan of salvation and offer to pray with patients. They even gave examples of specific prayers they would lead people to pray. 'Before the class was over,' Ernie told me, 'the sisters were drinking it all in. They got so excited!' They were saying, '*Now we know what to do! We can do more than administer last rites! We can explain to people how they can find Jesus before they die!*' They took the handouts Ernie and David provided and told them, 'We're going to use this to teach the staffs at our hospitals.'

"Some time later Ernie received a letter from one of those Catholic sisters," Sue said. "The nun thanked him for all that she'd learned and wrote, 'I love you, Dr. Steury.' Ernie got such a kick out of that letter." And the fact that Tenwek's newest ministry was to have such a widespread and unlikely impact was, in Ernie's mind, just another reason to give God all the glory and praise.

But his friend David Kilel believed Ernie was due some of the credit as well. "It is difficult to sum up all of Dr. Steury's contributions at Tenwek Hospital. There was so much growth—in facilities and staff—over the years. But I think the most important thing to him was the spiritual achievement. How many people walk with God today because of Dr. Steury! And he led many of those people to Christ himself. He was a God-fearing man, so God blessed his ministry. The people who came to the hospital, those who lived around it, and the government officials always honored him and respected the hospital because of that."

A Leader for the Future

As the end of the Steurys' term approached, the question remained: Who was going to carry on that legacy and lead Tenwek into the future? Ernie, however, continued to plan for the future. He began a campaign to raise money for a larger oxygen concentrator to provide adequate oxygen for pulmonary and cardiac patents. In early 1994 he also applied to USAID for a large financial grant to fund construction on two new large ward buildings to replace the outdated wards he helped plan and build decades before. Tenwek received the grant, but who was there to spearhead such an expansion as the hospital's chief executive officer?

Over a matter of weeks and months, as Ernie thought and prayed about it, one name kept coming up as the best possible person to take over as executive officer of the hospital. Not one of the doctors, but a nurse: Susan Carter.

As director of community health, Susan had built that program and overseen its incredible growth and ministry. She and Dave Stevens had used it as an incubator to try new management and administrative techniques and then exported the new systems into the hospital. Susan had proven her leadership and administrative skills and earned the respect and the affection of her large and scattered national staff. She had helped to formulate and then articulate to staff, donors, government officials, and others, the vision and the reality of this dynamic new ministry. And if she could accomplish all that with community health, Ernie felt confident Susan could handle the oversight of the entire medical operation at Tenwek.

When he called her into his office to tell her he wanted to recommend that the hospital board name her executive officer when he retired, Susan expressed a real reluctance to accept the position. But as they talked and Ernie voiced his faith in her and his belief that she was the best candidate for the job, Susan agreed to think and pray about the possibility. Eventually she told Ernie she would accept what she felt was God's calling. The hospital board favored the idea and voted to make her interim executive officer for a two-year period while they considered a long-time successor. Susan Carter took over as executive officer in June of 1994, a couple months before the Steurys' scheduled August departure.

"My Time Is Coming to an End Here"

Throughout his latest term Ernie had been saying to people, "I feel my time is coming to an end here." When the Kipsigis people understood that he meant to leave and retire in America, many people insisted he stay. "We will build you a house," they told him. "Where would you like it?"

When he tried to explain that as he grew older he needed to move back to America to be near his children and family, his African friends would argue, "You can tell your children to come here and visit you. We want you to stay!"

As flattering as it was that people didn't want him to leave, Ernie told Sue, "I want to go out when I can walk out, rather than be carried out or run out. I certainly don't want to overstay my time."

He assured his Kipsigis colleagues, "I will come back to visit."

The plan was that Ernie and Sue would spend a year in deputation, traveling, speaking, and continuing to raise support for Tenwek's ministry as they decided where to settle for their retirement years. And they would continue to serve World Gospel Mission in some capacity as long as they were able. They might even return to Kenya for another year or two, but certainly not as head of the hospital ministry again. Ernie would be turning sixty-five the following January, and he was ready to shift the leadership load onto younger shoulders.

Those final weeks in Tenwek were an emotional roller coaster of packing, planning, and painful goodbyes. Ernie and Sue sorted through thirty-five years of accumulated possessions, selling some of it, giving away a lot to colleagues and friends, and trying to decide the best means to transport the remainder back to America. And of course there were many bittersweet dinners, receptions, parties, and teas where speeches were made, accomplishments cited, gifts bestowed, memories recounted, laughter shared, and more than a few tears shed. Yet nothing that was said or done seemed, to those friends and colleagues of the Steurys, adequate honor for all their years of dedicated service. Ernie, on the other hand, always uneasy with compliments and praise, used every opportunity he was given to direct any praise to God for His faithfulness and provision and to challenge those who would carry on the work at Tenwek to remain faithful to the Lord and the calling He had given each of them.

Chapter 17

Kenya Is Still in Our Hearts

Reconciliation

In June 1995, Ernie and Sue went to Denver for the annual meeting of the Christian Medical & Dental Society. Since Ernie had been a member and a vocal booster of the organization for decades, he and Sue expected to see many old friends among his fellow physicians attending the convention, including David Stevens, the newly appointed executive director of the organization.

The previous year Dave had called and asked Ernie for advice and to pray for him about a decision he was facing. Dave explained that he was considering leaving World Medical Mission after just a little more than two years, during which Dave had helped mission hospitals around the world and pioneered sending medical relief teams into war zones and disaster areas such as Somalia, Sudan, Rwanda, and Bosnia. Ernie had even traveled to Mogadishu to work with Dave in the midst of violent chaos.

Despite his commitment to and love for the ongoing work of World Medical Mission, Dave had told Ernie he was considering an offer from the board of the Christian Medical & Dental Society to become that organization's executive director. Dave, like Ernie, had belonged to CMDS since medical school and was excited about leading and mobilizing thousands of Christian doctors to make a bigger impact in the world.

Ernie had promised he would pray with and for Dave as he weighed his decision. No sooner had Ernie finished their phone conversation than he told Sue, "Dave is the very man we've needed in that position for years." (CMDS had never before had a physician as executive director.) "He would do a wonderful job of leading the organization." So Ernie had prayed and been excited for Dave when he accepted the position.

Now, months later, Ernie had come to see Dave in action at his first national convention as executive director. Ernie had never been prouder of his young colleague than he was when David gave a wonderful, Spirit-filled keynote address to that roomful of doctors. David simultaneously introduced himself to the members, laid out his vision for the future of the CMDS, and then challenged his listeners to a deeper commitment to Christ and His service. He warned them of the things that could draw them away from God—power, prestige, and money—and how they as individuals and as an organization needed to be totally committed to Christ. At the end of his message, Dave gave an invitation, and there was a wonderful response as many doctors came forward to pray and seek spiritual counsel.

Ernie was moved by all that he witnessed that evening. He knew he needed to speak to Dave afterwards, but so many people were crowded around him that Ernie decided he would do it later. He and Sue made their exit. But as they inched their way through the crowd in the corridor outside the ballroom, a side door opened, and David Stevens stepped out. Surprised to suddenly find himself face to face with Ernie, Dave's face lit up with a broad smile, and he greeted both Steurys with warm hugs.

When Ernie told Dave what a wonderful job he had done with his message that evening, Dave reacted the same way he had seen Ernie respond to praise over the years. He graciously accepted the kind words with thanks, even as he deferred the credit by acknowledging that it was wonderful to see God's hand at work and that he felt privileged to be a part of what the Lord was doing.

Ernie smiled in acknowledgment, and then his expression and tone turned serious. David Stevens recounted what happened next:

"Ernie stepped closer and put his arm around my shoulder. And he said, 'David, I need to ask you to forgive me.' I said, 'Forgive you for what?' But I suddenly realized what he was talking about. 'If anyone needs forgiveness, it's me," I told him. 'For leaving you in Tenwek with all that work.'

"Ernie smiled, shook his head a little, and went on, 'No, David, I need your forgiveness for the resentment I felt about you leaving. I thought you were making a big mistake. I kept saying you needed to do what God would have you do because I didn't think you were listening to Him. I thought you were leaving Tenwek to come back to the States because you thought it would be easier or because of the prestige of working with Franklin Graham. I didn't think you were listening to the Lord. I never said that to you, but that was how I judged you in my heart.

"'Now I see so clearly what God was doing. Without your time and experience at World Medical Mission, you wouldn't have been asked to come to CMDS. And David, you are so clearly God's man for this job. And I want you to know I am so glad tonight that you did what He asked you to do. Can you please forgive me?'

"By this time," Dave recalled, "we were both bawling our eyes out and hugging each other right there in that crowded hallway with all these people walking by and wondering, *What in the world!* But I didn't give anyone else a thought at that time. All that mattered in that moment was that Ernie and I finally had closure on what had been so difficult for both of us."

Sue agreed. "Ernie had always loved Dave. He'd felt so hurt when he left. He'd gotten over most of that. And it had meant a lot when Dave had called and asked him to pray about his offer from CMDS. But that encounter between the two of them in Denver was so wonderful and meant so much to Ernie."

It meant just as much to David, who added, "No man, other than my dad, ever meant as much to me as Ernie did. I realized I'd disappointed him when I left Tenwek, and no one else understood how hard that was for me. When I finally knew God was calling me to leave the hospital and go with World Medical Mission, I remember arguing with God and telling him that Ernie needed me to stay. That was when I felt God saying so clearly, *I took care of Tenwek before you came; I'll take care of it after you leave.*

"Still, it was so hard leaving Ernie and knowing how disappointed he was. He couldn't hide his disappointment; we knew each other too well for that. But I'd never sensed any resentment. He'd been so gracious to tell me again and again that I needed to do what God wanted me to do. And those words actually bolstered me and helped my resolve during those difficult times. I never would have known the depth of his hurt, his resentment. He would never have had to say anything about that. But that was Ernie. Never afraid to humble himself to set things right."

Two doctors healed a wounded friendship that night in Denver. And as so often happens, the bond between the two men was stronger than it had ever been before. And it would remain so for the rest of Ernie Steury's life.

As Sue explained: "Many were the times in the years to come when our life path would cross Dave's, or Ernie would hear David being interviewed on a national radio or television broadcast, or we'd get some report about the tremendous growth or the incredible impact of what is now called the Christian Medical & Dental Associations under David's leadership. And every time Ernie would smile and say to me yet again, 'Little did I know what God was doing.'"

Retirement Living

When Ernie and Sue had first returned from Kenya in 1994, they had made no definite long-range plans about where they would establish their retirement residence. Their Kipsigis friends were particularly concerned to learn that they didn't even own a piece of property back in America; land is so important to an African that the thought of Mosonik not having an ancestral home to return to was terribly disturbing to them. They thought their dearest friends would be destitute.

While Ernie and Sue found their African friends' perspective somewhat amusing, Sue acknowledged how surprisingly unprepared they were for the adjustments they did have to make. "I actually felt a lot like a refugee, without a home or even a home country. Suddenly, facing the reality of retirement was a real letdown. I remember looking around, feeling lost, and thinking, *What now, Lord? Where now, Lord?* We'd never owned a residence of our own, though we had lived for years in the same mission house at Tenwek. I knew that would never again be our home. We planned to go back and visit, but after almost forty years as missionaries, our adopted land of Kenya was no longer our home either."

Their handful of short visits "home" and the death of their parents made the Steurys realize that their American roots were no longer deep enough to bind them to a particular place. "We really didn't know where we ought to settle," Sue said. "We had a lot of details to take care of at headquarters and a number of meetings and speaking engagements scheduled around the Midwest. So we temporarily set up housekeeping in an apartment in Berne. But having spent most of our furlough time over the years in Indiana, I was in favor of retiring in my own home state. Ernie had always loved the Smokies, and after a lifetime in the highlands of Kenya, we were both leaning toward an eventual move to the mountains of western North Carolina."

However, when the Steurys mentioned those plans to their friends Joe and Marilyn Luce, Joe's surprised and disappointed reaction prompted them to begin reconsidering their plans. Joe had something else in mind. After he and Ernie had discussed the Steurys' lack of retirement plans out in Maasailand years earlier, Joe Luce realized there were probably a lot of missionaries who would finish their overseas ministries and return to America with few, if any, provisions for retirement. So he bought an orange grove in central Florida and began developing it as a Christian retirement community, offering affordable housing for retiring WGM missionaries, family, and friends. The whole idea had been born in Kenya, and Joe had pursued the vision with Ernie and Sue specifically in mind.

"To tell you the truth," Sue admitted, "I really resisted the idea of going to Florida at first. I just didn't know if I could deal with the summer heat. Our son Nate, who was living in Florida, pointed out that the year-round temperature would be more like Tenwek than we'd find anywhere else in America. But I worried about the humidity, which we hadn't had to deal with in Kenya."

The Steurys were torn. A number of other missionaries they knew were already living in the Oaks. And Joe Luce was even planning to build a home for himself and Marilyn on a lot right next to the one he'd reserved for them. So Ernie and Sue knew their dear friend would be terribly disappointed if they chose to go somewhere else.

Gradually the Steurys accepted the idea of retiring in Florida. But even though the house was being built and could be finished by summer, they put off the move until the fall of 1995, after they finished up a year of deputation travel.

By the time moving day finally came in October, Sue had gotten past the point of merely being reconciled to living in Florida; she had begun to embrace the idea. Unpacking their personal things, seeing familiar books on the office shelves, and being surrounded by memory-prodding pictures and a lifetime collection of African curios and gifts made their one-level, two-bedroom home seem a lot more like home and a lot closer to Africa than she had thought possible.

"Ernie and I kept looking at our brand new house and then looking at each other and saying, 'We don't deserve this! We just don't deserve this!' But it wasn't long before I was saying to Ernie, 'Okay, it's true. We don't deserve this. But we're certainly going to enjoy it!' The Steurys quickly realized that having a place of their own they could call *home* meant more than they had ever realized it would.

"It helped that even though we were new to the neighborhood, we weren't strangers to the community," Sue said. "Most of our neighbors were fellow WGM missionaries from around the world—dear colleagues we'd known and loved and prayed for over many years." Those friends helped them celebrate a special honor not long after Ernie and Sue moved in.

The Grand Warrior

The Steurys had just arrived home from a trip late one evening in mid-December, when the phone rang. Burnis Bushong, a longtime friend and retired WGM executive who lived just a few doors away, announced that he needed to speak with them as early as possible the following day. After he and Ernie made an appointment, the Steurys went to bed.

Assuming Burnis really wanted to speak with Ernie, Sue headed off to take a shower minutes before the appointed time the next morning. She had just turned on the water as the doorbell rang. When Ernie answered the door, Burnis asked if he and Sue could come outside for a minute. Ernie said he could come out; Sue was showering.

Burnis insisted Sue come out as well. His demand seemed a little odd until Ernie heard some whispering and shuffling of feet from over toward the front of the garage—out of his line of sight. Realizing that something was going on, he told Burnis he would see if he could get Sue.

When Ernie called into the bathroom to tell Sue her presence had been requested as well, she suggested Ernie go and just make apologies for her. Ernie said he didn't think Burnis would take no for an answer, that he had heard some of their other neighbors hiding out of sight in front of the garage, and he suspected they had some sort of surprise planned. Sue hurried and got dressed as quickly as she could. But neither of them had any idea what was going on as they walked out of their front door a few minutes later. Suddenly they were surrounded by neighbors cheering, clapping, beating spoons against tin pans, and generally creating an awful ruckus.

What is this all about? they wondered. As the noise finally subsided and their grinning friends found amusement in their confused expressions, Burnis pulled out an elaborately designed piece of paper and began to loudly read a proclamation with a number of "whereases, whosoevers and therefores." It wasn't until he got to the end that Ernie and Sue realized he was saying that on December 12 in Nairobi, Kenya's president, Daniel Moi, had announced he was awarding Ernie that country's highest award, the Order of the Grand Warrior of Kenya, for his outstanding devotion to duty and his many years of invaluable and meritorious service to the people and the republic of Kenya. The Steurys' neighbors applauded again and crowded around to shake Ernie's hand and congratulate him.

"You didn't know anything about this?" Burnis asked when he noted their surprise.

"We didn't have a clue," Sue laughed. "What had happened was that a Kenyan government official had called Tenwek the day before. Our son Jon had actually been the one to take the call for 'Dr. Steury.' When he explained that Ernie was out of the country, the man expressed his disappointment because the president planned to confer the Order of the Grand Warrior of Kenya on Ernie the following day. Jon then contacted Cindy, who'd heard nothing but tried to let us know. When she couldn't reach us on the road that day to give us the word, she phoned Joe Luce, who had then let our neighbors know of the honor the night before."

Someone from the mission contacted a Kipsigis official who served as an assistant to the president of Kenya to inform him that the Steurys were planning to come back to Kenya for a year, starting in January of

1996. The official assured them that His Excellency, President Moi, would undoubtedly want to personally bestow the award upon Dr. Steury. If they would only let him know when they returned to Africa, a special ceremony would be arranged.

Coming Home Again

Spending 1996 in Kenya was a very different kind of experience for the Steurys. One more year at Tenwek seemed like a precious gift. In a way, it felt like coming home again. And yet it was no longer home. Another family occupied their old house. "So we lived out of our suitcases in the apartments of missionary friends who were gone on furlough or in mission residences temporarily unoccupied," Sue laughed. "We actually lived in four different places during that year. People kept apologizing for uprooting us. But they had a new family coming in that needed one place and then a missionary returned from furlough and needed her apartment back. It was so ironic we had to laugh. We'd moved into our retirement home in Avon Park the previous fall thinking we were through with moving. Then the very next year we moved four times!"

Other than the Tenwek transience, which they endured with customary humor and grace, Ernie and Sue's plans for that curtain-call year in Kenya went pretty much as anticipated. They thoroughly enjoyed the fellowship with missionary colleagues and national friends alike. As proud grandparents they also relished the opportunity to live at Tenwek with seven of their grandchildren. Jon and Vera were stationed there temporarily. Cindy and Daniel lived there most of that year prior to moving to Kijabe.

A Presidential Honor

That the promised personal audience with President Moi didn't materialize during 1996 was something of a disappointment. But then, just three days before Ernie and Sue were scheduled to return to the states in January 1997, word came from Nairobi that "President Moi requested the presence of Dr. and Mrs. Steury at the State House" the next day.

Fortunately, an Africa Inland Mission plane delivered a visiting doctor that same day, so Ernie and Sue caught a cross-country flight back to Nairobi with the pilot. And the following day they showed up at Kenya's state house in Nairobi at the appointed hour.

Ernie had been to the state house on previous occasions. But Sue took special note of their palatial surroundings as they were led into an elegantly appointed sitting room and served tea, just before His Excellency, President Moi, appeared to usher them into his personal inner office. "Everything seemed as luxurious, as exquisite, as you'd expect to find at our American White House," Sue recalled. "So it was reassuring that the president's welcome was so gracious and warm."

Not that the Steurys were surprised. They had known President Moi for decades since Ernie had first treated him at Tenwek for a throat infection during one of his early election campaigns when he was vice-president. He had toured the hospital on more than one occasion and had taken part at the dedications of both the N'getich Medical Center and the hydro plant. Ernie had occasionally visited him in Nairobi on official business for Tenwek Hospital, the mission, or on behalf of Africa Gospel Church. And another time or two President Moi had summoned Ernie to Nairobi just to discuss the general state of affairs at Tenwek and around the country.

Once, years earlier, President Moi had even inquired about the possibility of Ernie's serving as his personal physician. Ernie had respectfully declined that opportunity, explaining that while he was honored to be considered, it would take too much time away from his responsibilities at Tenwek and the much-needed ministry among the Kipsigis people.

"So there was much for us to cordially chat and reminisce about," Sue said. "We even prayed together before the president eventually moved to the point of the visit and led us out into the beautifully manicured lawn and garden behind the state house. There began what turned out to be a brief and very private ceremony just for Ernie and one other man who was also receiving an honor that day. His Excellency expressed both his personal respect and gratitude, along with that of the entire country, for Ernie's dedicated and distinguished service to the people of Kenya over so many years. An aide produced a large, elegantly simple medal (without any words on it at all), strung on a long ribbon, which the president placed over Ernie's head and around his neck. The two of them shook hands. The president's personal photographer snapped a photo, and the ceremony was over," Sue reported. "We said our goodbyes. He thanked us for coming. Then we were ushered out by an aide who took down information on where to send the pictures. And that was that."

No lights. No television cameras. No applause. No fanfare at all. In some ways the whole experience seemed almost anticlimactic. To have the highest honor a nation can bestow presented in such a low-key, private way seemed something of an oddity. At the same time, the subdued ceremony seemed particularly befitting someone who had labored and served so selflessly for so long.

"We obviously felt honored by the president's presentation," Sue said. "But the greater honor may have been the following day back at Tenwek when Ernie's award was publicly acknowledged at a hospital staff meeting." The entire roomful of doctors, nurses, aides, and other hospital staff broke into loud cheers as Ernie held up the medal for them to see. Everyone wanted to hear about the ceremony at the state house, so Ernie described in detail what had happened. When he demonstrated how he had leaned forward so the president could place the medal over his head and around his neck, the whole crowd broke into cheers again. And when Ernie told the assembled staff that he didn't consider this great honor from the president of Kenya his personal award, but that it really belonged to Tenwek Hospital and all of those in the room who ministered at Tenwek Hospital, the whole place exploded with the loudest cheers and applause of all.

That celebration with their friends and hospital family would echo in their memories as Ernie and Sue headed back to the States the next day. They knew that their final extended stay in their adopted homeland was now over. Ernie summarized their year in Kenya in a letter to friends and supporters:

"The year was different in many ways from our previous years of ministry. I had the privilege of working for a time in the hospital in surgery and outpatient. Being able to work with patients is always a joy, a challenge, and a blessing. It is often shocking to see the extent to which disease has progressed before the patients come for medical help. Tuberculosis, AIDS, and malnutrition are all too common and are often associated with each other. I was shocked to see how common cancer is becoming.

"The greatest joy was being able to pray with patients who had spiritual needs. I also had the privilege of speaking to several church conferences. God is working in and through the Africa Gospel Church and WGM in Kenya.

"Sue was involved in many activities. She was happy to teach evangelism to Community Health Helpers again. She was also able to spend some quality time with our grandchildren in Kenya. Assisting with the entertainment of visitors at Tenwek also kept her very busy.

"Many of you have asked when we are going to officially retire. We have arranged with the Mission to retire at the International Celebration of Missions in June 1998. In the meantime, we plan to return to Kenya in August of this year [1997] for approximately three months. Before we left Kenya in 1994, I wrote a proposal to the American Schools and Hospitals Abroad, a division of USAID in Washington, D.C., asking for a grant to replace the remaining old, dilapidated wards at Tenwek. They gave us a grant for $698,000, and the new construction is now being completed. We praise the Lord for providing this wonderful grant. The hospital board of governors asked that we return in August or September for the dedication of the new buildings. So we are planning to be there for that event. Kenya is still in our hearts."

Dedication and Recognition

The Steurys did indeed return to Kenya once again in mid-August of 1997, accompanied by their dear friend and long-time Tenwek colleague, Marilyn Van Kuiken, who was making her first visit back to Kenya since her own retirement.

Saturday, October 18, 1997, was the day set aside for the dedication of Tenwek's two newest buildings. A grand new ward building would increase the hospital's capacity to more than three hundred beds, making it one of the largest mission hospitals in Africa. The matching services building would house a library, educational rooms, hospital kitchen, dining room, and assorted other facilities.

The crowd began gathering early as thousands of people packed into the hospital courtyard to sit and stand on the sidewalks, in the grass, between and alongside other buildings—anywhere they could find a space from which to view the festivities.

"I was off to the side as usual," Sue recalled, "chatting with friends and family as we waited for the official ceremonies to begin. Ernie's sister and brother-in-law, Ruth and Gerry Sprunger, were with us. Jon and Vera were there. Even Cindy and Daniel had come up-country to be with us at Tenwek for the day. Cindy and I were talking when Susan Carter and a long line of dignitaries began filing through the crowd, down toward a roped-off area right in front of the new buildings. Ernie was in that group with Kenya's minister of health, the deputy ambassador from the American Embassy in Nairobi, a long line of other national and local officials, Africa Gospel Church leaders, members of the hospital's governing board, and assorted other bigwigs. The procession was making its way down through the crowd and would soon be passing right by us. As I watched for Ernie, Susan Carter told me, 'Sue, when the dignitaries pass by here, I want you to get in line with your husband.'

"My instant thought was, *I'm not going to do that! Ernie needs to participate in the dedication, of course—he got the whole project funded by applying for the grant. But they don't need me down there.* I started to make my protest to Susan when she interrupted to say, in a most insistent tone, 'Here comes Ernie. Go with him, Sue. Right now!'

"She gave me a nudge as Ernie was passing by. It was now or never. I had no opportunity or time to argue without making a public scene. Evidently that was Susan's strategy—to leave me no choice but to step out and join Ernie, which I did. To his surprise as well as my own, we walked together down to the very front of the crowd."

After the Steurys took their place of honor with all the dignitaries, the program officially began with the usual long litany of welcomes, introductions, and assorted prayers, declarations, and speeches that always mark such occasions. Finally Reverend Jonah A. Cheseng'eny, moderator of the Africa Gospel Church and chairman of the hospital's governing board, stood and asked Ernie and Sue to join him next to the entrance of the new ward building. He offered a dedicatory prayer of thanksgiving for Tenwek Hospital, for God's blessing on its great ministry in the community and throughout that part of Kenya, and for Ernie's leadership and commitment over the years. When Reverend Jonah said his amen, he unveiled a three-part plaque, the top panel of which read:

This building is dedicated in honor of
"Mosonik"
Ernest M. Steury, M.D., O.G.W. [Order of the Grand Warrior]
For his faithful and exemplary service
To God and the people of Kenya
at Tenwek Hospital from 1959 to 1994
He came to serve, not be served.
18 October 1997

The second panel of the plaque declared: "This building was opened by Kenya's Minister of Health, the Hon. Gen. (RTD) J. K. Mulinge, E.G.H., M.P. on 18 October 1997."

Panel three proclaimed: "This building is a gift from the people of the United States of America, Construction initiated 1995, Bill Clinton, President."

"Ernie was not merely surprised," Sue reported. "He was stunned. And overwhelmed. We both were. We had no idea our friends were going to honor him in that way."

But before the reality had a chance to truly sink in, Reverend Jonah led the Steurys over to the entrance of the second building. There he began another dedicatory prayer.

"I don't recall now whether he was praying in English or Kipsigis," Sue said. "But I was startled when I heard him use my Kipsigis name in his prayer. And I remember thinking, *What's going on . . .*"

Another plaque was unveiled. And the dedicatory inscription on the services building matched the first one on the ward building. Only the top panel was different. It read:

This building is dedicated in honor of
"Tapkigen"
Mrs. J. Sue Steury
For her faithful and exemplary service
To God and the people of Kenya
At Tenwek Hospital from 1959–1994
She was a teacher in word and deed.

According to Sue, "Ernie was more thrilled and I was more stunned by this honor than the previous one. I couldn't believe it. I kept thinking, *They should have dedicated this second building to someone else, someone who spent a lot more time at the hospital over the years than I did."*

As the crowd erupted in applause and cheers for the Steurys, the official ceremony concluded. But the congratulations of friends and colleagues, the shaking of hands, and kind words of countless well wishers went on and on and on, throughout the remainder of the day.

International Pastors

Still basking in the glow of that great honor, Ernie and Sue returned once again to the States in November to make preparations to assume new responsibilities as "international pastors" to other missionaries in WGM fields throughout the Americas and the Caribbean.

However, soon after that assignment started in January of 1998, an insignificant heart irregularity, which Ernie had known about for years, suddenly became more pronounced. His heart rate was so irregular and slow that a cardiological work-up determined he needed a pacemaker. He had the operation in Fort Wayne, Indiana, on January 28 and recovered well enough that he and Sue made their first trip as international pastors in March 1998.

In their new role they visited, counseled, encouraged, and ministered to WGM missionaries in Argentina, Paraguay, and Honduras.

Ernie and Sue officially retired from World Gospel Mission and were honored for their forty-two years of service at the organization's annual International Celebration of Missions on June 28, 1998. All four of their children were there—Jon and his family were on furlough, and Cindy and her two youngest girls, SaraBeth and Anna, flew home from Africa for the occasion. That was the first time the Steurys and all of their children had been together for six years.

But official retirement didn't mean the end of Ernie and Sue's service with WGM. "They retired us, then retreaded us," Sue laughed. "We continued in our duties as international pastors with plans to travel to visit our missionaries in Bolivia in August and September of that year."

Throughout the years of serving in this capacity, Ernie and Sue traveled to Arizona, Mexico, the Texas border, California, Bolivia, Argentina, Chile, and Central America.

In early November 1998, Ernie spent two and a half days in a hospital in Greensboro, North Carolina, when he developed a bowel obstruction due to adhesions from his previous cancer surgeries. Both Sue and Ernie were grateful it cleared up quickly with the proper medical care. Sue had arthroscopic surgery on her left knee in December for two torn cartilages.

Shortly after a mission trip to Arizona, Ernie was hospitalized yet again for a bowel obstruction due to more of those troublesome adhesions. But two and a half days of treatment cleared up the problem. So when a regularly scheduled check-up confirmed that he was still free of cancer, he and Sue were encouraged.

Return to Kenya

The Steurys journeyed to their beloved Kenya once again in July 1999 to attend their eldest granddaughter Rachel's high school graduation from Rift Valley Academy. They helped Cindy, Daniel, and the family pack up and leave two days later for a year's furlough back in the States.

No sooner had they finished helping one family move out than they went to Olderkesi in Maasai to help Jon and Vera and their family move into a newly constructed house at the mission station there. Sue sewed curtains and helped unpack. Ernie hung towel bars, installed medicine cabinets, and took on assorted other odd jobs to get the younger Steury family settled.

From there Ernie and Sue went to pay another visit to Tenwek, about which Ernie wrote: "Our time at Tenwek was very special. One morning as I sat in the doctors' meeting, I was almost overwhelmed. There were twenty-two doctors, medical students, and clinical officers in the room! What a contrast this was compared to all those years I was alone, or when Dick Morse and I were the only two doctors there! God is doing great things at Tenwek and its outreach ministries—and we praise Him for it."

Some weeks after their return from overseas, Ernie awakened Sue one night to tell her, "I think you need to take me to the hospital!" Severe pain in his chest was radiating down his arm.

Ernie's diagnosis: congestive heart failure. His long-standing condition was gradually getting worse with the wear and tear of age. There was some thought of implanting a defibulator, but his cardiologist eventually decided to see how Ernie fared with an adjustment of his pacemaker, some new medications, and alterations to his diet.

When Ernie came home from the hospital, Sue decided to do what she could to start cooking and even baking bread without any salt. For a short while Ernie steadily regained his strength and health. Then he seemed to peak and begin steadily losing strength and mental sharpness.

At times he couldn't think of a word he wanted to use, or he would have moments of incoherence. Ernie realized it when it happened. "I'm either getting Alzheimer's or I'm losing my mind," he told Sue. And either prospect scared him.

Ernie grew physically weaker and mentally fuzzier by the day, until one evening he picked up the phone and called David Stevens to describe what was going on, seeking his advice. David asked a lot of questions. When he called back he told Ernie, "Get yourself a big bag of potato chips and start eating! You don't have to eat the whole bag, but eat as much as you can. You're out of salt! Quit taking that diuretic prescription until you start feeling better," Dave told him. "And remind Sue you need *some* salt in your diet, and not to try to cut it out completely."

Within a couple of days, Ernie got his electrolyte level back in balance and was amazed at how much stronger and better he felt. Assured that he wasn't losing his mind after all, Ernie's spirits recovered even faster than his physical strength. But that experience, on top of all his other recent health episodes, served as a sobering reminder that his earthly body was slowly—or maybe not so slowly—wearing out.

Tenwek's Nursing School

Ernie and Sue journeyed once again to Kenya in August of 2000 for the opening and dedication of the new building for Tenwek's nursing school. Instead of making do with crowded and rather dingy basement offices and classrooms in one of the older hospital buildings, the staff and students of the growing nursing school would enjoy an expansive new structure that boasted some of the best workmanship of any building ever constructed at Tenwek. "Ernie was so thrilled to see what the local national contractor had done," Sue said. "He commented on everything from the quality masonry on the outside to the gorgeous woodwork throughout the interior of the building. What a wonderful place for our nursing students to work and learn."

Ernie had always believed great things would come of the nursing school. This new, fully equipped facility would support their upgraded official Kenya-registered community nurses training program and carry the school well into the twenty-first century. Many people congratulated and praised him for his vision and his role in getting the program started years before, but as usual, Ernie reminded everyone they needed to give God the glory for all that was happening at Tenwek.

The Steurys took the opportunity to visit with many Kenyan friends and spent several days at Olderkesi in Maasai with their son Jon and his family. There they were particularly encouraged to see the great number of committed Christians who were now part of the Africa Gospel Church in Maasai.

Chapter 18

WORTH IT ALL

Failing Health

Soon after Ernie and Sue returned home from Kenya, Ernie had to be admitted to the hospital with yet another bowel obstruction. Once again he was successfully treated without surgery, but this time his hospitalization lasted five days.

Ernie had regained much of his physical strength, but in June of 2001 he noticed what he thought was significant memory loss. When he mentioned it to Sue, she assured him, "Everyone forgets things," and it was probably just the natural result of aging. But Ernie sensed a growing mental fuzziness that alarmed him. When he got up one morning and noticed that his body listed a little to the left, he called his doctor and made an appointment for a CAT scan. The images clearly revealed a growth on the left side of his brain. And Ernie, who knew very well what a brain tumor looked like, called Dave Stevens to share the bad news and ask his recommendation on the best possible neurosurgeon in the Orlando area.

As concerned as Dave was to get this news, he said later he wasn't surprised. "I was doing a review for my family practice boards at the time," he said. "When I'd gotten to the area on astrocytomas where it said *Risk factor: Radiation*, I knew. Ernie had been exposed to a lot of radiation over the years in his practice. He had had radiation dermatitis on his hands for years from using old fluoroscopy technology in the early days at Tenwek. Any time he had to check for foreign bodies inside a patient, and a lot of times with certain bone fractures, he would utilize what was called a rare earth screen enlightened by a high-dose X-ray from underneath the patient. He would be looking down at the beam through the screen, which he moved around with his hands to get a clearer perspective.

"Brief, one-or-two-time exposures posed no significant threat to patients. But Ernie endured thousands of such exposures over the years. And not all of that radiation stopped at his hands. His head was also exposed. So while I could never prove it medically, I think there is every reason to believe Ernie's brain cancer was a direct result of his service and commitment as a missionary doctor. And if that's true it means that he truly sacrificed his own health and his own life for his patients."

As executive director of the Christian Medical & Dental Associations, Dave had instant access to a membership list of more than fifteen thousand doctors around the country. But his personal knowledge of the Orlando medical community was limited. "I do know, and so do you," Dave assured Ernie, "someone who would know who you need to see. Mike Cheatham is practicing in Orlando now. Let me give him a call and make some inquiries."

Mike had been a college student when Ernie and Sue had first become acquainted with him. Dr. Mel Cheatham, Mike's dad, had served as a visiting doctor at Tenwek for a few weeks and brought his family along. Mike had returned later during medical school to gain some short-term missions experience. So when Dave Stevens called Mike to explain the health crisis Ernie was facing, Mike set up appointments for Ernie with the best specialists in central Florida.

When Ernie and Sue tried to express their gratitude for his personal concern, Mike surprised them by saying how indebted he was to Ernie. He went on to explain that when he had come out to Kenya as a medical student, he had planned on specializing in neurosurgery and going into practice with his father. But after working alongside Ernie at Tenwek Hospital, he had decided he could help more people as a general surgeon, so that's what he had decided to do. "I wouldn't be here, doing what I am today, if it wasn't for you, Ernie. So I'll do anything I can to help."

"We were practically overwhelmed by what Mike told us," Sue said. "Ernie had no idea he'd played such an important role in this young doctor's life. He was truly humbled by Mike's words of respect and affection. We both were."

The doctors who looked at Ernie's CAT scan couldn't believe he wasn't in any pain. "Then how did you know to come in for a scan?" they wondered. He told them he had noticed a loss of memory and just knew something was wrong.

Once the experts looked at his scans, they told him what he already knew would be the standard protocol in a situation like his. Step one would be surgery—to remove as much of the tumor as possible and to biopsy it in order to decide what additional treatment would be dictated.

Ernie didn't need the experts to tell him the prospects didn't look good. Yet he found reason to be positive and hopeful in the fact that the specialists Mike Cheatham had contacted who had agreed to take his case were not only highly respected for their medical competence, but also were Christians. "I'm so thankful for doctors of faith, who trust the Lord and are willing to give him credit," Ernie told Sue. After praying for, and with, hundreds of thousands of his own patients over the decades, he found great comfort in having a surgeon who prayed with him at every appointment.

Still, Ernie and Sue approached this brain surgery with real apprehension. And for good reason.

"Each of our children was there. Debbie and Nate were in the States," Sue said. "Cindy and Jon flew over from Kenya to be with us at this time. I don't know how I would have managed without all their love and support." The Steury children stood with Sue before surgery as she watched Ernie being wheeled off to the OR. They waited with her during surgery while there was nothing to do but hope and pray. And after surgery they sat with her as the surgeon gave them a grim report.

"He explained they had removed as much of the growth as they felt they could," Sue said. "But the tumor had been so deep and so intertwined with the brain, that in his words, 'If we'd taken any more, we wouldn't have Ernie.'"

The cancer was inoperable—a grade-three astrocytoma—malignant, aggressive, and ultimately fatal. Treating it with radiation could buy some time. But the prognosis wasn't promising.

"That was a pretty dismal day," Sue confessed. "But at least I had the children there to cry with me." They bolstered one another's spirits and, at the medical staff's suggestion, managed to get a quick meal at a nearby restaurant before they were finally allowed back into the recovery room to see Ernie. According to Sue, "Despite the bandages, he was his usual, smiling, cheerful self, wanting to know if we'd all gotten something to eat. More concerned about our condition than his own . . . so like Ernie."

Jon Steury recalled, "A little later that day, I was with him in recovery when one of his surgeons first came in to talk with Dad about the results of the surgery. As soon as the doctor began explaining what they had found, Dad obviously knew what that meant, and he remained very quiet as the man laid out the options that would need to be considered. When he drew his comments to a close, Dad finally spoke up to ask if he could pray with the surgeon before he left. Then Dad offered a short prayer, asking for blessing on the doctor and committing his own health into the Lord's hands. When he finished, the surgeon in a choked-up voice announced, 'I'd better be going now.' "

The bad news weighed heavily on the entire Steury family over the next couple of days. Ernie himself wasn't exactly chipper on the morning of August 20, when Sue walked into his hospital room to greet him with a cheery, "Happy anniversary, honey! Forty-seven years!"

"Happy anniversary to you!" Ernie replied. Then he added, "I certainly didn't expect to be celebrating it like this."

"I'm just thankful you're still with us," Sue assured him.

That was the same day Sue remembered the primary surgeon, Dr. Bailey, stopping by on his rounds to check on Ernie. "As always he took time to pray for Ernie," she said. "But this time when he finished his prayer, Ernie asked him, 'Could I pray for you?'

"The surgeon nodded, 'I can use all the prayer I can get.' So Ernie began thanking the Lord for his doctor, for the man's faith, for his medical skills, for his compassion and concern for patients. And he prayed for God's blessing as well as divine wisdom and strength for him in his life, his career, and all that he had to do that day. When Ernie finished and this young doctor thanked him, I could tell he was deeply moved."

Ernie was soon well enough to go home to Oaks Village and what Sue referred to as "the best neighbors in the world. The day of Ernie's surgery they had all gathered in the village clubhouse for a prayer meeting. They prayed us through! And then when we got home they showered us with food and offers of whatever help we needed."

Five days a week, for six straight weeks that fall, Ernie endured radiation treatments. "They created this waxy, mesh-covered mask that went over his face and head," Sue recalled. "Every day they screwed that contraption to the table to hold him absolutely still so they could direct the radiation to the precise points of the tumor they wanted to target."

Despite the ordeal Sue never heard one word of complaint from Ernie during those treatments. The two of them joked about using the mask for trick or treating on Halloween. And his routine answer to anyone who asked how he was doing was a repetition of what he regularly said to Sue and the family: "I just praise the Lord I'm not suffering. He is faithful."

He said the same thing to the psychiatrist his doctors referred him to in order to assess his emotional state as he faced the reality of his terminal illness. But after that appointment he did admit to Sue, "I just pray that Jesus takes me quickly."

He knew very well what death from brain cancer could be like. "That was one way in which being a doctor was probably a disadvantage," Sue acknowledged. "He wasn't at all afraid of death. But he had witnessed the suffering some of his patients had been through. And part of him couldn't help dreading that prospect."

However, any final timeframe became more uncertain a few weeks after Ernie completed the course of radiation when a follow-up CAT scan revealed the positive results of his treatment. The image showed his tumor was still there. It hadn't even noticeably shrunk. But it had definitely stopped growing.

Though no one could say for how long.

Journey to Kenya

The decision to journey to Kenya for Christmas wasn't an easy one. Both Jon and Cindy wanted one last chance to spend time with their dad and their children to have an opportunity to say their goodbyes to their grandpa. Naturally, Sue and Ernie also wanted that time with Cindy's and Jon's families in Africa. And, of course, Sue understood that one more visit home to Tenwek to see all their friends would mean the world to Ernie.

Packing for their trip was a sobering reminder to Sue that this last visit would be very different from the other flights she and Ernie had made to Kenya over the years. Before, Ernie had always handled all the logistics—from passport and plane reservations to the details of who was going to meet them at the airport. The responsibilities for all of these details would fall on Sue this time.

After the Steurys landed in Nairobi in mid-December, they stayed at Cindy's home in Kijabe until Christmas. The flight had drained Ernie, but being with Cindy, Daniel, and the Tolan grandchildren seemed to rejuvenate him fairly quickly.

Sue's first reaction to the fact that Ernie seemed to be getting worse was to think, *Maybe we shouldn't have come after all* . . . But then she noted how much he seemed to enjoy being with the grandchildren, and she decided the trip had been important enough to Ernie to be worth it. Yet the deterioration of his communication skills greatly bothered her. And it obviously frustrated Ernie that more and more of the time when he'd want to say something, the right words simply wouldn't come to him. He clearly loved being with family and listening to the grandchildren talk about friends, school, and other activities. But he was becoming less and less conversant with Sue or the others around him.

The Steurys celebrated Christmas morning with the Tolans in Kijabe. Then, part way through the day, Cindy and Daniel and the children drove them out to Olderkesi in Maasai to stay with Jon and Vera and their family for a time. They all had a second Christmas celebration there.

According to Jon, it was an emotional and memorable time, sitting together as a family around the Christmas tree, singing carols by candlelight. "The next morning, Boxing Day in Kenya, we all decided to celebrate by fixing Dad's famous barbecued chicken. We marinated the meat for hours in his secret-recipe sauce. Then late in the afternoon, I went outside and lit the fire in the cement block fireplace I'd built to accommodate the big three-foot by three-foot metal grill top I'd inherited from Dad when he left Tenwek—the same grill he had used for years when he'd had his big backyard cookouts for missionary colleagues and hospital staff.

"No sooner did I get the fire started than a light rain began to fall. I wondered if we would need to change plans and cook the chicken inside. But it never did do more than mist. So Dad and I put on ponchos and stood side by side to initiate my new barbecue pit, using his old grill, to cook what every WGM missionary in Kenya knew as 'Ernie Steury's Famous Barbecue Chicken' for the entire family. Dad didn't say much. But so many wonderful memories flashed through my mind as we stood over that grill, that I will never forget what a special day that was for me."

Tenwek Hospital planned another special day early in January of 2002, and Ernie was invited. The occasion was a huge banquet to celebrate the hospital board's appointment of Stephen Mutai to replace Susan Carter as the first African to serve as Tenwek Hospital's executive officer. Ernie smiled proudly when Jon informed him about the occasion.

No one knew better than the Steury family how the nationalization of Tenwek Hospital had been Ernie's goal since he came to Kenya more than forty-two years before. The hospital's matron of nursing (head nurse) for years had been an African. Kenyan doctors had served at Tenwek for almost two decades. The Steurys' old friend Ezekiel Kerich had been the longtime hospital administrator before Ernie had hired Stephen for that position when Ezekiel retired in the early 1990s.

At last the day Ernie had dreamed of and worked for had come. This young man he had hired and trained and advised had finally been selected to serve as Tenwek Hospital's executive officer. So Ernie would have enjoyed nothing more than to be at that celebratory banquet.

"I would love to go," he told his family. "But I won't. This should be Steven's night."

Cindy explained, "Dad understood that if he showed up at the banquet, everyone's focus would be on him. And he didn't want to take anything away from the honor due Steven."

Grand Rounds at Tenwek

Ernie did go to Tenwek for a very memorable visit just a few days after the banquet. One of the first staff people to see and welcome him with open arms was Geoffrey Lang'at, former assistant (and currently the new) hospital administrator. Geoffrey was as excited to see Ernie as Ernie was to see him. "I have always remembered the two things you said to me before you left, Dr. Steury," Geoffrey said. "You told me to be honest and faithful. I have always tried to do that, and the Lord has helped me."

Geoffrey then insisted on escorting Ernie and his party around the hospital. He took one of Ernie's arms and Cindy took the other as Mosonik made his grand rounds one last time. "It was amazing how just being at Tenwek energized Ernie," Sue said. "For weeks he'd had no physical stamina whatsoever, yet we were on our feet for three hours that day, as he was determined to visit every part of the hospital. For weeks he'd been struggling to carry on conversations, yet he greeted most of the longtime employees by name. And every staff person he encountered, whether missionary or national, he stopped to thank for their faithfulness and their service to Tenwek and to the Lord. Cindy and I kept looking at each other and shaking our heads in amazement as he conversed with the nationals in Kipsigis and at one point even used an obscure word for *pincher ant* in the local dialect."

"Again and again, as Ernie thanked staff members for their work, he would challenge them to 'be faithful. Stay true to the Lord. Because He's coming back.'"

What a wonderful day Ernie had greeting and saying goodbye to many old friends. It meant so much to him to see and hear how the new administration was carrying on the spiritual legacy of Tenwek by continuing to make evangelism a priority. "That last visit to the hospital felt like an incredible gift from God," Sue said.

As much as the day had lifted Ernie emotionally and spiritually, it seemed to take its toll physically. Instead of going to Maasai where Jon lived, Ernie and Sue decided to go back with the Tolans to Kijabe to be near a well-staffed mission hospital. The wisdom of that decision was soon evident to Sue and the Tolans, because the high Ernie had experienced during his visit to Tenwek was about to be followed by some very definite new lows.

Declining Health, Surprising Rallies

Several times a night Ernie would awaken Sue as he tried to get out of bed—confused about where he was and having to be reminded by Sue that he couldn't go to the bathroom by himself without risking a fall.

Interaction during the day also became more difficult. Much of Ernie's communication began with a word or two that trailed off into a sudden and awkward silence without the sentence ever being completed. Sometimes Ernie seemed oblivious to what had happened—as if he'd forgotten he'd even said anything. But in many other instances, Ernie would first look confused, then frustrated, to find himself wandering wordlessly in the conceptual wilderness, uncertain how or where he'd lost his trail of thought.

"I think the hardest part was seeing how much Ernie was aware of, but couldn't do anything about," Sue said. "There were times when his mind was so fuzzy that he may have been completely out of it. But most of the time, on some level, I think he not only recognized what was happening, but he also realized his own helplessness in dealing with it."

Sue believed that Ernie still retained enough of his lifetime of medical knowledge and experience to anticipate and dread what is often an extremely difficult and painful end stage with brain cancer. Back in the fall, when he'd been better able to articulate his thoughts and fears, he had indicated to Sue his concern that whatever happened, whatever he might have to go through, he prayed that God would be glorified in his actions and his attitudes—that he would do nothing to dishonor the Lord.

No doubt Ernie had seen many instances over the years with patients where pain, fear, and frustration led to uncharacteristic anger, sometimes belligerence, toward those around them. Just thinking about that possibility would have greatly disturbed this gentle man.

Fortunately those concerns never materialized. According to Sue, "Ernie was so careful to thank me or the girls or anyone else for everything we did for him—whether it was to bring him a drink, help him walk from his easy chair to the table at mealtime, or just cut up his meat to make it easier for him to eat. He remained the same sweet, gentle person he'd always been, for which we were extremely grateful. What a blessing that he wasn't suffering the kind of pain that might have changed his personality and made him difficult to handle. I don't know how I would have dealt with that. The mental and emotional anguish was enough as it was."

The deterioration in those weeks after Christmas was so rapid and so severe that Daniel Tolan, with the consent of the entire family, decided to do another CAT scan to see what was happening with the tumor. Ernie had the scan done in Nairobi, and the images were sent to his doctors in Orlando for a comparison with the last scan they had done in the fall.

The findings were revealing, if not encouraging. The reason Ernie seemed to be losing ground was that the tumor was growing again—and fast. This meant there was nothing to do but wait, and that wait probably wasn't going to be long.

While the report wasn't surprising, it was still such a disappointing blow for Sue and her children that the family wasn't sure how to tell Ernie. But that night during family devotions—after Scripture reading and prayer—Daniel simply came right out and asked, "Dad, would you like to know the results of the CAT scan?"

Ernie didn't hesitate. "Of course I would," he replied. So Daniel explained how much and where the tumor was growing. He also reported the consensus of the doctors in Orlando: There was nothing more to be done.

Even as the Steury family struggled to deal with their issues of suffering and loss, shocking news reached Kijabe from the States. Their dear friend and next-door neighbor Marilyn Luce had died suddenly from a heart attack. She had gotten out of bed one morning and walked into the kitchen to run water for some tea. Joe had come in a few minutes later and found her slumped over the sink.

Just that quickly she was gone.

"I wasn't sure how Ernie would react to that news," Sue recalled. "But I knew I had to tell him. When I did, he groaned in grief, and then with great sadness, longing, and pain in his voice he exclaimed, 'Oh, how I wish I could see Joe right now and give him a hug!'"

Joe Luce did place a call to the Tolan house in Kijabe right after the funeral. "He tried to be so chipper," Sue said, "keeping his spirits up for our sakes. But we knew, and Ernie knew, Joe was hurting inside. So Ernie tried to encourage him by telling him how sorry we were, how we were praying for him, how much we were all going to miss Marilyn, and how we wished we could be there with him and for him in Florida."

"Ernie," Joe told him, "You need to get back here. There is no place like Avon Park to go to heaven from!"

The idea of going home to Florida and being among their friends there certainly appealed to Sue. She even raised the possibility with Ernie after that. "I don't think there is any way I can make the trip," Ernie told her. He was still certainly aware enough to realize the distance and the ordeal that would be involved.

But despite her daughter's help and care for Ernie, Sue felt more and more isolated there in Kijabe where the people inside the Tolan house were the only people she really knew. Most of the active WGM missionaries still in Kenya were halfway across the country at Tenwek. Most of their oldest friends, their peer group, colleagues they had loved and served with over the years were now retired in the States; many, like the Lewtons and the Morses, were neighbors back in Avon Park. Sue missed those friends.

Even more she missed the man she had been married to for forty-seven and a half years, because every week, sometimes every day, she realized a little more of him was slipping away. When their old friend Marilyn Van Kuiken called to talk with her, Sue tearfully acknowledged, "He's just not Ernie any more."

He spent more time each day sitting alone in the easy chair in the Tolan living room. Seemingly unaware of his surroundings, seemingly unaware of anything—except that occasionally when Sue or Cindy or Debbie would go in to check on him, they would hear him mumbling in prayer, humming some hymn, or just raising his right hand in silent praise to his Lord.

The remainder of February 2002 saw little change in Ernie's condition, except maybe a slight continuing loss of strength and communication. Yet there were some surprising rallies.

One Saturday a contingent of old friends from Nairobi—a representative of MAP (Medical Assistance Program) International, a Christian obstetrician and her husband, and a couple officials from CHAK (Christian Health Association of Kenya)—all folks Ernie had known and worked with on joint projects over the years—came out to Kijabe for a visit. Daniel

Tolan had warned them not to expect much, if anything, in the way of conversation. So they and the entire family were shocked when Ernie greeted them all by name and said, "It's so good to see you. I love you and have been praying for you." He told them, like he explained when Sue put him on the phone to speak with friends and family who called, "I'm very confused sometimes. But I'm not in any pain, and I praise the Lord for that." Then he went on talking for several more minutes, encouraging his visitors in their important work: "Don't ever give up. The Lord will always be there to help you when you need it."

Sue laughed at the memory. "Our mouths were just hanging open. When I walked our friends out to the car at the end of their visit, I said to the visitors, 'This has just blown my mind. He not only knew you, but that's the most he's talked in weeks.'

"Our obstetrician friend smiled and said, 'The Lord did that. He knew we needed Ernie's encouragement.'"

Not many days after that, missionary doctors from throughout Kenya, Africa, and that half of the world gathered outside Nairobi at Brackenhurst, a large Christian retreat center, for several days of continuing medical education. Ernie had played a role in these conferences since their beginnings over twenty-five years before, so virtually everyone attending this Nairobi session knew him, had been praying for him, and wanted to hear the latest update from Daniel Tolan.

As Daniel had talked about the conference ahead of time, Ernie expressed his desire to go and see the many friends he knew would be there. Sue had told him if he was feeling up to it, they would see what they could do about making a short visit one of the days. But when the time finally came, Ernie seemed so weak that she decided against going the first day. And the next. And the next.

"On the morning of the last day I realized it was now or never," Sue said. "I told Daniel we could try. We took Ernie to Brackenhurst and into the auditorium where everyone had gathered for the final worship service, which was about to start. Ernie was too weak to stand, so Daniel pushed him in his wheelchair up near the front where he could see and hear everything. As the session came to a close, the emcee announced a time of special prayer and asked Daniel if he would bring Ernie to the front. Daniel stepped behind the wheelchair to begin pushing when Ernie shook his head and told him, 'I want to walk.'

"Daniel took one arm. Someone else the other. And Ernie moved slowly, almost painfully to the front of the entire roomful of missionary doctors who all rose to their feet and applauded. Many of them had tears streaming down their faces.

"When he reached the front and turned to face the crowd, an old Indiana University friend of Ernie's and one of the conference organizers, Dr. Charles Kelly, made ready to offer a prayer. But Ernie indicated he wanted to speak first.

"Daniel had inquired ahead of time: 'Mom, should we ask Dad to say something at the conference?' I'd told him no," Sue said, "because I didn't want to do anything that might create pressure or worry Ernie about going. But here he was, stopping the proceedings and starting to make a speech. It was difficult for me to hear everything he said. But he told everyone how great it was to be there and to see so many old friends. He also encouraged this auditorium full of missionary doctors to 'be faithful' and know they could trust the Lord to be with them whatever challenges or problems they faced."

Many familiar faces swarmed around Ernie as the meeting concluded. "I didn't know if we would ever get away from that conference," Sue said. "The morning totally exhausted Ernie. But what an incredible memory that was!"

Going Home

As the days and weeks passed with the occasional ups and downs but only a gradual overall decline in Ernie's condition, Sue couldn't help but wonder how long his ordeal was going to last. She asked Cindy, "What happens if Dad continues to hang on when June comes and you have to pack up, get out of this house, and head back to the States for furlough?"

Neither of them had a workable answer to that question. They both knew it wouldn't be practical to take Ernie to Jon's place way out in Maasai. Not with the rest of the family and all their friends back in America. So Sue again began to toy with the idea of taking Ernie home.

Sue just didn't know what would be best—to stay in Kenya or try to get back home. "I just knew if he and I didn't go back to Avon Park together, it would be a long time before I would ever want to walk into our home alone."

Sue discussed it with the children, then sought some additional counsel with a call to her longtime friend Marilyn Van Kuiken, who assured her, "If you do decide to come home, I'll meet you in Florida and help you take care of Ernie."

But Sue remained torn and still prayed, *Lord, I need your guidance, because you can see the whole picture.* She also longed desperately for some input, some feel from Ernie that would help her more clearly know what she ought to do.

Sue remembered one day when she had been sitting with Ernie out on the porch swing and had asked, "Honey, do you miss our friends back in Avon Park?"

Ernie had admitted, "I sure do!"

"Would you like to go back?" she had asked him.

"Oh, do you think we'll ever get back there?" he had responded longingly.

Wondering if he still felt the same way or if he even remembered they had another place where they had lived, Sue asked again, "Do you miss our home in Florida, honey?"

Ernie replied with emphasis, "I sure do!"

"How 'bout our friends? Do you miss them?"

"I really do," he said, with even more feeling.

According to Sue, "That was what I needed to hear. Even if he didn't realize the full implication of what he was saying, I knew that response was from his heart. So I asked Cindy to go ahead and get the tickets."

The goodbyes at the airport on March 17, 2002, were especially painful. Cindy was flying back to Florida with Ernie and Sue to help them manage the logistics of the flights and to assist with her dad's medical and physical care during the trip. Daniel and the Tolan grandchildren were there to see them all off. So were Jon, Vera, and all their children.

Daniel explained the situation to the airport authorities, who allowed the whole family past security to wait together in the restricted departure area near the airline check-in desk. "I realized this would be the last time I'd ever see Dad on this earth," Jon said. "He obviously didn't have many days left. But as we said our goodbyes, it seemed that on some level, though he remained confused, he sensed the significance of what was happening. Because after the entire family had circled around and prayed together, just before Mom and Cindy wheeled him past the security checkpoint and out to the plane to leave Africa one final time, Dad looked around at everyone and said the very last words I ever heard him say, 'It's been worth it all.'"

Homecoming

Landing uneventfully in Orlando gave Sue an almost overwhelming sense of relief and gratitude. It served as one more reminder to her of the promise in Psalm 48:14: "For this God is our God forever and ever: he will be our guide even unto death." "The Lord gave Ernie and me this special verse when we first left for the mission field," Sue explained. "And it was still our promise for this day. The previous few months had been difficult for us, but the Lord had been our hope and security. We were safe at home at last."

When they entered the house in Oaks Village, Ernie obviously knew he was home. He finally seemed to relax in a way he hadn't been able to do for weeks in Kenya. He happily greeted and embraced the stream of friends and neighbors who stopped in.

Ernie especially brightened up when Joe Luce visited. "Joe bent over Ernie's easy chair to give him a welcome-home hug, and Ernie just held on and held on," Sue recalled.

A local hospice group had set up a hospital bed and all the other equipment they thought would be necessary in the sunroom at the back of Steurys' house. They visited as necessary and offered twenty-four-hour caregivers. With all the friends around, plus the family who came, Sue had all the loving help she needed to care for Ernie.

After a long drive down from her home in Illinois, Marilyn Van Kuiken reached Avon Park the day after the Steurys returned. Her decades-long friendship, her extensive nursing experience, and her promise to stay as long as she was needed greatly heartened Sue, who certainly needed encouraging.

As low as his dad now seemed to Nate and to the Oaks Village neighbors who hadn't seen Ernie since the Steurys had left for Kenya back in December, Ernie was about to go lower. The hopeful burst of energy prompted by the return home and the pleasure of seeing so many family and friends again merely seemed to trigger a slow but noticeable decline in Ernie's health and strength.

Before long, most of Ernie's communication was limited to words rather than sentences. And he finally began evidencing signs of serious discomfort; whenever he had to be moved, he would hold his head and quietly moan, "Oooh, oooh, oooh!"

One day he said, "That thing in my head is getting so big! It feels like it's gonna explode!"

Thinking maybe it was time to start administering some stronger medication, daughter Debbie asked, "Dad, are you having a lot of pain?"

"Not pain," he told her, "just pressure."

Ernie became less and less responsive over the next couple of days. His eyes seemed to focus when he heard a deep voice, but when Sue spoke to him, she saw no indication he even heard her.

"I knew how much that was bothering Sue," her friend Marilyn recalled. As nurses, both she and Debbie recognized this lack of responsiveness as evidence that the end was very near. "I felt so badly for Sue that I remember praying and praying to God Tuesday evening that He would let Ernie speak to her one more time," Marilyn said.

"I walked into Ernie's room Wednesday morning to open the window blinds," Sue recounted, "and I greeted him, 'Good morning, sweetheart. I love you!' His eyes remained closed, but he turned his head toward me, smiled, and echoed my words, 'Good morning, sweetheart. I *love you*, too.' He said it with such feeling.

"Those were the last words I ever heard Ernie speak."

The next day, April 4, 2002, just two and a half weeks after the Steurys had arrived back in the States from Kenya, Ernie's sister Ruth sat at his bedside, holding his hand. She felt her brother squeeze her hand.

His eyes came wide open, and he raised his hand as if he were greeting someone.

Then Ernie was gone.

In Remembrance

A memorial service took place in Avon Park the following Monday, April 8, 2002. A second service was scheduled the week after that at Ernie's home church in Berne, Indiana. And naturally, the largest and longest service of all was held at Tenwek in Hotchkiss Memorial Church, where Ernie's Kipsigis friends and missionary colleagues from all over Kenya gathered to celebrate his life and memory.

Sue attended only the Florida service—the one Ernie helped plan—and for which he selected some of his favorite hymns and Scriptures. The first Scripture reference Ernie had chosen to be read started with Isaiah 41:10, "Do not fear, for I am with you; do not anxiously look about you, for I am your God. I will strengthen you, surely I will help you, surely I will uphold you with My righteous right hand." The passage ended with verse 13, which Ernie had claimed as his life verse: "For I am the LORD your God, who upholds your right hand, who says to you, 'Do not fear; I will help you.'"

During that memorial service, numerous Christian leaders and friends testified to God's hand of blessing on Ernie's ministry.

Dr. Mel Cheatham, an old friend and noted surgeon, represented World Medical Mission. He said he'd never operated with a more gifted doctor than Ernie and brought greetings and condolences from Franklin and Billy Graham, "two men who have loved and admired Ernie so much."

The former president of Ernie's alma mater, Asbury College, Dr. Dennis Kinlaw, said, "I don't know that I've ever met another man who better fulfilled this passage from Ephesians 5: 'Be imitators of God, therefore, as dearly loved children and live in love, just as Christ loved us and gave himself up for us, as a fragrant offering and sacrifice to God.' There was a delightful fragrance about the life of Ernie Steury."

Of all the people who would have been glad to preach at Ernie Steury's funeral, the family knew Ernie would have wanted them to ask Dave

Stevens. Dave caught a red-eye flight from the West Coast, where he had a speaking engagement the previous day, in order to speak at the service.

Dave said he hadn't struggled with so much emotion and so much uncertainty about knowing what to say since his own father's funeral. But that day as he had made notes and tried to decide what to say, he commented, "I realized Ernie has already preached the sermon. I just need to remind you" of his message.

Dave noted that the world measures a man by three things: wealth, power, and achievement. He said Ernie might not have had a lot of money, "but he owned things money couldn't buy—things he possessed in his character and his nature. In terms of integrity, gentleness, and wisdom, Ernie Steury was the richest man I ever knew."

He had seen a different kind of power, a greater power, in Ernie Steury, who knew what it was like to work every day, all of his life, with the Great Physician. "He was the most competent physician I ever worked with," Dave said, "and perhaps the most humble." Recognizing the power of his mentor's example, Dave acknowledged, "Ernie had a servant heart."

Dave said what impressed him most about Ernie and what was the greatest accomplishment of Ernie Steury's life was that "he stayed faithful. Because I know how hard that was for him over the years. But he always kept the faith, and being faithful . . . that's real accomplishment."

When Ernie had called him the previous summer to say he had been diagnosed with brain cancer, Dave admitted his first reaction had been to question God: *Why? Just when Ernie finally has some time to spend with Sue, to enjoy his children and grandchildren, to look back and reflect on his life, to relive the memories. He's already given and sacrificed so much over the years. Why would you take him now?*

The answer to his why question didn't come, David said, until he was on his way to the funeral and thinking about what to say. "Then it hit me why. It was because God couldn't wait to give Ernie his reward!"

When Dave Stevens concluded his remarks, people who weren't on the platform were given opportunity to share. A number of folks did, including several family members who gave beautiful eulogies.

Cindy, who had just gone back to Africa after accompanying her folks home, couldn't return for the funeral. The Tolans and Jon's family would represent all the Steurys at the memorial service for Ernie in Kenya. Cindy's college-aged daughter, Rachel Tolan, was at her grandfather's funeral in Florida, representing her parents.

Rachel read this tribute, written by her mother:

> One of my most vivid memories of Dad is of him on his knees in his office. Every morning for as long as I can remember, if I rose early, I would see him there praying before he would start his day. It didn't matter if he'd been up part of the night, or all night on call, he would still take time for his own quiet time with God. This made such a huge impression on me as a child—and still does to this day.
>
> Many people have asked how Dad ever survived being the only doctor at Tenwek for so many years. I know how he made it. He spent time with his source of strength, every single day.

Nate Steury also memorialized his father, building on one of David Stevens's points:

> The sermon has been preached. The life has been lived.
>
> Three things make Dad the greatest man I have ever known. The first was his deep commitment to Christ—demonstrated in his compassion.
>
> The second thing was his amazingly humble spirit. There are many great people in this world, but very few of them are humble. I thank God that my dad was one of those.
>
> The third thing that made Dad the greatest man I have ever known . . . is Mom. Perhaps the only thing harder than being a great person in this world is being the spouse of one. They pay the price.
>
> I think of that song titled "Wind Beneath My Wings." Mom was that for Dad. Thank you, Mom.
>
> And I just thank God that I had the privilege of being Ernie Steury's son.

The service concluded with the congregation singing one of Ernie's favorite songs, the tune his mother always sang around the house when he was a boy: "My Jesus I Love Thee, I Know Thou Art Mine."

When the music stopped, everyone headed to the fellowship hall to console Sue and the family. "I saw so many friends and loved ones that it was wonderful," Sue said. "It 'just so happened' that most of the WGM field directors from around the world, those who headed up the mission's work in their particular region or country, had been together in Orlando for a leadership conference over the weekend. Some of them switched their return flights so they could stay over an extra day and come to Ernie's funeral. As a result, we had a huge WGM crowd—executives from headquarters, longtime mission colleagues now serving as field directors around the world, numerous people who'd worked with us in Kenya over the years, and quite a few missionaries from some of the fields we had served in retirement as international pastors. What an amazing reunion it was!

"It wasn't until later and I had a little time to reflect on the memories of that wonderful day that it struck me: That meeting of all those missionaries in Orlando wasn't a coincidence at all. The righteous right hand of the Lord was in that, just like the Lord's hand had been in Ernie's and my life since the beginning. Since I'd felt the call to missions as a little girl of eight; and His hand had been there beckoning when I felt the specific call to Africa at the age of thirteen. The Lord's hand had been on Ernie that long-ago morning in Fort Wayne—to turn him around and send him home instead of getting on that bus and joining the navy. The hand of the Lord had provided Ernie with a minister who "just happened" to have graduated from and recommended Asbury College. God's hand had to be in the selection of Ernie's roommate, who talked Ernie into considering joining him in premed, though he never went on to become a doctor himself.

"I know God's hand was there when I was looking through my brother's college annual, picked out Ernie's picture to ask about, only to have my brother tell me, 'He's the one for you, Sis.' The Lord's hand was certainly with us during med school—first prodding Joe and Marilyn Luce to make a scholarship available and then enabling Ernie to get into the program at IU despite not having a premed degree.

"Looking back now I can see how often God's hand worked in our lives. How often He took our right hand and led us when we didn't know where to go. During surgeries. When we were tired and discouraged. In sickness and in health. When we faced danger. When we celebrated and when we grieved. And in recent months when Ernie had walked through the valley of the shadow of death.

"I could see it now. How the 'coincidence' that all those missionary friends 'just happened' to be in Orlando so they would be with us for Ernie's funeral at Avon Park was just one more proof for me. And I could only stand in awe of our God who can be trusted to orchestrate not only our lives but also our deaths."

Afterword

That isn't the end of the story. Even here on earth Ernie Steury's legacy continues.

Tenwek is now the largest evangelical mission hospital in Kenya, perhaps in all of Africa. Today it is considered by many people to be one of the premier mission hospitals, if not *the* premier mission hospital, in the whole world. Health experts, government officials, and missionaries from dozens of countries have traveled to this rural African hillside to study Tenwek's successful model of community-based health care to borrow training materials, to learn how volunteers are motivated, and to see how to duplicate the same thing elsewhere.

The nursing school continues to grow and improve—from an enrolled community nursing school at the outset to one of the top registered community nursing schools in all of East Africa. Recently, when annual licensing exams were administered for all the graduating registered nurses in Kenya, three of the top ten scores in the entire country were awarded to Tenwek students.

Dave Stevens said, "In all my years traveling around the globe with World Medical Mission and the Christian Medical & Dental Associations, I have never met another doctor who had such a passion for the gospel or such an ability to communicate it as Ernie had. He made evangelism the most important thing at Tenwek from day one, when Tenwek was only him. And that emphasis continues today. I don't know of another hospital anywhere that has had such a direct spiritual impact on so many thousands of souls."

The L. Nelson Bell chaplaincy school has become both cause and effect of that emphasis. It has grown to the point of planning a campus of its own, just across the river from the hospital. It not only develops and equips Tenwek chaplains but also continues to train men and women from throughout Africa to develop chaplaincy ministries in their own countries.

The ongoing impact of Tenwek Hospital and of Ernie Steury continues far outside the bounds of medical ministry. Proof can be seen today in the broader outreach of the Africa Gospel Church. The current moderator of the AGC, Reverend Joseph Rono, said, "We knew Dr. Steury loved and was committed to the hospital—it was in his blood. But he also loved Christ and was committed to the ministry of God's church, preaching to congregations whenever he could, and always encouraging our people in their church ministry." The Africa Gospel Church now boasts over seventy thousand members in more than thirteen hundred congregations throughout Kenya and several neighboring countries. While many factors have contributed to the denomination's remarkable growth, the single greatest and most consistent source of converts and new members over the past half a century has resulted from the spiritual outreach of Tenwek Hospital and its various ministries.

However, the true measure of Ernie Steury's legacy is not to be found in buildings, facilities, institutions, or even outreach programs. The greater impact of Ernie Steury's life has been on people.

All four of his children, their spouses, and their families are currently serving the Lord in a variety of ministry settings. Sue continues to spend as much time as possible encouraging and ministering to her friends in Avon Park and visiting her children and grandchildren whenever she can.

Daniel, Cindy, and their four children, son-in-law, and grandson all live in Johnson City, Tennessee. They are still serving under World Gospel Mission but are seconded to the Christian Medical and Dental Associations, where Daniel is the associate director of the Center for Medical Missions. They are actively involved with local college students, challenging them to be involved in missions and taking one or two teams a year to mission fields.

Jon, Vera, and their two boys are still serving with World Gospel Mission in Olderkesi, Kenya. Jon is doing community health with the

Maasai people in that area, and Vera is homeschooling the boys. Their oldest child, Bethany, is a freshman at Asbury College.

Nate, Elinda, and their four children reside in Indialantic, Florida, where Nate is senior pastor for St. Mark's United Methodist Church. Elinda, a nurse, works part time at Palm Bay Hospital.

Debbie, Ajit, and their three children live in Fort Wayne, Indiana, where Ajit teaches physical education at an elementary school and Debbie works as a nurse at Parkview Hospital. They are involved in a college ministry in their church.

Hundreds of fellow missionaries, visiting doctors, interns, and medical students worked with Ernie in some capacity during his years in Africa. They are now spread out around the world in ministry. Even today, new ones who flock to Tenwek for rotations of a month or two of service are touched by Ernie's legacy. As a result, life will never be the same for most of them, and many will go on to career missionary service somewhere in the world.

Mosonik's work at Tenwek not only saved thousands of Kipsigis lives and revolutionized health care in that region of Kenya; it led to transformed living conditions for hundreds of thousands of people. The effect of the hospital's community health program can be illustrated with this mere sampling of statistics over twenty years: from 63 volunteer health workers in 1983 to 1,000 volunteer health workers in 2003; from 559 cases of measles (including 19 fatal cases) at Tenwek Hospital in 1983 to only 68 cases of measles and no fatal cases in 2003; 1,101 cases of diarrhea diseases treated at Tenwek in 1983 versus 97 such cases in 2003; and 30 deaths from whooping cough in 1983 and none in 2003.

But the best example of the ongoing influence of Ernie Steury's life and ministry is not to be found in groups of people but in the lives of individuals with whom he served.

When Steven Mabatu graduated from high school, he found his first job working for the tea industry in the highlands of western Kenya. Picking tea in the hot fields and laboring in the processing plants was rough duty. Although he was a good worker, his supervisors often beat or verbally abused Steven. But because that was his first job, Steven assumed such treatment was an accepted part of the working world.

During morning and afternoon break times, hot tea was served to employees. Only the supervisors were allowed to use company teacups. Steven made do by drinking his tea out of a cardboard milk carton. He considered that too just a part of life.

Soon after he came to know Christ through the influence of a coworker, Steven also heard of a place called Tenwek Hospital. Because it was closer to his family's village, he applied for and was hired as an attendant in the surgical ward.

In typical British style, Tenwek also served tea to employees at break time. So Steven brought his cardboard milk carton to drink from.

One day soon after that, when Dr. Steury took tea with the surgical staff, he noticed Steven's worn milk carton, which had sprung a few leaks by this time. "Where is your cup, Steven?" Ernie asked.

"This is the only one I have," Steven replied.

Ernie, who had finished his tea, took his own cup, washed it out, handed it to Steven, and said, "This can be yours. From now on, Steven, you take your tea from this cup."

Ernie probably didn't give that gesture a second thought. But years later Steven would say, "At that moment, I saw Jesus. I knew this was a man I could trust, a man I could pattern my own life after, a man to learn from." And that's just what he did. For the next seventeen years, Steven worked his way up through the ranks to become supervisor of the OR and a valued hospital staff member. He left Tenwek only after he was appointed as assistant chief in his home area of Kipsigisland.

Already a longtime Christian leader at work and in his church, Steven assumed a position of even greater leadership responsibility for his people. And it all started with a cup of tea. A simple act of kindness. And one man's example.

Yet another Kipsigis leader, the top administrator in the Africa Gospel Church, Reverend Joseph Rono, tells about the influence Ernie had on him.

"Dr. Steury was the first Christian white man I ever knew. I had grown up on a white settler's farm where my father worked. But the man who owned that farm was not a Christian. So when I met Dr. Steury at a youth camp in 1969, I noticed that he was just as white as other white men I'd seen. But I realized, *Here is a white man who can talk with a black man and love a black man. There is something different about this man.* The next year I became a student at Tenwek High School and got to see him on a regular basis. Then when I became an officer in the Christian Union Group at school, we had more interaction. Together we even planned a retreat out in Masai for the student leaders. Dr. Steury spoke at the retreat, shared his own Christian testimony, and challenged us to consider serving God by going into the ministry. He also spent individual time talking to each of our students.

"Because some of the teachers at my school saw me as a leader, they advised me to enroll in the university and go into government service. But just before I graduated, Dr. Steury talked to me and said, 'If you would go to a Christian college, you could become a leader in the church. I think God is going to use you. Please think and pray about that.' His words moved me.

"When I did pray about it, I felt a strong pressure to do as he said. So you could say I went to college through the influence and challenge of Dr. Steury. I became a pastor and a Christian leader because of him!

"Dr. Steury knew who he was. And he knew who had sent him. He was a true missionary. As the apostle Paul would say, 'Follow me, as I follow Christ.' Dr. Steury could say the same thing. He was a Christian example to so many people."

One of history's great evangelists, Dwight L. Moody, used to challenge his listeners in the late nineteenth century by saying, "The world has yet to see what God can do with one man, totally committed to Him."

Those who knew and loved Ernie Steury during the last half of the twentieth century and have heard of his work at Tenwek Hospital in Kenya have now seen what God can accomplish with one committed Indiana farm boy.

But because that statement would have embarrassed this humble man, we close with the words from the sign at Tenwek Hospital:

"We treat. Jesus heals. To God be all the glory."

Author's Note

When Dave Stevens called me, a longtime friend who had co-authored a book with him a couple of years before, he asked one simple question: "How soon could you leave for Africa?"

"How soon did you have in mind?" I asked.

"How about tomorrow?"

Four days later I sat at the Tolans' supper table in Kijabe, Kenya, listening as Ernie, with Sue's regular prompting, haltingly recounted his feelings on that long-ago morning at the recruiting station in Fort Wayne, Indiana, when his life changed course—when, without understanding why, he had turned and walked away from the bus that would have taken him to basic training at the Great Lakes Naval Training Station in Chicago.

Perhaps that memory was easier to access for Ernie because he had told that story so often over the years. The details of other incidents seemed buried a little too deep for him to pull out.

Later Sue recalled, "That may have been the first time Ernie truly realized how much of his long-term memory was gone. That he wasn't going to be able to help with this book. And for some reason, that really seemed to get to him that night."

The next morning I headed for Tenwek to spend the next week and a half asking numerous missionaries and nationals for their favorite Ernie Steury stories. Everyone interviewed was asked this question: *If our book is going to capture and present an accurate picture of Ernie/Mosonik, what characteristics and personality traits of the man need to come through?* Answers varied, of course, as people listed a variety of characteristics. But without fail, every person I spoke with—from Ernie's son Jon to missionary colleagues and Kipsigis friends alike—all included two words. At or near the top of this list, everyone said that for readers ever to get a true picture of Ernie Steury, this book would need to convey two primary traits: his humility and commitment.

What a testimony that is! What a fitting epitaph those two words would make!

On my return to Kijabe, I sensed a noticeable decline in Ernie's physical mobility and mental sharpness had taken place since I'd left ten days before. I couldn't help thinking this might be the beginning of the final descent to the end. But as I bid Ernie a last goodbye before heading for the airport, he rallied enough strength to pray a powerfully memorable, meaningful, and moving blessing on me, my life, and my work on this book.

It has been my great privilege to write this book for him. I have been blessed because of Ernie's life. I am grateful that I had the privilege of meeting this servant of God, and I hope I have captured the true essence of his life while fulfilling his desire—"to God be the glory."

Thanks to David Stevens for encouraging the Steury family to bring this story to others, and for spearheading the creation and publishing of this book; it was a labor of love for both of us. And special thanks to the late Joe Luce, who underwrote the financial aspects of this project.

—GREGG LEWIS
2007

Additional Information

Websites

www.tenwek.org
www.wgm.org

Books

1901 Sketches from the Dark Continent. (early history of Tenwek)

Come Walk with Me, Melvin L. Cheatham, M.D., Thomas Nelson, Nashville, 1993.

The Hill of Vision: The Story of the Quaker Movement in East Africa 1902–1965, Levinus King Painter, Nairobi, The English Press, 1966.

Kindled Fires in Africa, Laura Cammack Trachsel, Marion, Indiana, World Gospel Mission, 1964.

Jesus, M.D. David Stevens and Gregg Lewis, Grand Rapids, Zondervan, 2001.

The Place of Songs: World Gospel Mission, Africa Gospel Church, Burnette C. Fish and Gerald Fish, Marion, Indiana, World Gospel Mission, 1990. (detailed history of Tenwek)

Then and Now in Kenya Colony: Forty Adventurous Years in East Africa, Willis R. Hotchkiss, Old Tappan, New Jersey, 1937, Fleming H. Revell Company. (early history of Tenwek)

Christian Medical & Dental Associations

As a medical student, Ernie Steury joined the Christian Medical & Dental Associations (CMDA). He was involved in the creation of CMDA's continuing medical and dental education conferences for missionary doctors in Kenya, which he regularly attended.

Founded in 1931, CMDA exists to motivate, train, and equip Christian doctors to glorify God. With over seventeen thousand members, its vision is to transform doctors to transform the world. Today it has over eighty outreaches that teach doctors how to address their patients' spiritual needs, grow stronger in their Christian walk, and serve the poor in the United States and abroad.

Its Center for Medical Missions works with over one thousand career missionary doctors around the world and helps them meet the enormous challenges they face. CMDA sponsors the Global Missions Health Conference at Southeast Christian Church in Louisville, Kentucky, the second week of November (*www.medicalmissions.com*) with over 80 workshops, 120 mission exhibitors, and 2,500 in attendance. CMDA also equips healthcare professionals and their patients with books, conferences, and other educational resources. The organization also regularly speaks out on ethical and healthcare policy issues to the government, media, and church.

Ernie Steury was recognized by CMDA as a "Servant of Christ" in 1989 for personifying the compassion, servanthood, and ministry of the Great Physician.

If you would like to learn more about the Christian Medical & Dental Associations, including how healthcare professionals can join this movement of Christian doctors, go to *www.cmda.org* or call 1-888-230-2637.

World Gospel Mission

When Ernie and Sue Steury arrived as World Gospel Mission (WGM) missionaries at Tenwek in 1959, there was only a small cottage hospital from which Ernie, the first resident physician, sought to meet the medical needs of the people of the Bomet District of Kenya's Rift Valley Province. Two of Ernie and Sue's four children serve with WGM today: Jon and his wife Vera serve among the Maasai people of the Olderkesi District in Kenya; and Cindy and her husband, Daniel Tolan, worked in Kenya for years and are currently seconded to the Christian Medical & Dental Associations.

By the time Ernie left for heaven in 2002, Tenwek had become a major referral center of East Africa with more than three hundred beds. Today Tenwek Hospital has a nursing school and a hospital chaplaincy training program. Tenwek also offers internships for medical and clinical officers and cooperates with other hospitals in a family practice residency program. More than six hundred thousand people live in the thirty-two-kilometer radius served by Tenwek.

Medical professionals of all types are needed short- or long-term at Tenwek, the hospital with the motto We Treat—Jesus Heals. You may learn more about this major Christian ministry committed to excellence and offering compassionate health care, training for service, and spiritual ministry by visiting *http://www.tenwek.org*.

For more information about becoming a partner with WGM through prayer, donations, and service, please contact us at:

World Gospel Mission
P.O. Box 948
Marion, IN 46952-0948
765-664-7331
wgm@wgm.org
http://www.wgm.org

Note to the Reader

The publisher invites you to share your response to the message of this book by writing Discovery House Publishers, Box 3566, Grand Rapids, MI 49501, USA. For information about other Discovery House books, music, or videos, contact us at the same address or call 1-800-653-8333. Find us on the Internet at http://www.dhp.org/ or send e-mail to books@dhp.org.